Clinical Neuropsychology and Brain Function:

Research, Measurement, and Practice

Master Lecturers

Maureen Dennis

Edith Kaplan

Michael I. Posner

Donald G. Stein

Richard F. Thompson

THE MASTER LECTURES

Edited by
Thomas Boll
and Brenda K. Bryant

AMERICAN PSYCHOLOGICAL ASSOCIATION
WASHINGTON, DC 20036

Library of Congress Cataloging-in-Publication Data

Clinical neuropsychology and brain function: research, measurement, and practice/master lecturers, Maureen Dennis . . . [et al.]; edited by Thomas Boll and Brenda K. Bryant.

p. cm.—(The Master lecture series; v. 7)

ISBN 1-55798-038-1

1. Brain damage—Diagnosis. 2. Clinical neuropsychology. 3. Neuropsychological tests. I. Dennis, M. (Maureen) II. Boll, Thomas J. III. American Psychological Association. IV. Series.

[DNLM: 1. Brain—physiology. 2. Neuropsychological Tests. 3. Neuropsychology. W1 MA9309V v. 7/WL 103 C6418]

RC387.5.C554 1988

152—dc19

DNLM/DLC

for Library of Congress 88-14558

CIP

Copies may be ordered from:
Order Department P.O. Box 2710
Hyattsville, MD 20784

Published by the American Psychological Association, Inc.
1200 Seventeenth Street, N.W., Washington, DC 20036

Printed in the United States of America.

CONTENTS

MASTER LECTURES

Self-Study Instrument

Each year the Master Lectures are presented at the APA Convention, and attendees have an opportunity to receive credit. If you were unable to attend the Master Lectures, you may obtain Continuing Education Credit through a self-study instrument (SSI) developed to accompany each volume of this series, beginning with Volume 2. For further information about this or previous years' SSI, please write or phone:

MLS-SSI
CE Program Office
American Psychological Association
1200 Seventeenth St., N.W.
Washington, D.C. 20036
(202) 955-7719

PREFACE

The annual Master Lecture Series of the American Psychological Association (APA) is designed to inform, stimulate, and educate psychologists from diverse backgrounds as regards developments in areas of topical importance. For 1987, the lectures were on neuropsychology. As typifies this series, five internationally recognized psychologists were chosen to present. Their lectures, reporting on progress in neuropsychological research, span a broad range of topics, addressing current basic and applied issues in the field, including localization of learning and memory in the brain, effects of brain injury at different stages of development upon subsequent mental functioning, recovery from brain injury and the use of transplants to facilitate recovery, the analysis of the way persons with different types of brain injury approach and solve tasks, and the identification of neural structures and systems involved in visual attention.

The selection of neuropsychology as the central theme for the lectures was timely. There are few areas of psychology that have shown as remarkable a growth in such a short period of time. Although there has been an interest in brain–behavior relations dating back to the Egyptians and Greeks, and physiological psychologists have always had a strong commitment to research in such relations, the great explosion of interest in neuropsychology has occurred in the last several decades. Although there are many reasons for this upsurge, there are three major influences that I would like to note: First, technological advances in biomedical techniques such as single unit recordings, EEG quantification, computed-average evoked potentials, cerebral blood flow measurements, and the development of computerized tomography and magnetic resonance imaging provided new valid and reliable criteria against which behavioral changes could be measured. Computers, as they have in most phases of science, opened new doors for rapidity of measurements and analyses of complex brain–behavior relations.

Second, the mid-century "cognitive revolution" in psychology (Baars, 1986) gave rise to models of information processing, decision making, memory, and other cognitive processes that provided new paradigms for exploring neuropsychological relations. In a similar fashion, in the basic neurosciences, the importance of the neurotransmitters and their receptors rapidly became established and their relations to brain function were explored. Psychopharmacological studies provided new tools (in the form of drugs) to study behavioral effects and provided new sources of data for inferences concerning brain–behavior relations (Bloom, 1986; Feldman & Quenzer, 1984; Lister & Weingarter, 1987).

A third major influence was the rapid development of clinical neuropsychology. In 1970, I described the development of a new specialty—"clinical neuropsychology" (Parsons, 1970). By 1973 the International Neuropsychological Society was formed, and in the late 1970s the APA Division of Clinical Neuropsychology (Division 40) was established. Each of these organizations now has over 2,000 members. In 1970 I could identify two journals that were primarily neuropsychological in nature, *Neuropsychologia* and *Cortex*. By 1987 there were at least a dozen more journals that met this criterion (e.g., *Brain and Cognition*, *Brain and Language*, *Journal of Experimental and Clinical Neuropsychology*, and *Archives of Clinical Neuropsychology*). Similarly, whereas in 1966 Luria's seminal work *Higher Cortical Functions in Man* was the only major text, today there are scores of books devoted to the many aspects of neuropsychological research and practices such as, Filskov and Boll's (1981) *Handbook of Clinical Neuropsychology*; Grant and Adams' (1986) *Neuropsychological Assessment of Neuropsychiatric Disorders*; Kolb and Whishaw's (1985) *Fundamentals of Human Neuropsychology*; Parsons, Butters, and Nathan's (1987) *The Neuropsychology of Alcoholism: Implications for Diagnosis and Treatment*; and Levin, Graffman, and Eisenberg's (1987) *Neurobehavioral Recovery From Head Injury*.

Paralleling the growth of journals and books has been the establishment of courses in neuropsychology in graduate programs throughout the country. Whereas in 1970 there were, at most, one or two universities that had such courses, in 1987 almost every graduate program in clinical psychology had at least one and often more than one course in human neuropsychology. By 1987, postdoctoral training programs in both basic and applied neuropsychology had become commonplace whereas in 1970 they were few and far between. The American

Board of Examiners in Psychology in 1986 started offering the diplomate examination in clinical neuropsychology. The demand for the services of clinical neuropsychologists has mushroomed; as rapidly as neuropsychologists are trained they are recruited for service and academic positions.

Considering all of these developments, it was indeed appropriate to select neuropsychology as the topic for the Master Lecture Series and, given the diversity of the area, it was also appropriate that the lecturers who were selected were conducting research in quite different domains of neuropsychology. Thus, although the contributors to this volume address substantive topics that are legitimately subsumed under the rubric of neuropsychology, the chapters have little overlap. This point is dramatically illustrated by the fact that only one of the contibutors cites the work of any of the other four; indeed, only one such citation is present. Each author has focused upon different salient questions in today's neuropsychology and uses his or her own research questions to frame the answers to these questions. Inevitably, however, in one form or another, the authors deal with what is perhaps the oldest, most debated, and most important issue in neuropsychology—localization of function.

The first chapter, by Donald G. Stein, is a carefully crafted and challenging delineation of the problems and issues in our current understanding of the recovery of function from neural insult. He directly assails the notion of localization of functions held by many neuroscientists and neuropsychologists, that is, that higher mental functions are invariantly localized in specific circumscribed regions or interactive regions of the brain. Rather, he proposes that the context in which damage to the brain occurs and individual organismic factors, such as age at time of injury, nutritional status, and hormonal status, lead to wide variability in responses to injury. Stein's long-term research program in one-stage versus two-stage operations clearly sets the problem. Deficits due to the lesions in one-stage operations are not found in two-stage operations even though the amount of tissue removed or destroyed is the same in extent and location. From a strict localization point of view, how could this be?

These findings and many others lead Stein to the investigation of factors that promote recovery of function. Although this research area is in its infancy, he cites his own work and that of others that indicate the numerous probes that have promise, for example, fetal tissue transplants, glial tissue grafts, and injections of nerve growth factor and gangliosides (important constituents of cell membranes). To repeat, although this work on recovery of neural function must be considered in its early stages, Stein's review of progress hints at intriguing possibilities that could have important scientific and clinical implications for neuropsychology and for rehabilitation medicine.

In the next chapter, Richard F. Thompson systematically explores the question of brain substrates of learning and memory in the best of the localization tradition that Stein inveighs against. Thompson believes that it is now possible to localize the sites of memory storage and analyze the cellular and molecular mechanisms of that storage! Citing Lashley's (1950) inability to locate engrams of memory traces in cortical brain centers of rats, Thompson points out that lower brain structures such as the hippocampus, amygdala, and cerebellum may be important in certain aspects of memory and learning. Citing the work with amnesics, he describes experiential ("time-tagged") memory, declarative memory, and procedural memory as three memory systems that are selectively affected by different types of neural insults. Thus amnesics who have limbic (subcortical) system damage may do quite well in tasks involving procedural learning and memory but be impaired on tests of declarative and, particularly, experiential memory.

In the latter portion of his chapter, Thompson presents an elegant program of research on the neural basis of associative learning (eyelid conditioning in the rabbit). Step by step we are inexorably led to the location of the neural center, the interpositus nucleus of the cerebellum! Lesions made in that area permanently abolish the conditional response but have little effect on the unconditioned response. Further, if the lesion is made before training, no learning occurs. This and other evidence leads Thompson to conclude that the development of computational models of cerebellar learning hold promise for the future not only in terms of the basic science of neuropsychology but also for application to control and guidance systems such as seen in robotics.

The first two chapters deal primarily with research using animal models. In the next three chapters, the focus is on human research. The first of the three researchers, Maureen Dennis, asks whether there are differences in the behavioral effects of damage to the brain as a function of stage of development in children. She provides a comprehensive affirmative answer to this question by focusing on language development and its vicissitudes as a result of brain injury. She first shows us how research in this area has been impeded by faulty assumptions, for example, language is a unitary behavioral function, child language is a simplified version of adult language, and adult aphasia distinctions can be used as a framework for analyzing child language loss. She then provides us with a number of revised assumptions that emphasize that problems associated with the acquisition of language skills must be approached differently than problems in maintaining such skills as one would see in adults. In this context she presents "heuristics" or frameworks that serve as guides for identifying the important variables in developmental research. Although applied to language variables, these heuristics could be used to study any developmental function. Dennis exemplifies her approach with interesting data and conclusions derived from her factor analytic studies of language functioning in a large sample of children with different types of brain damage. Variables that help define the outcome of brain injury over the developmental course are: chronological age at which the lesion occurs, age of the lesion, age at time of testing, location of lesion (left or right hemisphere, anterior vs. posterior), type of lesion (e.g., trauma, cerebrovascular, and congenital), electrophysiological disturbances as in epilepsy, and cortical and subcortical involvement. What are the implications of the research? It is clear that in children the kinds of brain damage that affect the emergence and development of a skill are different from the kinds of damage that disrupt maintenance of a skill once acquired; therefore, a developmental framework must be used. It is also clear that traditional psychological assessment does not necessarily reveal the presence of language deficits, thus, new techniques are called for. Finally, in some instances early brain damage can have delayed effects on language functions that are not apparent until some years postinjury, that is, the deficit can be established only at the time when, in the course of development, it should have emerged.

The tremendous growth of clinical neuropsychology has been based in part on the development of standardized instruments or batteries of a "fixed" nature (i.e., some tests given every patient) or a "flexible" nature (tests vary as a function of deficits identified). These approaches obviously have served us well. However, in the book's fourth chapter, a wise and articulate clinician, Edith Kaplan, in her chapter, points to some serious problems in relying only on achievement or final test scores as the end product of neuropsychological assessment. She graphically makes the case for examining how the patient with suspected or actual brain damage goes about solving the problems or tasks presented to him or her. In other words, the "process" by which the patient masters the task may give as much relevant information or more than an "achievement" score. Said somewhat differently, a qualitative analysis of performance rather than a quantitative approach is emphasized. Importantly, however, the qualitative process approach can be quantified and subjected to statistical analysis. In Kaplan's hands this approach lends itself to improved diagnostic accuracy and increased specification of affected processes and adaptive strategies used by the patient. The result, Kaplan avers, is a higher probability that effective treatment may be instituted in the rehabilitation of the patient.

Kaplan provides a rich series of exemplars. Particularly impressive is her analysis of task dimensions that elicit different strategies or approaches by brain-injured patients. For example, in reproducing block design patterns, right hemisphere lesion patients differ from left hemisphere lesion patients in whether they start on the left or right side of their reproduction of the design, whether they break the overall configuration of the design, and whether they make more errors in one visual hemispace or the other. These behaviors can be quantified and used for either diagnosis or isolation of the specific error pattern. If, for example, the patient has many more errors in the left hemispace than right, not only is a right hemisphere lesion likely but a sub-clinical problem of left hemispace attentional neglect may be identified. On test after test, Kaplan gives ingenious examples of how the process approach can enrich the understanding of the nature and extent of the deficits in brain injury. In many instances this leads her to modifications of the standard tests so as to identify more specifically the processes that are affected. The variations used in the Digit-Symbol subtest of the Wechsler Scales, one of the tests most sensitive to brain injury, should become part of every clinical neuropsychologist's examination. Indeed, this chapter can be read with profit by every clinical neuropsychologist, no matter how skilled or experienced.

In the last chapter, Michael I. Posner masterfully integrates methods of experimental psychology with biomedical techniques such as the Positron Emission Tomography (PET) scan, and does this in groups varying from normal controls and brain-damaged patients to schizophrenics! Posner's delineation of the neurocognitive systems involved in attentional control presents us with a view of the brain as an integration of specific systems. His work is based on a rather simple paradigm: The subject is given a central target to fixate on and then given a cue as to which visual field he or she should shift attention. Cues can be valid (correctly indicate the location of the new target) or invalid (the new target appears in the field contralateral to the cue). When the subject detects the new target he or she presses a button and reaction time is recorded. In this seemingly simple task (one that would warm the cockles of every experimentalist's heart), the following stages are thought to be present: alerting by change in stimulus, interruption of current attention, disengaging from first target, movement of attention, engagement with new target, and inhibition of return to that target.

Using this paradigm in patients with left and right parietal lesions, patients with lesions of the midbrain, and patients with thalamic lesions, Posner shows that visual attentional control involves at least three neurocognitive systems: a parietal system that is related to the attention disengage stage, a midbrain system that is involved in the movement of attention stage, and a thalamic system that is salient in the engage attention stage.

Posner extends his methods to address problems of visual pattern recognition, language processing, and their interrelations. He concludes that visual–spatial attention and language processing are separate functions but that they share a more general attentional system. This general system, he suggests, lies in the frontal areas of the brain, thus the subsystems are integrated and controlled by the area of the brain most closely connected to the motor systems.

How can this approach be applied to problems in psychopathology? Posner chooses to exemplify such application by studying schizophrenia. Using the cueing method described earlier he found schizophrenics to have attentional deficits characteristic of patients with left hemisphere lesions, especially those with lesions in the left anterior frontal area. These findings are consistent with recently articulated theories of brain dysfunction in certain types of schizophrenia (Weinberger, 1987).

Finally, where does Posner stand on localization? He is explicit. He writes, "The nervous system localizes cognitive operations in widely separate neural systems that are then orchestrated in performance."

In summary, the master lecturers in neuropsychology have presented us with stimulating accounts of their empirical and theoretical advances in neuropsychology ranging from the highly specific identification of the neural systems involved in particular cognitive processes to the clinical neuropsychological process examination of patients with suspected or established brain damage; from the question of the differential effects of brain injury as a function of stage of development to the current question of what biological factors (e.g., fetal transplants) will stimulate recovery of neural function; from the classic experimental method of lesion studies using animal models to the use of the accidents of nature (i.e., groups of patients who have specific kinds of brain lesions); from a strict localization of function point of view to a broad multifactorial interpretation of brain function; and finally, from the systematic accumulation of empirical data to frameworks and models that, taken together, expand our current knowledge of brain–behavior relations and our understanding of brain function.

Oscar A. Parsons

References

Baars, B. J. (1986). *The cognitive revolution in psychology*. New York: Guilford Press.

Bloom, F. E. (Ed.). (1986). *Handbook of physiology: Sec. 1. The nervous system: Vol. 4. Intrinsic regulatory systems of the brain*. Bethesda, MD: American Physiological Society.

Feldman, R. S., & Quenzer, L. F. (1984). *Fundamentals of neuropsychopharmacology*. Sonderland, MA: Sinauer Associates.

Filskov, S. B., & Boll, T. J. (Eds.). *Handbook of clinical neuropsychology*. New York: Wiley.

Grant, I., & Adams, K. M. (Eds.). (1986). *Neuropsychological assessment of neuropsychiatric disorders*. New York: Oxford University Press.

Kolb, B., & Whishaw, I. Q. (1985). *Fundamentals of human neuropsychology* (2nd ed.). New York: W.H. Freeman.

Lashley, K. S. (1950). In search of the engram. *Society of Experimental Biology, Symposium 4*, 454–482.

Levin, H. S., Grafman, J., & Eisenberg, H. M. (Eds.). (1987). *Neurobehavioral recovery from head injury*. New York: Oxford University Press.

Lister, R. G., & Weingartner, H. (1987). Neuropharmacological strategies for understanding psychobiological determinants of cognition. *Human Neurobiology*, *6*, 1–10.

Luria, A. R. (1966). *Higher cortical functions in man*. New York: Basic Books.

Parsons, O. A. (1970). Clinical neuropsychology. In C. D. Spielberger (Ed.), *Current topics in clinical and community psychology* (Vol. II, pp. 1–60). New York: Academic Press.

Parsons, O. A., Butters, N., & Nathan, P. E. (Eds.). (1987). *Neuropsychology of alcoholism: Implications for diagnosis and treatment*. New York: Guilford Press.

Weinberger, D. R. (1987). Implications of normal brain development for the pathogenesis of schizophrenia. *Archives of General Psychiatry*, *44*, 660–669.

DONALD G. STEIN

IN PURSUIT OF NEW STRATEGIES FOR UNDERSTANDING RECOVERY FROM BRAIN DAMAGE: PROBLEMS AND PERSPECTIVES

Donald G. Stein is currently a professor of psychobiology, Dean of the Graduate School, and Associate Provost for Research at Rutgers University, Newark. He received his bachelor's and his master's degrees in experimental psychology from Michigan State University and his PhD in physiological psychology at the University of Oregon in 1965. He then worked as an National Institute for Mental Health Postdoctoral Research Fellow in Neuroscience at the Massachusetts Institute of Technology. Until January, 1988, he was a professor of psychology and the Director of the Brain Research Laboratory at Clark University.

Stein has received several Fulbright Scholar awards and awards from the Institute National de Sante de la Recherche Medical (INSERM) for travel and research in France where he studied with professors M. Jouvet and M. Jeannerod at the Universite Claude Bernard in Lyon. Since 1971, he has continued to maintain collaborative research contacts with colleagues in Lyon, Paris and Strasbourg, France. More recently, he has been developing research with colleagues at the National Hospital in Copenhagen, Denmark. His current research emphasis on central nervous system (CNS) plasticity began in 1972 when he secured an NIH Research Career Development Award and focused his time on studying functional recovery from traumatic injury to the CNS.

He is the author of more than 100 articles and books on the subject of recovery from injury to the brain and he continues to pursue this work with support from the National Institutes of Health, the American Paralysis Association, and the Fidia Research Foundation. In addition, he has organized a number of national and international meetings on nervous system plasticity and has lectured at many universities and research institutions in the United States and abroad.

In 1980 Stein received the American Association for the Advancement of Science Congressional Science and Engineering Fellowship, which permitted him to spend a year working in the United States Senate. As a result of that experience, he helped to found and chair the National Coalition for Science and Technology (NCST), a lobbying organization for scientists, educators, and high-technology businesspeople. He currently resides with his wife, Darel, in Maplewood, New Jersey.

DONALD G. STEIN

IN PURSUIT OF NEW STRATEGIES FOR UNDERSTANDING RECOVERY FROM BRAIN DAMAGE: PROBLEMS AND PERSPECTIVES

This chapter is organized around a historical and contemporary view of research on recovery from traumatic injury to the central nervous system (CNS). To understand this organization, readers should be aware of the fact that current thinking about how the nervous system functions is undergoing a quiet revolution. Not long ago it was thought that the adult, mammalian nervous system is basically a "hardwired" structure, with little or no regenerative capacity and virtually no real possibility for recovery from injury. Thus, the victims of brain damage were usually faced with poor prognoses and often limited to custodial care. For the most part, clinical therapies were designed to reduce further damage (e.g., bleeding, edema, etc.) rather than to repair nervous tissue directly or enhance new neuronal growth or re-form nervous connections.

I would like to thank the many graduate and undergraduate students at Clark University whose commitment to learning and research made much of this work possible. I am also indebted to Wendy Praisner who worked hard to type and recreate this manuscript from the scribbling she was given. The research done at Clark University was supported by grants and contracts from the National Institutes of Mental Health; the National Institute of Neurological, Communicative Disorders, and Stroke; the American Paralysis Association; and Fidia Pharmaceutical Corporation and I am very grateful for their generous support.

The older view of nervous system function derives from the classic paradigm that the nervous system consists of a collection of organs, parts or nuclei, each of which has a highly specified role in determining behavior. In this context, damage to any one part would lead to the loss of the behavior controlled by, or "centered" in, that part. The localizationist theory led quite logically to the belief that the behavioral functions of the brain could be mapped and labelled with great accuracy. Here are a few examples from recent sources that demonstrate my point. I have selected a passage from what may be the most widely read textbook in the neurosciences (Kandel & Schwartz, 1981). In discussing the issue of brain localization of function, these authors turned their attention to whether character and affective traits were anatomically localizable, and in this context they reviewed several clinical studies to support their position. From their perspective, "These clinical studies and their counterparts in experimental animals suggest that *all behavior* (italics mine), including higher (cognitive as well as affective) mental functions, is localizable to specific regions or constellations of regions within the brain. The role of descriptive neuroanatomy is, therefore, to provide us with a functional guide to localization within the three-dimensional neural space—a map for behavior. On the basis of this map we can use the patient's behavioral performance, as elicited in a clinical examination, to infer where the difficulties are located" (p. 11).

Although Kandel and Schwartz do modify their position slightly by talking later about "parallel processing mechanisms" and shared functions, the localization paradigm they employ cannot account for the kinds of neural and behavioral plasticity I discuss in this chapter.

The localizationist doctrine has not and will not be easy to change because it does, in fact, lead to easily testable hypotheses (e.g., damage to the hippocampus will produce a specific deficit in short-term working memory) that permit inferences about structure–function relations with apparent face validity. Sometimes, even in the face of data that contradict the paradigm, it is not easy to give up a well-established set of beliefs and attitudes (Rokeach, 1960). I will take the liberty of using a personal anecdote to illustrate because it demonstrates the point I wish to make and because it was the precipitating event which focused all of my research efforts for the last 21 years.

I was a new assistant professor at Clark University and was presenting my first talk on recovery from brain injury at an American Psychological Association (APA) meeting in San Francisco. Afterwards, a very distinguished neuropsychologist came up to me and said, "You know, I don't believe you." Knowing the reputation and stature of this very senior person, I was very upset. I had all of my raw data with me because I wanted my former professor to re-examine it with me to be certain I had made the right interpretation. I said to my adversary, "If I've done something wrong, I have all my results with me. If I could take a few moments and show you, I would be willing to repeat the experiment again if you find anything wrong." He looked at me again and said, "I don't want to see any data; I just don't believe it." Then he turned and walked away.

In this context, Kuhn (1970), who has written extensively on paradigms and revolutions in science, says, "Normal science, the activity which most scientists inevitably spend all of their time, is predicated on the assumption that the scientific community knows what the world is like. Much of the success of that enterprise derives from the community's willingness to defend that assumption, if necessary, at considerable cost. Normal science, for example, often suppresses fundamental novelties because they are necessarily subversive of its basic commitments. Nevertheless, as long as these commitments retain an element of the arbitrary, the very nature of normal research ensures that novelty shall not be suppressed for very long" (pp. 1–7).

I will suggest that the prevailing paradigm of functional localization as currently used may not be the most appropriate for explaining recovery from brain injury. What can be offered as a viable alternative? I think that the context in which damage to the brain occurs may be just as important in determining behavioral sequelae as the site of the lesion itself. For me, the context in which CNS trauma occurs not only implies that environmental influences are important, but also that individual, organismic factors (e.g., age at time of injury, nutritional status, hormonal influences, learning history, and general health of the subject) are also critical in predicting how the subject will respond to injury and any subsequent therapy.

The important point to emphasize here is that although neural plasticity and behavioral recovery from brain injury may occur spontaneously in some instances, it cannot be taken for granted that it will always occur as an inherent and "automatic" capacity of the nervous system. Although the potential for recovery or plasticity has to be a component of neural organization (else it would never occur), there is mounting evidence that special manipulations or conditions must be present to induce it. This is the task of the researcher and clinician—to find the keys to unlock the potential for recovery.

Contextual Factors in Recovery From Brain Injury

What follows is one example of how contextual variables affect recovery from general surgery. Ulrich (1984) examined the records of 46 patients who had all received cholecystectomies between 1972 and 1981. Half of the patients were assigned to rooms with windows that faced out onto a small cluster of trees. The other 23 patients had windows that faced on a brown brick wall. The patients were matched, as closely as possible, on all other relevant variables.

For the most part, the patients who had a view of the trees had shorter recovery times, took fewer doses of pain-killers, and received less negative comments from nurses than patients who faced the brick wall. Although Ulrich was unable to determine the specific components of the scene that led to the better recovery, his study demonstrates that psychological factors, in this case sensory stimulation, influence the healing processes that follow traumatic tissue injury.

Is there good reason to suspect that the healing of brain tissue would be subject to a completely different set of rules? If anything, the evidence suggests that enriched environmental stimulation can also enhance recovery from brain injury in adult animals. To give a brief example, Kelche and Will (1978) damaged the dorsal hippocampus in mature rats and then exposed the animals to "enriched" housing (a large group cage filled with novel objects, ladders, tunnels, etc.) or standard housing (i.e., isolated, no stimulation, constant conditions) for up to six months after the surgery. The rats were then tested on all twelve problems of the Hebb–Williams maze as a measure of their learning ability (Hebb & Williams, 1946). In this situation, the differential housing had no effect on the performance of the intact control rats; however, postoperative exposure to the enriched environment significantly reduced the severity of the learning impairment that typically results from the simultaneous, bilateral removal of the hippocampus.

The role of an enriched environment in the enhancement of recovery from CNS injury has recently been reviewed in detail by Dalyrimple-Alford and Kelche (1985). The point I wish to make here is that, although the issue is complex and the mechanisms for recovery not yet well understood, there is sufficient evidence to show that environmental factors play a role in determining the outcome of brain damage. This fact emphasizes the point that the inherent "plasticity" of the nervous system in response to injury can be tapped by environmental influences, and, therefore, the outcomes of such injury are not as invariant as one might suppose. If they are not invariant, then under what specific conditions is it possible to predict the outcome of brain injury? Under what specific conditions following brain damage is it appropriate to infer structure–function relations from lesion data? The current localizationist and reductionist paradigm does not place much emphasis on the kinds of contextual and organismic factors (such as differential housing conditions) that I believe need to be considered in thinking about neural functions and CNS organization, especially in the light of attempts to localize functions in specific brain regions.

In turning now to some of my own research, I would like to provide another example of how the context in which a CNS injury occurs can have a significant impact on behavioral outcome. My initial work on recovery was based on clinical and experimental observations that had been reported from time to time beginning well over 100 years ago. Here, I am referring to work showing that slow-growing brain lesions usually do not produce the severe symptoms associated with the same extent of injury that occurs after rapid onset (see Finger & Stein, 1982 and Stein, Rosen, Graziadei, Mishkin, & Brink, 1969, for a detailed review). Although the "momentum" of brain lesions hardly receives any attention at all in contemporary neuroscience textbooks or journals, the serial lesion effect (Finger, Walbran, & Stein, 1973) has been recognized as an important feature of brain localization doctrine. For example, Riese (1950) argued that "the time a lesion needs for originating, growing, and spreading is an essential element in cerebral localization. Sudden changes such as traumata, vascular accidents, etc., . . . are most likely to produce symptoms, although sometimes only temporary ones . . . this chronological factor has not been given the full credit it deserves in our attempts to correlate lesions with symptoms" (p. 138). John Hughlings Jackson coined the term "momentum of the lesion" (1879) to describe the fact that lesions caused by sudden injury were much more likely to have enduring effects than those due to slowly developing damage.

What triggered my research more directly was a report by Adametz (1959), who examined eighty adult cats that had received large electrolytic lesions of the midbrain reticular formation (MBRF). When the lesions were performed in a single stage, the cats went into a coma and usually died within several days after the surgery. Another group of cats received a series of eight lesions throughout the core of the MBRF, spaced one to two weeks apart. After each operation the animals awakened and were soon able to walk, groom, and feed themselves. Adametz also reported that the animals maintained normal sleep–wake cycles, and this despite the fact that postmortem histology revealed almost complete destruction of the MBRF.

As noted elsewhere (Finger & Stein, 1982), Adametz' data represent a clear anomaly—in the context of the classical localizationist paradigm—because the area designated as the "control center" for arousal and conscious attention had been virtually obliterated without serious loss of either consciousness or attention. Based on Adametz' findings, my students and I decided to examine whether cognitive and learned behaviors could also be spared in the absence of the areas thought essential for their mediation and organization. Here it seemed as if, once again, the context (in this case, the temporal sequencing of tissue removal) in which an injury occurs would have dramatic implications for the outcome of that injury.

Our work at Clark University was based on the following question: If, according to the localizationist paradigm, a structure is necessary for the mediation of behavior, then what could be inferred if removal of the structure does not cause the expected deficit? Can one argue that a structure is essential for mediation of a given behavior if its removal does not produce any impairment? In our first series of studies, we created a unilateral lesion on one side of the brain, gave a four-week rest interval between surgeries, and then removed the contralateral structure. The experimental procedures we employed to test the serial lesion paradigm are shown in Figure 1.

Briefly stated, one group of animals served as a sham-operated control group; the second group received simultaneous, bilateral dam-

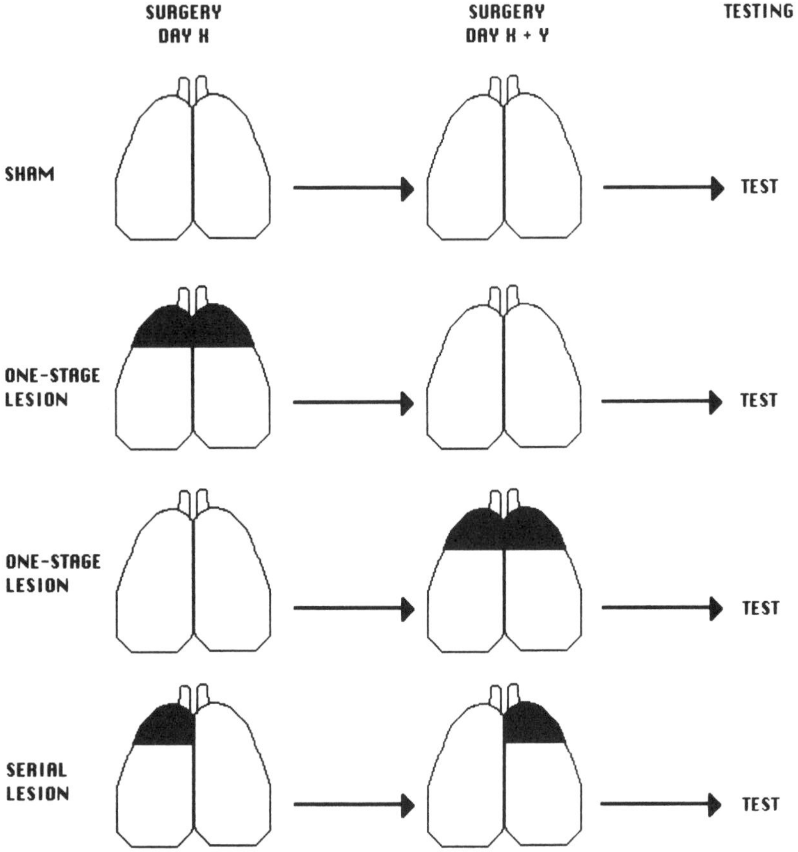

Figure 1. How serial lesions are created in experimental subjects. One group receives no brain injury although it may receive anesthesia, bone flap removal, and dural puncture at several different times corresponding to the surgery of the other groups; this is the sham-operated group. One group will receive the aforementioned plus bilateral removal of the target brain tissue in a single sitting; this is the one-stage operated group. (One-stage groups may receive surgery either at the time of the first or the second surgery of the serial group). The serial group receives damage first to one hemisphere and then, after a suitable delay, the contralateral structure is removed. All groups then begin testing after they have received the same "recovery" period. Adapted from Finger et al. (1971) by permission.

age or removal of a structure; and the third group was given the same extent of injury, but with a delay between the surgical operations. When behavioral testing began, all of the brain-injured subjects had bilateral injuries of the same extent. No special handling, testing, or training was provided prior to surgery or during the intervals between the staged surgeries. In the case of animals receiving one-stage surgery, the actual postoperative recovery period is longer because the animals have about six weeks of recovery before testing, whereas those with the two-stage surgery begin testing only two weeks after their last operation. As a case-in-point, we can examine the effects of serial lesions of the frontal cortex in adult rats on their ability to learn spatial and visual discrimination tasks. Figure 2 shows performance on spatial alternation; light–

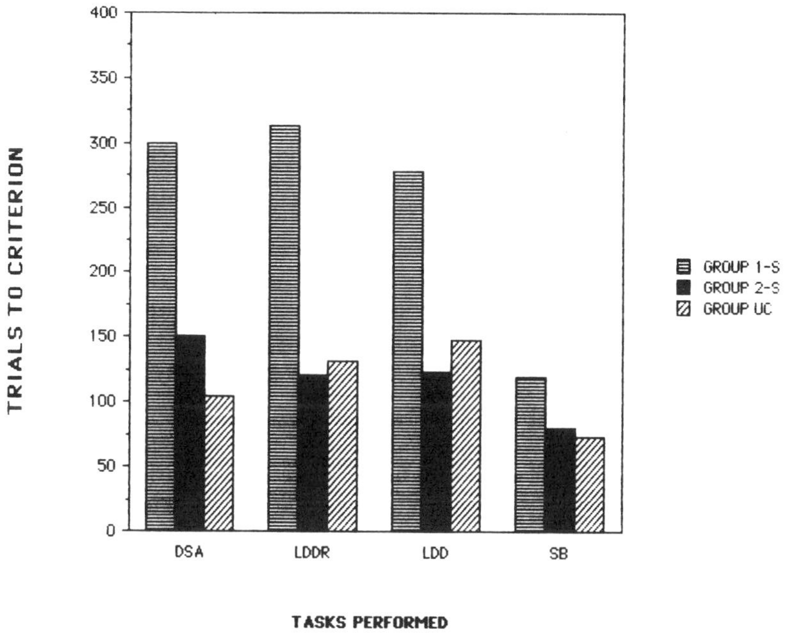

Figure 2. Trials to criterion learning performance in rats with single or two-stage frontal cortex lesions. The rats were tested on spatial alternation and brightness discrimination tasks. In each test, the animals with serial lesions performed significantly better than counterparts with single-stage lesions and their performance was often indistinguishable from sham-operated controls. DSA is delayed spatial alternation, LDDR is light–dark discrimination reversal, LDD is light–dark discrimination, and SB is successive brightness discrimination. Adapted from Stein, Rosen, Graziadei, Mishkin, and Brink (1969) by permission.

dark, successive discrimination; light–dark discrimination reversal and simultaneous discrimination learning. Detailed descriptions of these tasks can be found in Stein (1974).

The results of the behavioral testing were quite dramatic. On the first three tests of performance, it was apparent that the animals with one-stage surgery were significantly impaired with respect to the animals in the control group and to those with two-stage lesions (2-S). In marked contrast, the 2-S group performed as well as their control counterparts—despite the fact that the extent and locus of the injury were the same for both groups of brain-injured rats. The simultaneous discrimination task did not appear to be sensitive to frontal cortex damage. From the localizationist perspective, this should give some pause for thought. In the 2-S group, the specific, neural structure was gone at the time of testing. Yet, there was almost complete sparing of the functions thought to be mediated by the mature frontal cortex. One might argue that the frontal cortex of the rat may have some unusual characteristics that predispose it to such dramatic plasticity. However, that cannot be because the serial lesion paradigm has been applied successfully to a number of different brain areas such as the hippocampus and amygdala (Stein, 1974), the caudate nucleus (Schultze & Stein, 1975), motor cortex (Gentile, Green, Nieburgs, Schmeltzer, & Stein, 1978), somatosensory cortex (Finger et al., 1971), visual cortex (Ades, 1946; Barbas & Spear, 1976), reticular formation (Kesner, Fiedler, & Thomas, 1967), and, even more recently, to recovery from damage to the lumbar region of the spinal cord (Alstermark, Lundberg, Pettersson, Tantisira, & Walkowska, 1987).

More important, perhaps, is the fact that sequential injury to the fully mature primate brain also produces significant recovery from injury to the frontal cortex. For example, in one series of experiments, Butters, Rosen, and Stein (1974) were able to demonstrate that serial removals of the sulcus principalis (dorsolateral frontal cortex) led to significantly better performance on retention of a delayed alternation task, acquisition of delayed response task, and on a position reversal learning task. The monkeys with one-stage injuries were significantly more impaired than the serially operated animals, despite the fact that the lesions in the serial group were actually much larger than the one-stage group. Butters et al. (1974) speculated that the serial operations (there were four surgeries spaced three weeks apart: left upper bank of principalis, right lower bank, left lower bank, and right upper bank) caused more gliosis and dural adhesions after each surgery. Thus, even in the face of more extensive damage to the cortical regions surrounding the sulcus principalis, the monkeys with serial lesions had much less symptomatology than their one-stage counterparts with less injury. I should note, however, that the same authors did not obtain any evidence for better recovery when they performed serial removals of the orbito-frontal cortex in adult monkeys, using the same temporal parameters. As we shall see, the time between surgery may be one important factor in determining the success or failure of the serial lesion technique.

Nonetheless, the main point to emphasize is that the way in which surgery is performed (i.e., contextual factors) can determine the extent, type, and duration of the symptoms and deficits produced by injury to a specific brain region. Simply stated, the outcome of injury to the brain need not be an invariant characteristic, wholly predictable on the basis of localizing that injury to a specific CNS region. If this proposition is true, and if recovery does occur, then can one be completely certain of current inferences concerning the localization of specific behavioral functions in specific brain regions? If one accepts the proposition that functions can "shift" as a result of trauma or injury, is it less logical to assume that such functions could shift in the intact brain—as environmental demands require? Or is it more logical to think that complex behavioral functions are a characteristic of the whole brain and not really to be found residing in specific nuclei or anatomically defined CNS regions?

Even in the case of human neuropsychology, we should at least begin to question the concept more thoroughly. For example, with respect to mnemonic ability in humans, many of the inferences about localization of memory are made on the basis of examination of the same few individuals who have been tested in many different laboratories by investigators who share the same paradigm (e.g., the cases of HM and NA).

HM was a patient with what has been described as a total retrograde amnesia that resulted from bilateral, surgical removal of the medial temporal region performed to control severe epileptic seizures. According to the many investigators who have tested him (see Squire, 1987, for a review), HM cannot learn anything new despite the fact that he seems to recollect older memories and has a reasonable vocabulary. NA is another patient that was first described around 1968. He received an accidental stab wound directly into the forebrain and also shows a profound retrograde amnesia and an inability to learn new facts.

However, in a recent review of the clinical literature, Markowitsch (1984) examined a large number of cases in which amnesia did not accompany damage to thalamic, mammillary, or hippocampal regions. Markowitsch suggests, "Both the findings in humans and nonhumans may be viewed as biased by two common failures in interpreting brain–behavior relations in amnesics, namely, the selection of one or two particular damaged structure(s) to the neglect of many others damaged as well, and the failure to take into sufficient consideration the widespread interconnections of brain regions with each other. Just considering the high degree of connectivity among different brain regions immediately points out the diversification and mutual interdependence of function communication in the brain and the consequently widespread changes of losing even a small and restricted region of the brain" (pp. 36–37).

What renders the issue of what can be localized where even more complex is the growing body of literature demonstrating that the behavioral effects of small, relatively well-localized lesions can often be completely eliminated by subsequently extending the damage or creating a larger lesion in the first place. The outcome of the injury will vary as a function of a number of different contextual factors (e.g., age, personality, and environmental factors). Earle (1987) has recently provided a comprehensive review documenting the idea that larger lesions may lead to disinhibition or unmasking of behaviors that are suppressed (rather than lost) as a consequence of injury to brain loci. She, too, emphasizes that current attempts to localize function in damaged structures (e.g., Squire, 1982) will not be appropriate without considering the many other organismic and environmental variables that can attenuate or exacerbate lesion outcome.

As Zangwill (1963) wrote:

> There can be no doubt that a variety of behavior patterns may be evoked by stimulation, or lost after ablation, of limited parts of the brain. But I do not think we should therefore postulate special 'centers,' that is to say, assemblies of neurons whose function it is to generate the behavior in question. As Sherrington (1906) clearly saw, behavior does not spring ready-made from the brain, like Athena from the head of Zeus. Rather it must be regarded as an integration of a large number of component activities. . . . No one level, not even the highest, can properly be regarded as the exclusive seat of a behavior pattern (pp. 338–339).[1]

Despite Zangwill's and Markowitsch's admonitions, the paradigm of localization is still cause for active debate as it was when it was first argued more than 100 years ago by Broca and Flourens (Finger & Stein, 1982). As an example, Thompson (1986) described his thoughts on the localization of memory by writing, "It now seems possible to identify the circuits and networks that participate in learning and memory, *localize the sites of memory storage* (italics mine), and analyze the cellular and molecular mechanisms of memory." About four weeks after Thompson's article appeared, John, Tang, Brill, Young, and Ono (1986) presented a feature article describing their work on functional localization of visual discrimination learning in adult cats, using isotopic markers of metabolic activity in neurons during learning and retention as measures of neuronal information processing. John et al. summarized by saying, "Our results do not fit well with the general computer-like model of the brain, with information stored in discrete registers, no matter how many in number. *No conceivable neuron or set of neurons* (italics

[1]Reprinted from Zangwill (1963) by permission.

mine), no matter how diffuse its synaptic inputs can evaluate the enormous amount of neural activity here shown to be involved in retrieval of even a simple form discrimination. Memory and awareness in complex neural systems may depend on presently unrecognized properties of the system as a whole and not upon any elements that constitute that system" (p. 1175).

The issue here is not whether one should agree with either Thompson or John (or Kandel & Schwartz, 1981), but rather that competing paradigms concerning the question of localization of function in the CNS still remain to be resolved! The different paradigms will employ specific techniques to demonstrate and support the hypotheses that derive from the paradigms; so the question of what is localized where may be more a function of the method applied to the study of the problem than to the inherent characteristics of the brain itself.

I believe that coming to grips with the issue is of more than academic importance. The beliefs and attitudes (paradigms) held by the scientific community at any given time have important implications on social (and medical) policy. Given the prevailing mechanistic reductionism of the neurosciences (including neurology), it should come as no surprise that, until very recently, there has not been much research on functional recovery from brain injury. Thus, if "centers" (or aggregates of centers) are lost or damaged, leading inevitably to permanent impairments, why spend money for research (or treatment) on an area with so little promise for success? Normal science takes its paradigms for granted and the enterprise "seems an attempt to force nature into the preformed and relatively inflexible box that the paradigm supplies" (Kuhn, 1970, p. 24).

Perhaps one small step in the right direction may be taken by at least giving more consideration to the role of the past history of the organism, as well as existing context and environment, when manipulations (recording, surgery, or diagnostic testing) are made to determine brain functions.

Taking a more contextual framework in evaluating brain function does not necessarily mean that, when appropriate conditions are specified, one cannot ascribe symptoms of the result of injury to a given hemisphere or brain region. It is also very likely that even independently of environmental context, certain brain regions may be genetically more vulnerable to the consequences of injury than others and that certain symptoms will appear when these areas are damaged. The symptoms resulting from brain injury need not necessarily be taken as reflecting the specific functions of the damaged region, especially in light of the fact that the symptoms often vary as a function of a broad array of factors acting on the organism at the time of the trauma.

Riese (1977), who himself disagreed with the theory of localization, argued for the concept of vulnerability as I have outlined it earlier. For example, he stated, "To make clear the greater vulnerability of a given nervous region of the brain and its distinction from the seat of this function at the same region, the analogy with the famous heel of Achilles may be used. Although the heel is the most vulnerable region of the hero's body, and although its injury would be fatal for his life, life cannot be understood to be localized at the heel; it pervades the whole body" (p. 65).

Throughout the remainder of this chapter, I will try to provide specific examples of experiments that are designed to demonstrate that the symptoms of brain damage do not necessarily reveal how a given part of the brain works in the healthy, intact organism. Rather, what is reflected in posttraumatic performance is the attempt of the brain-damaged subject (human patient or laboratory animal) to adapt, as a whole, to a radically changed nervous system. Although it may seem too obvious to mention, posttraumatic behavioral performance reflects not so much the function of the damaged part as much as what the remaining brain can do in the absence of that part.

It should also be remembered (however obvious) that over time, neural processes in the intact or damaged brain will change. For example, in the case of an initially severe deficit that gradually disappears, what inferences could then be made about the localization of that function in the zone of injury?

Temporal Factors in Recovery From Brain Damage

What role do temporal factors play in influencing the outcome of brain injury? This question may have important clinical implications for diagnosis and treatment of brain injury. Although time itself is not a variable, posttraumatic, chemical, physiologic, and anatomic changes are known to be critical in brain injury repair (see Nieto-Sampedro & Cotman, 1985, for an excellent and detailed review).

The serial lesion phenomenon I described earlier can serve as an example of how temporal factors can influence the outcome of bilateral cortical injury. Using the frontal cortex as a model (Patrissi & Stein, 1975), adult rats had bilateral aspiration lesions made either simultaneously or with a 10-day, 20-day, or 30-day interoperative interval between the first and second lesion.

Figure 3 shows what might be called a window of opportunity to promote sparing of function after serial lesions. If one compares the animals' performance with the sham-operated controls, it can be seen that the 20- and 30-day interoperative interval groups are not significantly different from the shams in their postoperative performance. No special handling and no training is given; the rats are simply maintained in their home cages. Yet their performance is equivalent to the sham control group. The animals with a 10-day interoperative interval are also significantly better than the one-stage group, but they are still

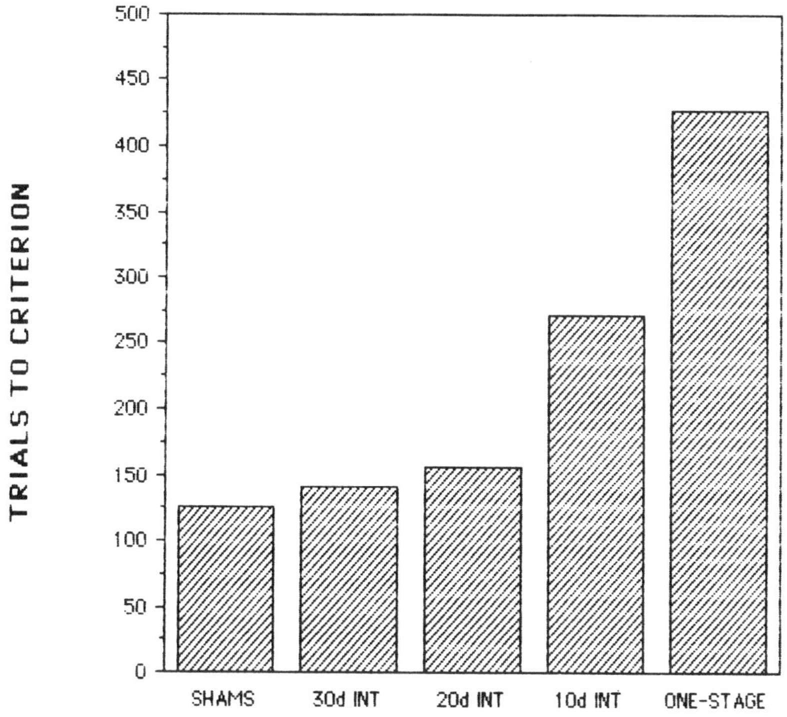

Figure 3. Mean spatial learning performance in adult rats with simultaneous or serial lesions of frontal cortex. The serial lesions were made with 10-day, 20-day, or 30-day intervals between the first and second operations. The performance of rats with simultaneous lesions is shown at the far right of the graph. Adapted from Patrissi and Stein (1975) by permission.

impaired with respect to the control group. In this particular study with the frontal cortex, the "critical period" for sparing of behavioral functions appears to have been between 10 and 20 days. However, one cannot assume that the same critical period would hold for all brain regions. Just as some brain areas might be more vulnerable to injury, it might also be the case that the healing processes would take greater or less time depending on the structure involved and the type and extent of injury it sustained.

When we conducted the critical period study in the early 1970s, we had no direct notion of what physiologic factors could have accounted for the better recovery seen in animals with "slowly occurring" central nervous system lesions. However, the field of neuroscience has made dramatic advances in our understanding of CNS repair processes over the last ten years.

In explaining our results, one of the first ideas that comes to mind is that anomalous or redirected neuronal growth (neuronal sprouting) might be induced by the progressive damage such that afferents to the frontal cortex would be redirected to other targets in the absence of the target tissue. There is some evidence indicating that serial brain damage does, in fact, accelerate axonal sprouting in the adult rat. For example, Scheff, Bernardo, and Cotman (1977) created one- or two-stage unilateral lesions of the entorhinal cortex (EC), a part of the classic limbic system, in mature rats. Unilateral EC lesions will remove nearly all of the input from the EC to the dorsal hippocampus and will stimulate the proliferation of afferent fibers from the septum to the dentate gyrus of the hippocampus. The proliferating septal fiber terminals (this is one definition of "neuronal sprouting") re-occupy the synaptic spaces that were vacated by damaging the EC inputs. Using special stains that identified cholinergic fibers, Scheff and colleagues demonstrated a 30% increase in the spread of the new collaterals in animals with the sequential EC lesions. There was also sprouting in the one-stage EC group, but it took longer to occur and the proliferation of the septal fibers was not as great as it was in the two-stage lesion group.

What factors may have accounted for the enhanced growth in the serial group? Is new growth as critical as the enhanced survival of neurons that would ordinarily die as a result of the injury? We now know that there is a specific, temporal sequence of biochemical and morphological events that follow cerebral injury (Nieto-Sampedro & Cotman, 1985; Schoenfeld & Hamilton, 1977). Figure 4 (taken from Nieto-Sampedro & Cotman, 1985) provides a convenient schema of the temporal order of events that are involved in the adaptive response of the brain to trauma.

In examining the chart, one can see that sprouting and the formation and maintenance or survival of new neural connections in the brain are actually the end-stage mechanisms leading to behavioral recovery, rather than initiating events. The first response of the brain is to eliminate toxic by-products of the injury itself and then, through vascularization, to provide appropriate nutritional factors to surviving neurons. Next, according to Nieto-Sampedro and Cotman (1985), the brain "has to protect itself against indiscriminate influences from the rest of the organism by forming a blood CNS barrier (glia limitans—pia arachnoid systems)" (p. 442). Nieto-Sampedro and Cotman (1985) have shown that new capillary growth and macrophage invasion of the lesion site begin almost immediately after the lesion. Glial proliferation starts at 2–3 days postlesion. Secondary neuronal death continues up to about 4 days after the injury, "whereas maximum neurotrophic factor induction takes about 8–10 days after the injury" (p. 419).

This last point is important, and I will come back to it later in this chapter. For the time being, however, it is worth noting that neurotrophic factors are substances that sustain neurons in culture and promote their

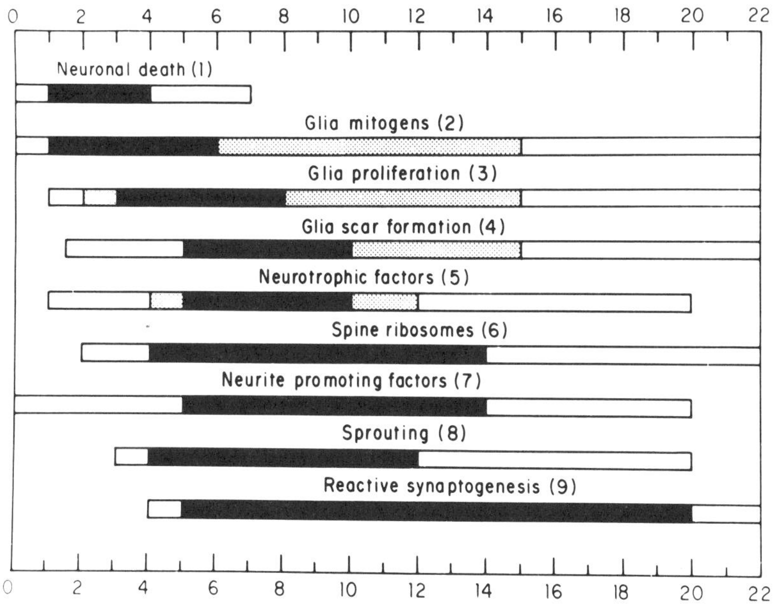

Figure 4. The time course of primary and secondary events following traumatic injury to the brain. Adapted from Nieto-Sampedro and Cotman (1985) by permission. The intensity of shading is meant to show the intensity of the reaction over days postlesion.

growth toward specific target sites both in vitro and in vivo. Cotman's group has now documented the fact that trophic factors occur naturally in the developing nervous system, and they can also be induced by damage to the brain. Although it is only corollary evidence, it is nonetheless interesting and significant that the first instance of our behavioral recovery in animals with serial lesions occurred in the 10-day interoperative group, which is the time course for the maximal quantities of injury-induced neurotrophic factors (NTFs) appearing in the damaged brain.

Why should serial lesions be better than one-stage lesions in affecting the process? First, and most obvious, is that serial lesions by their very nature, are smaller than one-stage—at least initially. If there is a limit to how much can be repaired (or spared) by the presence of NTFs, then smaller initial damage would mean fewer cells requiring trophic support during the critical, early stages of injury. Second, the serial lesions may produce less toxic substances than more massive damage, and, also, the dynamics of revascularization would proceed more rapidly. Thus, the longer the delay between successive injuries, the more effective and efficient each adaptive process—including elimination of toxic debris and glial cell production of neurotrophic factors (Whitaker-Azmitia, Ramirez, Noreika, Gannon, & Azmitia, 1987).

Having now said this, I do not wish to imply that recovery is strictly dependent on whether or not an injury is inflicted slowly. Other processes may also play a role in recovery, and they may be latent or very slow. The capacity or potential for recovery and neuronal repair are present in the adult brain, but they may have to be induced by special manipulations that are just beginning to be studied. Another hypothesis is that unaided neuronal repair processes in the mature organism may simply take far longer to occur than we have previously suspected.

Very often in clinical cases of head injury, subjects are rarely followed or tested for years, much less decades, after their injury. In particular, it is very unlikely that patients who are refractive to the initial regime of "rehabilitation" therapy are continued in the program for a number of years. Yet, sometimes total recovery has been observed many, many years after initially profound deficits that were assumed to be permanent.

For example, Geschwind (1985), in one of his last papers suggested, "There must be many cases in which the capacity for recovery is latent and revealed only by some further manipulation. But experimenters have only rarely been zealous in their search for the right maneuver" (p. 1). Geschwind argued that the time needed for recovery in adults may be much longer than those seen in infants. He said, "Most neurologists are gloomy about the prognosis of severe adult aphasia after a few weeks, and pessimism is reinforced by a lack of prolonged follow-up in most cases. I have, however, seen patients severely aphasic for over a year, who then make excellent recoveries, one patient returning to work as a salesman, the other as a psychiatrist. Furthermore, there are patients who continue to improve over many years. For example, a patient, whose aphasia is still quite evident six years after onset, cleared substantially by eighteen years" (p. 3). A fact that rarely emerges in the experimental analysis of brain damage is that there is usually great variation in the severity of the deficit as well as in the extent of recovery. At present, investigators can do little more than speculate about the reasons for such variability. The main point here is that there are factors that occur over time that are rarely examined thoroughly in the context of a post-operative or posttraumatic neuropsychological workup.

Sex Differences and Recovery From Brain Injury

Throughout this chapter, I have been emphasizing the fact that the outcome of brain injury depends on a multitude of factors that sometimes may have very complex or subtle interactions. The ability to predict the extent to which an organism may suffer from the effects of brain damage will depend on our understanding the environmental and organismic factors that contribute to, or block, the repair processes. In this context, for example, one question that has not received very much attention in the experimental or clinical literature concerns sex differences in response to brain damage or other disorders of nervous system function. Is it possible that the gonadal hormones could play a significant role in affecting the cognitive deficits that often accompany brain damage or other forms of neuronal loss? If there are differences in recovery from brain injury, are there any implications for potential therapy or posttraumatic care?

Unfortunately, there is not a lot of literature on this subject, but there are some reports hinting that there are sex differences in brain malfunction, although the specific reasons for the differences are not well understood. For example, McGlone (1978) found that aphasia following stroke in the left hemisphere was three times more frequent in men than in women.

Geschwind and his colleagues also began to re-examine the question of sex differences in brain disorders in a series of clinical case studies. For instance, in one report, Geschwind and Behan (1982) found that dyslexia and stuttering may be affected by androgen levels. Behan and Geschwind (1985) also examined hyperkinetic and hyperactive children and found more than twice as many boys than girls afflicted with this childhood disorder. Others have reported that male fetuses are generally less viable than female fetuses and are slower to develop (Ounstead & Taylor, 1972). It seems that sex differences and exposure to gonadal hormones during development play an important role in shaping brain morphology, although most studies appear to be limited to areas concerned with sexual and emotional behaviors.

Recently, Juraska (1986) examined whether exposure to enriched or isolated environments could alter CNS morphology in male and female rats. She maintained littermates in each of the two environments from weaning to postpuberty and then examined cell types and structures in the visual cortex and hippocampal dentate gyrus.

The results showed that although the environment does shape cerebral morphology, sex differences were more subtle and the effects depended on the specific neuronal population examined. Thus, in layer III of the visual cortex, male rats were more affected by the enriched conditions than female rats (longer, more complex dendritic fields) but not in the other cortical layers. In contrast, female rats had more extensive dendritic branching than male rats in the hippocampal granule neurons of the dentate gyrus, if they were exposed to the enriched environment.

This work is important to the present discussion because it demonstrates that early environment and sex differences in response to the environment can alter the complexity and structure of CNS neurons. Presumably, such structural alterations would play a role in the ability of the organism to process information, to adapt to its environment and probably in its response to brain injury or disease as well.

The effects of gonadal hormones on sex behavior and on early morphology of brain tissue have been given a lot of attention, but much less work has been concerned with whether sex differences can affect recovery from brain injury. In one report bearing on this question, Goldman (1975) studied male and female monkeys given orbital prefrontal lesions at 50 days of age, and then began behavioral testing on an object discrimination reversal task at 75 days of age. The male monkeys with brain lesions were impaired on this task whereas the female monkeys were not. In animals operated upon as juveniles or adults, there were no sex differences in response to the injury. As Goldman noted, it is generally assumed that sex differences in brain injury disappear once maturity is reached; however, data from our laboratory suggest that this notion may also be subject to modification. Once again, I have to stress that outcome of brain injury may depend on how and when lesions are made and that sex differences in such outcomes (or hormonal effects) may be emphasized or reduced, depending upon the specific conditions at the time of injury. For example, in an early serial lesion study (Stein, 1974), we subjected male or female adult rats to one- or two-stage removals of frontal cortex and then tested them on a spatial alternation task. All of the brain-damaged rats were compared to age-matched and sex-matched normal control rats.

First, we noted that intact female rats learned the alternation task more rapidly than intact male rats, which in some respects was consistent with other experimental findings that women may be better at certain learning tasks than men (Broverman, Klaiber, Kobiash, & Vogel, 1968). Our results with the brain-damaged animals were more surprising. Although both male and female animals with one-stage lesions were equally impaired, only the male rats with two-stage lesions showed clear evidence of functional sparing; female rats with the same type and extent of injury were as impaired as animals with one-stage removal of frontal cortex. Thus, the female rats, as intact animals, showed more rapid learning, but serial lesions conferred no benefits whatsoever on post-operative performance. At the time, we speculated that the failure to obtain two-stage recovery in the female rats may have been due to higher circulating levels of adrenocorticotrophic hormone, thus reducing the animals' ability to cope with stress.

We are only a little closer to understanding some of the possible bases for sex differences in brain function, but there are now more tantalizing clues to study. Recently, my colleagues and I tried to determine whether the failure to find recovery in adult female rats was related to the relative amounts of circulating estrogen present at the time of frontal cortex surgery (Attella, Nattinville, & Stein, 1987). In our first experiment, we attempted to manipulate estrogen levels directly by subcutaneous implants of silastic tubing containing estradiol. This procedure resulted in very significant impairment in the estrogen-treated rats, but our results proved to be inconclusive because so many of the animals given the hormonal supplements developed large pituitary tumors (adenomas), which probably contributed to the severity of their impairments. We decided to examine the question of whether estrogen was contributing to the recovery from brain damage (or making the impairment worse) by physiologically manipulating the estrous cycle at the time of injury. We noted in our review of the literature that there were no direct experiments designed to determine whether hormonal changes during estrous could influence the outcome and symptoms of brain damage in other than reproductive behaviors.

Accordingly, we shifted our strategy by going to a more indirect manipulation of circulating estrogen and progesterone. It had been previously established that mild, vaginal stimulation in the mature female rat causes the animal to become pseudopregnant. In this condition, which can be maintained for long periods of time, circulating estrogen levels decrease and circulating progesterone levels increase. Before any surgery was done, we carefully measured the different stages of the estrous cycle (metestrous, proestrous, and estrous) by taking samples of vaginal epithelial cells and examining their shape under the microscope. Once the estrous cycle was precisely determined (see Attella et al., 1987, for details), the rats began testing on the acquisition of a spatial alternation task identical to the one we have used in our previous studies of recovery from frontal injury. As Figure 5 shows, the performance of normally cycling (N/C) and pseudopregnant (PP) intact female rats on the learning task is practically identical. It seems that mature, normal, and healthy female rats are unaffected by differences in hormonal state. In contrast, Figure 6 shows what happens after PP or N/C rats have received bilateral injury to the frontal cortex and are tested for retention of the learned alternation.

Although both groups were impaired in comparison to intact PP or N/C controls, the N/C female rats with frontal lesions were extremely impaired with respect to their PP counterparts. After all behavioral testing had been completed, we removed and examined the brains to see if we could detect any morphological differences resulting from the manipulations we had made. The most obvious and dramatic effect we noted was that the dilation of the cerebral ventricles was much greater in the N/C than in the PP animals. Ventricular dilation is one measure of cerebral edema, and so we reasoned that extensive edema seen in the N/C female rats could have been the basis for our failure to obtain recovery in the N/C rats. The mechanism is complex, but the effects of estrous cycling on recovery from brain damage may be related to the effects of estrogen and progesterone or angiotensin or vasopressin—hormones that are directly involved in water balance and retention.

We discuss this relation in detail elsewhere (Attella et al., 1987). These results demonstrate that, once again, environmental and contex-

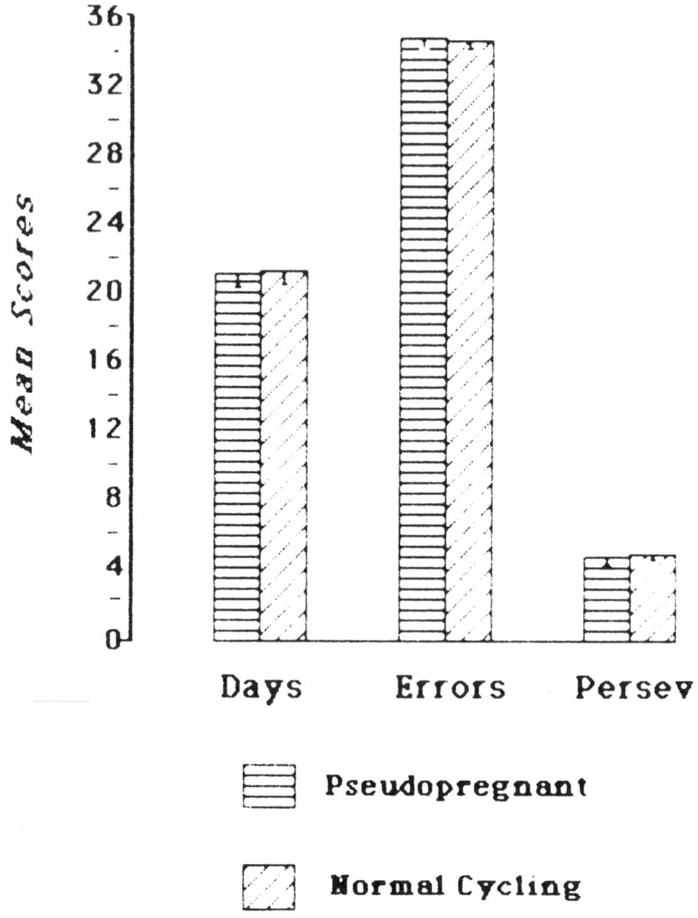

Figure 5. Preoperative learning scores (days, errors, and perseverations) in pseudopregnant or normal cycling female rats on a spatial alternation task to a criterion of 30 out of 30 successively correct trials. The scores represent the average number of days the rats took to reach criterion. Adapted from Attella, Nattinville, and Stein (1987) by permission.

tual (organismic) factors have a major role to play in determining the outcome of brain injury and the long-term ability of the organism to adapt to trauma. In this particular instance, our results can be taken to suggest that underlying hormonal differences in response to brain injury may not be apparent unless the symptoms are correlated with the onset and phase of estrous. If this factor is not considered, important data about brain and behavior relations could be lost or simply (and cor-

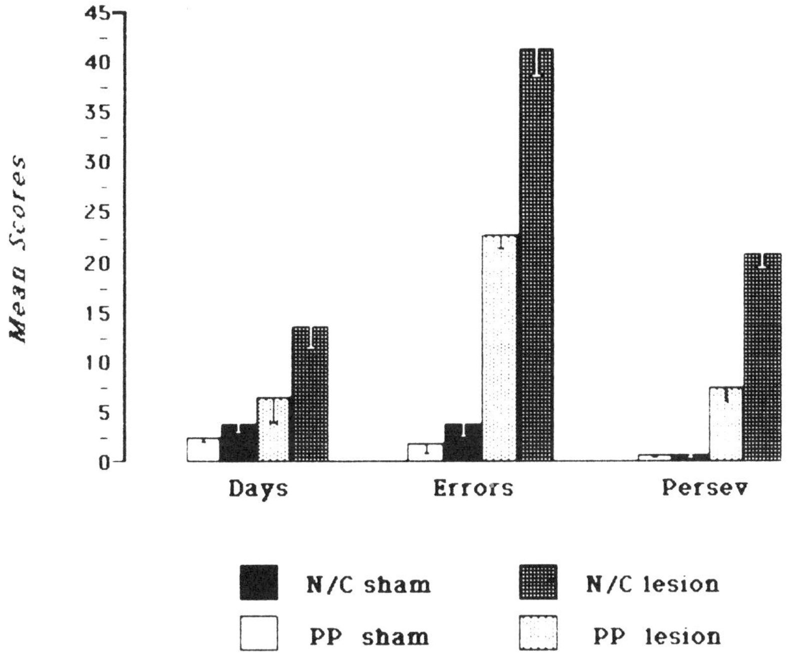

Figure 6. Postoperative learning scores (days, errors, and perseverations) in pseudopregnant (PP) or normal-cycling (N/C) female rats with bilateral lesions of the frontal cortex. Although the PP groups with lesions were significantly better than the N/C lesion group, they were still impaired with respect to the control group. Adapted from Attella, Nattinville, and Stein (1987) by permission.

rectly) attributed to measurement error or other unknown factors contributing to normal variability or individual differences.

Although there may be important species differences in the outcome of manipulating the estrous cycle, our data suggest that some caution might be taken in deciding whether and when to perform brain surgery in women. It might also be appropriate to ask whether the state of estrous should be directly manipulated to produce the least severe side effects following neurosurgery. At present, only more research on this important, but virtually unexplored, topic can answer these questions.

Enhancing the Recovery From Brain Damage

We have now seen that a number of different examples of the outcome of injuries to the central nervous system follow a specific progression of events that can result in either dramatic functional recovery or severe and often permanent impairments. In each individual case of brain injury, the prognosis for recovery will depend upon the specific historical and contextual factors affecting the organism at the time of the injury or onset of disease. Obviously, the question of where the injury occurs will be important in determining symptomatology. But equally as important will be the question of how the damage has occurred and what the functional state of the nervous system is at the time of the injury. The influence of the injury on the remaining CNS determines the type and severity of the symptoms that will be seen.

As I discussed in previously published work (Finger & Stein, 1982), Jackson, one of the founders of modern neurology, was very aware of the importance of the condition of the brain at the time of injury in determining functional outcome. For example, he stated, "One advantage of considering numerous maladies as dissolutions is that in doing so we are obliged in each case to deal with the diseased part as a flaw in the whole nervous system; we thus have to take into account the undamaged remainder and the evolution still going on in it" (Taylor, 1898/1958, p. 422). In other words, after an injury, the remaining nervous system should be considered as a new, reorganized structure and not just as a structure minus one part. In my view, the symptoms that follow brain damage do not stem from the missing or damaged part, but rather from the organism's attempt to adapt, cope, and survive.

Depending on conditions, symptoms may be severe or mild and recovery may be rapid, or prolonged, or simply not occur (consider serial versus one-stage lesions, for example). Describing and cataloging deficits has been useful in developing theories of localization of function, the importance of cerebral asymmetries, and of how memory and cognition may work. However, for the victims of brain damage, such theories are of small comfort, especially if they lead to the conclusion that the prognosis for their eventual recovery is hopeless and that there is no satisfactory treatment available to them. As I mentioned earlier, because it has been the prevailing paradigm, the pessimism inherent in the localization doctrine has probably been an important factor in blocking a major commitment to research in the development of effective treatments for brain injury, until very recently. This is not an insignificant problem when one considers that in the United States alone, over 500,000 people each year fall victim to brain damage. It is worth noting that, at the present time, there is no clinically effective treatment for brain (or spinal cord) injury, despite the tremendous economic and social costs to the nation. However, there are now several lines of very promising research that may offer new hope for repair of nervous system injuries. There are already a number of reviews available (Nieto-Sampedro & Cotman, 1985; Dalyrimple-Alford & Kelche, 1985; Earle, 1987; Feeney & Sutton, 1987; Marshall, 1984; Stein & Sabel, in press) that describe current research so I will present only a few examples to highlight what is being done directly to promote behavioral recovery from brain injury.[2]

One of the most exciting and provocative areas of research in promoting behavioral recovery from brain damage concerns the use of fetal brain tissue transplants directly into the damaged nervous system of an adult host. Although such transplant experiments were done even before the turn of the century (Thompson, 1890), they were generally not well received and they were more concerned with whether such grafts could simply survive than whether or not they had any benefit for the organism. It is really only within the last ten years that serious attention has been paid to the question of whether xenografts (i.e., tissue taken from a donor) could successfully ameliorate the deficits caused by traumatic brain injury or other forms of neuronal loss.

One of the first contemporary reports demonstrating that embryonic brain tissue transplants could enhance learning ability in brain-damaged rats came from Dunnett and his colleagues in Cambridge, England (Dunnett, Low, Iversen, Stenevi, & Bjorklund, 1982). Dunnett et al. first made bilateral lesions of the fimbria-fornix, the band of fibers that make up the primary connections of the hippocampal formation with other parts of the brain. Bilateral fimbria-fornix lesions alone usually result in disruptions of maze learning ability requiring spatial or working memory.

Groups of brain-damaged rats were given either solid grafts of embryonic septal tissue or suspensions of septal cells taken from 15–17-

[2]It is interesting to note that even though there is increasing interest in neural plasticity and the way it can be experimentally (and clinically) manipulated, there is very little concern with whether such plasticity has beneficial or maladaptive consequences for the organism. For example, Seil, Herbert, and Carlson (1987) is dedicated to "neural regeneration." Of the forty chapters in this volume, only one examines functional recovery using single-cell electrophysiological recording techniques. In Gilad, Gorio, and Kreutzberg (1986) only one of thirty-three chapters was concerned with any behavioral measure of recovery from CNS trauma.

Finally, within the last two years there were two major symposia on fetal brain tissue transplants in the mammalian CNS. In one sponsored by the New York Academy of Sciences (Azmitia & Bjorklund, 1987), there were only 5 out of 42 papers assessing the functional aspects of the tissue transplants. In the more recent Schmitt Symposium held at the University of Rochester in July, 1987, only ten percent of the speakers presented data having any bearing on whether the transplants promoted functional recovery, had no effect, or were potentially detrimental. This informal survey highlights two important facts: (a) the neurosciences in general are not really concerned with the behavioral aspects of recovery and, even when the studies are ostensibly directed towards remediation of brain and spinal cord injury, there are rarely careful and detailed functional assessments designed to determine whether the experimental manipulations do anything (good or bad) for the organism; and (b) there is an exciting and important opportunity for experimental psychologists to play a role in helping neuroscience researchers to recognize that the brain is something more than a convenient colony of individual neurons available for increasingly more in vitro and in vivo molecular assays that are unrelated to functional consequences for the behaving organism.

day-old embryos. The septal tissue grafts were chosen to restore cholinergic stimulation. In addition, one group of brain-damaged animals received grafts of E16-E17 grafts of locus coeruleus tissue to provide adrenergic input. The performance of the surgical groups was then compared to intact controls or lesion-alone animals, and all rats were allowed a 7-month postoperative recovery period to allow for sufficient transplant growth.

In Dunnett et al.'s hands, the normal rats were easily able to learn a rewarded alternation task in a T-maze, although the brain-damaged group remained very impaired. The animals with septal grafts showed significant improvement in learning, but this was not the case with the locus coeruleus transplants. The grafts were not effective in reducing disturbances in spontaneous activity or spontaneous alternation. Subsequent histology revealed that the behavioral recovery correlated significantly with the ingrowth of acetylcholinesterase (AChE)-positive fibers from the grafts into the host brain. Dunnett et al.'s results were the first to demonstrate that neural grafting could reduce learning deficits in adult brain-damaged animals. Based on their anatomical and behavioral findings, the authors were led to the conclusion that cholinergic reinnervation growing from the transplant into the host may have been necessary to induce the functional recovery they observed.

Dunnett et al.'s findings were followed by a virtual explosion of anatomical and histological reports (see Azmitia & Bjorklund, 1987; Bjorklund & Stenevi, 1985; Gash & Sladek, in press, for comprehensive reviews of this subject), the majority of which demonstrated that fetal tissue can, indeed, form reciprocal neuronal connections with the host brain.

In my laboratory, we decided to extend Dunnett et al.'s work to an examination of whether learned deficits caused by bilateral aspiration of the frontal cortex in adult rats could be attenuated by grafts of embryonic frontal cortex tissue (E-19) directly into the zone of injury (Labbe, Firl, Mufson, & Stein, 1983). Our study differed from Dunnett et al.'s (and many others) in several important ways. First, we were examining recovery in spatial learning ability after frontal cortex rather than subcortical lesions. Second, and more importantly, we only waited 7 days after the grafts were placed into the host brain to begin training our animals in the T-maze situation. The reason for this was that we wanted to test the hypothesis that the recovery was not due to the re-formation of specific, anatomically appropriate connections between host and transplant tissue, but rather to transplant-induced stimulation or release of neurotrophic factors at the site of the injury. We reasoned that 7 days would be too short a period for substantial reinnervation between host and transplant tissue to occur.

Accordingly, we tested a normal control group, rats with lesions of the frontal cortex only, rats with lesions of the frontal cortex with grafts of embryonic frontal cortex, and rats with lesions of the frontal cortex with implants of E-21 cerebellum as an additional control. Our results showed that grafts of embryonic frontal cortex, but not cerebellum, significantly improved postoperative performance of spatial alternation learning. Figure 7 shows that although the animals with frontal cortex grafts were not as good in the task as intact animals, they learned in about half the number of trials required for the lesion-alone or cerebellum implant group; the latter being as impaired as the lesion-alone group. In this experiment, all of the frontal transplant grafts survived but none of the cerebellar grafts did so. As was the case with the Dunnett et al. experiment, we were able to show that there was some penetration of the graft by cholinergic fibers coming from the host brain, but they were very sparse and they did not enter more than a few microns into

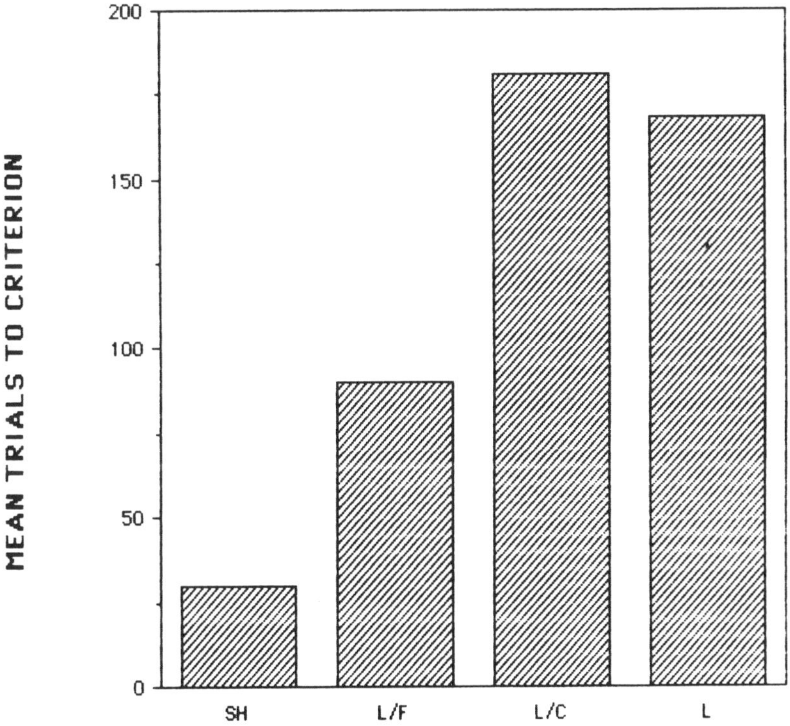

Figure 7. Average number of trials needed to reach criterion of 9/10 successively correct responses on spatial alternation in one testing session. SH is the sham-operated group, L/F is the group of rats with a frontal cortex lesion plus transplant of E21-22 frontal cortex, L/C is the group of rats with a frontal cortex lesion plus transplant of E21-22 cerebellum, and L is the group of rats with a frontal cortex lesion alone. Adapted from Labbe, Firl, Mufson, and Stein (1983) by permission.

the transplant (see Labbe et al., 1983, and Stein & Mufson, 1987, for more details). Although the transplants themselves had some characteristics similar to normal tissue (Stein & Mufson, 1987), the general morphology was quite atypical of the mature rodent frontal cortex.

Although there has been considerable discussion of the idea that functional recovery following neural grafts depends on reinnervation and restoration of specific connections in the damaged brain, our own data did not lend itself to this conclusion. Given the rapid behavioral recovery following grafting, and the fact that the reciprocal innervation between the host brain and the transplants was so slight (and abnormal), we became interested in the idea that transplants were promoting recovery by stimulating the production of nonspecific trophic factors rather than by forming new neural connections per se.

To test this notion as well as to determine if embryonic neural grafts could facilitate recovery of sensory impairments, we decided to study transplant-induced recovery from damage to the visual cortex in adult rats. The anatomy and connections of the occipital cortex have been studied in great detail, and bilateral lesions of this area often result in severe impairments on visual discrimination ability. If specificity of neuronal connections is critical in visual function, we reasoned that grafts of embryonic frontal cortex into the zone of injury would have no effect on recovery of any visual performance after occipital injury. In contrast, implants of fetal occipital cortex should facilitate recovery because the appropriate "visual" neurons would be grafted into the zone of injury.

In this experiment (Stein, Labbe, Attella, & Rakowsky, 1985), we tested a control group of adult rats that was sham-operated, a group with occipital cortex lesions alone, a group with lesions with grafts of fetal occipital cortex (E-18 or 19), and a group with lesions with grafts of fetal frontal cortex. Behavioral testing on simple brightness discrimination followed by pattern discrimination learning began two weeks after transplant surgery had been completed.

Our results were only partially successful; nonetheless, the data provided some interesting suggestions about the mechanisms underlying transplant-induced functional recovery. First, we were able to demonstrate that the grafts of E19 frontal cortex did enhance postoperative recovery of the brightness discrimination task, although the animals were not as good as intact controls. Surprisingly, the grafts of embryonic occipital cortex had no effect; animals with this tissue implanted into the damaged visual area were as impaired as the lesion-alone controls. On the pattern discrimination problem, neither frontal nor occipital neural grafts were successful in promoting functional recovery. Figure 8 summarizes these results.

Our histological analyses showed that both types of embryonic tissue survived and grew in the host cortex, so the failure of the occipital tissue to enhance recovery was not due to its lack of structural viability.

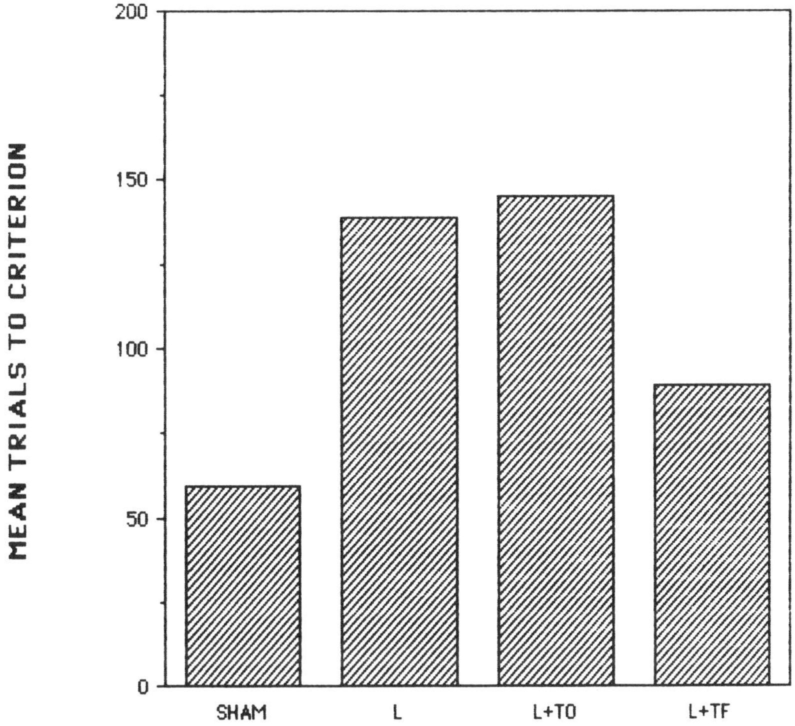

Figure 8. Mean trials to criterion on a brightness discrimination learning task in rats with lesions of the visual cortex given embryonic brain tissue transplants of frontal or occipital cortex. L is the lesion alone group, L + TO is the group with a lesion followed by a transplant of the fetal occipital cortex, and L + TF is the group with a lesion followed by transplant of fetal frontal cortex. Adapted from Stein, Labbe, Attella, and Rakowsky (1985) by permission.

In some of the animals we also injected the enzyme marker horseradish peroxidase (HRP), directly into the transplants. This substance can be transported retrogradely from axon terminals to the cell body and thus can be used to "label" neurons from the host tissue whose axons entered into the transplants.

Neither type of transplant tissue showed any retrograde labelling (see Stein, Labbe, Firl, & Mufston, 1985, for details) of host cortex or lateral geniculate body (LGN, the thalamic nucleus that projects to visual cortex). When, in a few cases, the HRP leaked from the transplant into the host cortex, some labelling was seen in the LGN. This told us that the failure to obtain labelling of neurons was not a failure of the technique per se, but rather was due to the fact that the transplants were not forming neural connections with the host brain. Yet, despite the lack of connectivity, there was some functional recovery.

This experiment addressed two important points. First, that limited functional recovery could be induced by the transplantation of tissue that was not homologous with the site of injury;[3] improvement was obtained with embryonic frontal grafts into the visual cortex. Second, our evidence suggested that specific (homotypic) connections between the host and transplant tissue are not essential for recovery, at least with respect to improvement in brightness discrimination. The clues were there, but we needed further experiments to pin down our growing suspicion that, at least in some instances of transplant-induced functional recovery, specific reinnervation was not the mediating factor.

A third experiment provided more indirect support for our tentative hypothesis that neurotrophic factors secreted by the transplant, or stimulated in the host brain by the presence of the transplant, were directly involved in promoting recovery from brain damage. This experiment was actually designed to study the question of how long after an injury transplants could be made and still facilitate recovery from brain damage.[4] However, the results we obtained had direct bearing on the issue of how grafts might mediate behavioral recovery (Stein, Palatucci, Kahn, & Labbe, 1988).

Because of the consistent success of the frontal transplants in enhancing recovery from frontal cortex injury, we decided to repeat the experiment but with varying delays between the initial frontal cortex lesions and the implantation of the fetal tissue. Thus, groups of mature rats with bilateral frontal cortex injuries received transplants of E-19 frontal cortex at 7, 14, 30, and 60 days after the initial injury. No special handling or training was given prior to surgery or during the interval between the lesions and the insertion of the grafts into the zone of injury. After all surgery had been completed (lesion and transplants), the animals were trained to learn the spatial alternation task used previously. Figure 9 summarizes the results of this experiment.

In looking at the long delays first (30 to 60 days), it is clear that the rats with delayed transplants were as impaired as their lesion-alone counterparts; no recovery of function was observed on any of the measures we employed. In contrast, the rats with transplants made at 14 days after injury or at 7 days postsurgically showed the typical, improved performance we noted in our previous work (Labbe et al., 1983).

[3]This same type of finding has now been demonstrated with transplants of autologous blocks of adrenal medulla directly into the brains of patients with Parkinson's disease. There are still many controversial issues surrounding this technique, although clinicians are reporting significant amelioration of the symptoms of the disorder (see Azmitia & Bjorklund, 1987, for recent reports).

[4]From a clinical perspective, it is important to know whether there is a limited period after injury during which transplants (or any other pharmacotherapy) could be effective. Thus, early after injury, transplants might enhance the rate of recovery, but could have no effect when placed in the brain weeks or months after the initial trauma had occurred.

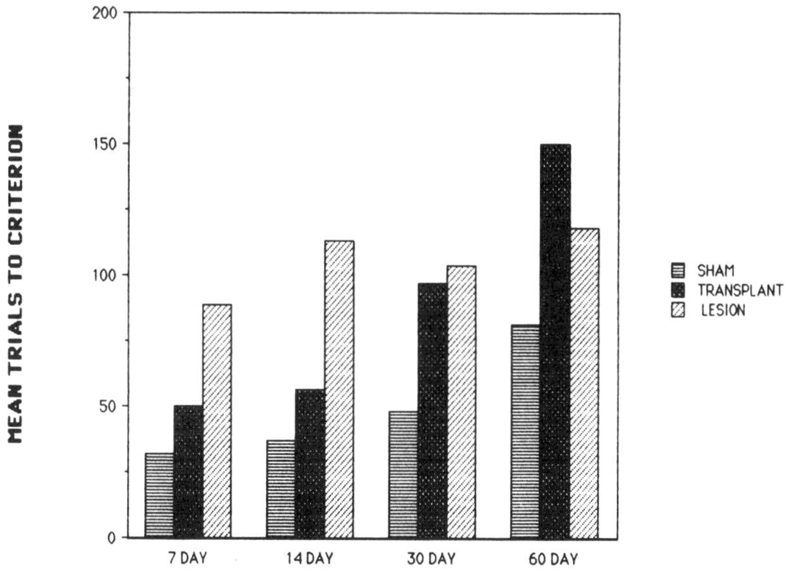

Figure 9. Trials to criterion on a spatial alternation task in adult rats with frontal cortex lesions given embryonic brain tissue transplants 7, 14, 30, or 60 days after receiving bilateral frontal cortex injuries. Adapted from Stein, Palatucci, Kahn, and Labbe (1988) by permission.

After all behavioral testing was completed, the rats were killed and their brains taken for histological examination. Based on our finding that the rats with postinjury transplants at 30 or 60 days had hardly any viable transplant tissue in the zone of injury, it was not surprising that these two groups evidenced no behavioral recovery on the learning task. We were surprised, however, to learn that the 14-day delay group also had only one or two viable transplants, yet this group's postoperative performance was, on average, as good or better than the rats with transplants made 7 days after the injury. It should once again be remembered that animals began behavioral testing only a few days after the grafts were introduced, and recovery was observed prior to the time that extensive regenerative phenomena could occur (see Stein et al., 1988, for a detailed discussion).

Based on these data, we became even more convinced that, at least insofar as recovery from frontal cortex injury is concerned, specific neural connections between host and transplant tissue were not essential. The argument that specific neuronal "reconnections" are not required for some kinds of cognitive recovery becomes more compelling, but the evidence could still be considered "indirect."

What would be the best test of the hypothesis that fetal brain tissue transplants mediate recovery by inducing, in one way or another, the release of neurotrophic or neuronal survival factors at the site of the injury? We reasoned that the most direct examination of whether the transplants are necessary to maintain functional recovery, would be to remove them after observing an initial effect and then retest the subjects on a new task.

This experiment essentially consisted of four groups of adult, male animals. Three of the groups (10 rats per group) received bilateral removals of the medial frontal cortex and one served as a sham-operated control. Two of the groups with lesions received transplants of E-19 frontal cortex directly into the zone of injury 7 days after the lesions were created. The remaining group with lesions received no further treatments.

When all surgery was completed, the animals began testing on the "standard" spatial alternation task. The animals with transplants tended to perform better than the lesion-alone rats, but not as consistently as in previous work. In addition, they were not as good as intact rats, which was as we expected.

After the spatial alternation learning was completed, the animals underwent a second surgery. Ten animals with transplants had them removed under visual guidance and the remaining brain-damaged rats had sham surgeries to control for bleeding, anesthetic, stress, and so forth. Within one week of this surgery, all of the rats began testing on a spatial navigation task in a water maze (Morris, 1981). Basically this task requires rats to locate a platform submerged in milky-colored water by using distal room cues to locate where the platform is in the tank. The time it takes to locate the platform and the distance swum in the water maze are the dependent variables we used to assess recovery. This task has certain advantages in that no deprivation is required to motivate the rats, and most animals with frontal lesions can eventually learn the task with repeated testing.

Looking at mean swimming distance over twenty trials in the water maze, it was clear that rats with lesions alone were more impaired than their counterparts with transplants intact or removed just prior to testing (see Figure 10). In fact, in the absence of the transplants, the rats were able to perform as well as the intact control rats.

Our results can be taken to suggest that transplants of embryonic brain tissue into damaged adult hosts may be sufficient to induce functional recovery but they are not necessary to maintain it. Once recovery of learned performance has occurred, the transplants may be removed without return of the initial deficit. Under these circumstances it is hard to argue that transplants induce recovery by restoration and maintenance of neuronal connections. The hypothesis that transplants may act by induction of substances that nourish remaining brain tissue becomes more tenable and interesting. We are currently reexamining the question in animals with occipital lesions given transplants of embryonic frontal cortex into the zone of injury.

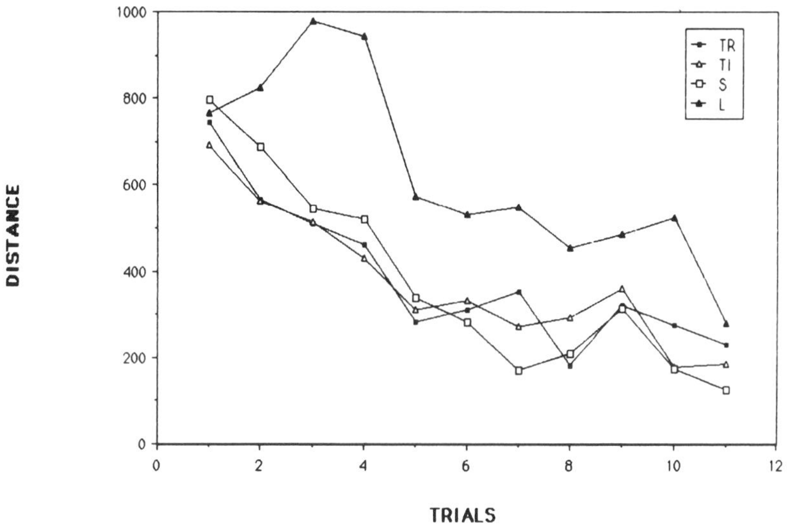

Figure 10. Distance required to find a submerged platform in a spatial navigation task in rats with transplants intact or with transplants removed just prior to testing. The groups with transplants were compared to lesion-alone and sham-operated controls. TR is the group with transplants removed, TI is the group with transplants intact, S is the sham-operated group, and L is the group with lesions alone.

One final (and unpublished) experiment from our laboratory provided the proof we needed to confirm our idea. My colleagues and I (Jorgenson, Labbe, & Stein, 1988) began to examine whether transplants of embryonic tissue could induce the production of diffusible trophic factors involved in neuronal guidance and survival (e.g., see Nieto-Sampedro & Cotman, 1985). One class of factors is known as neuronal cellular adhesion molecules (NCAM). NCAM and other markers of synaptic growth, such as D1 and D3 protein, are found throughout the central nervous system and specific antigens have been used to identify the presence and levels of these proteins in the brain.

To study the role of transplants on NCAM trophic factors, we created unilateral lesions of the frontal cortex and then implanted E-19 frontal tissue into the wound area 7 days later. Another group was given unilateral frontal cortex injury with no further treatment and a third group served as an intact control.

Twenty-seven days later, we took samples of transplant tissue, host brain tissue immediately adjacent to the transplant or to the lesion itself, and samples of host brain tissue in the homologous area of the contralateral, intact cortex. The samples of brain tissue were then subjected to immunoelectrophoresis in order to assay for amounts of NCAM and D3 protein at the sites we selected.

Our results were statistically significant and bear mentioning here. First of all, the lesion itself resulted in a clear decrease in NCAM and D3 protein in brain tissue adjacent to the injury, however, the animals with transplants had higher levels of NCAM in tissue near the damaged site. The same findings were generally true for the NCAM levels in the contralateral intact hemisphere; lesion-alone animals had lower levels on NCAM, whereas rats with transplants were within normal titers. The effect the transplants had on D3 protein was even greater; the levels of this protein were very elevated in the tissue contralateral to the lesion in comparison to lesion-alone rats.

Our results may be the first to demonstrate that brain lesions and transplants alter the production of neurotrophic factors like NCAM's not only in tissue near the injury, but even in tissue contralateral to the damaged site. Under these circumstances it becomes increasingly hard to argue that transplants need exert their beneficial effects by reestablishing neuronal connections with the host brain.

The series of studies we have conducted help to make the case for a more generalized, beneficial effect of transplants whereby they act to stimulate the production of "survival factors" in the host brain itself, rather than by forming new point-to-point connections. Although there may very well be circumstances in which transplant-induced recovery depends upon only specific neuronal connectivity, we have yet to see where they are essential in our experiments. I believe that this is why it is important to provide functional assessments in grafting experiments. One cannot assume that because transplants grow in the brain, or form synapses, that they are necessarily good for the organism. In fact, in some cases, excessive growth of transplants caused by hormonal alterations can lead to increased behavioral deficits in female rats with frontal cortex lesions (B. Kolb, personal communication, January, 1987).

This is not just a minor experimental point at stake here. Given all the attention to recent transplant surgery for treatment of Parkinson's disease in humans, it is clear that there are many critical technical and moral questions that need to be answered. If substances such as trophic factors rather than neural connections are the important variable, it might then be possible to administer such agents directly to the site of injury or even through systemic injections.

As a case in point, there is increasing evidence that transplants of nonneural tissue can be effective in promoting recovery from brain damage. The most dramatic cases are the clinical studies in which patients have received grafts of their own adrenal medullas into the dorsal caudate nucleus (see Gash & Sladek, in press, for details). Great symptomatic relief has been reported for these patients and despite great interest in the technique by the media and practicing neurosurgeons, there are still many unresolved questions concerning routine employment of the procedure (see also Azmitia & Bjorklund, 1987, for a discussion).

In the laboratory, there is now evidence that grafts of cultured glial cells can also induce recovery from frontal cortex injuries. Recently, Kesslak, Nieto-Sampedro, Globus, and Cotman (1986) cultured embryonic reactive astrocytes (they are one form of glial cells that occur in response to brain injury) and grafted them directly into rats that had previously received bilateral lesions of the frontal cortex. The animals were behaviorally tested in the spatial alternation paradigm identical to the one that we have used in many of our experiments.

Kesslak et al.'s results were quite dramatic. The adult rats who had received the glial grafts showed significant recovery of spatial alternation behavior in comparison to counterparts who had only pure gelfoam inserted into the wound area. The glial transplants were just as effective as solid grafts of embryonic frontal cortex.

On the one hand Kesslak et al. replicated our embryonic frontal cortex transplant data, and on the other, they extended and confirmed our hypothesis that neurotrophic factors and not specific neural connections are sufficient to promote functional recovery from brain damage. It is interesting to note in this context that glial cells are capable of secreting neurotrophic factors once damage to the brain has occurred (Barde, Lindsay, Monard, & Thonen, 1978; Lindsay, 1979). In addition, the brain itself responds to focal injury by the endogenous production of trophic factors, which, when isolated, can sustain colonies of neurons in culture. The amount of trophic factor present after injury decreases as one gets further from the site of the damage and also decreases over time. The highest amount of trophic titer occurs within 10 days after injury, and then begins to decline gradually for another 8–10 days (Nieto-Sampedro & Cotman, 1985).

The presence of trophic factors may do a number of things to promote functional recovery. First, they can "neutralize" the effects of injury-induced, toxic by-products that could destroy living, but injured, neurons. Second, they might act by sustaining neurons that might ordinarily die by retrograde degeneration. Third, trophic substances could act to prevent the injury-induced withdrawal of dendrites and synapses from their appropriate target sites. Fourth, trophic factors could also play a role in angiogenesis—the reestablishment of better microcirculation needed to provide nourishment to healthy as well as damaged neurons.

Based on these data, it is becoming more apparent that there may be two (or more) models of recovery from brain damage that need to be given serious attention. One is the more traditional anatomical model that assumes that reestablishment or replacement of neural connections is the key to functional recovery. In this context then, transplants are seen as a critical, clinical tool in restoring healthy function to damaged nervous systems. The second model is also deserving of attention even though it may be somewhat more controversial. This model assumes that specific reconnections are not essential for the induction or maintenance of functional recovery from CNS injuries. Under these assumptions a pharmacological approach to the treatment of brain and spinal cord injury becomes theoretically and practically more feasible. If a class of substances could be identified and could be systemically or intracerebrally administered with subsequent functional recovery, then the need for fetal tissue transplants might be reduced.

For a number of years, my colleagues and I have been concerned with finding and developing effective pharmacological treatments for brain injury. We began our initial series of investigations using direct, intracerebral injections of nerve growth factor (NGF) into the site of the injury itself (see Stein, 1981, for more detailed review). NGF was one of the first trophic (growth and survival-promoting) substances to be identified by Levi-Montalcini and her colleagues (Levi-Montalcini & Callissano, 1979), so it was logical to see if it would have ameliorative effects when injected directly into the brain. These early experiments met with some degree of incredulity because only 10 years ago, it was thought that NGF would have no central nervous system effects, because attempts to localize receptors for NGF in brain tissue had been unsuccessful, even though Bjorklund and his colleagues (Bjorklund & Stenevi, 1972) were the first to show that NGF injections into the brain could cause sprouting of noradrenergic fibers.

Bjorklund's work led us to try intracerebral NGF injections to promote behavioral recovery from caudate nucleus lesions in adult rats. In this experiment (Hart, Chaimas, Moore, & Stein, 1978), we showed that a single injection of NGF given within moments of the caudate injury could enhance postinjury performance of a spatial reversal learning task. This was one of the first reported demonstrations that NGF treatment could produce recovery of a complex learned behavior following brain injury. In subsequent research with colleagues in France (Eclancher, Ramirez, & Stein, 1985; Stein, 1981; Will & Stein, 1981), we were able to demonstrate that single intracerebral injections of NGF, if administered at the time of injury, could partially or fully enhance long-term recovery from severe, bilateral brain damage.

In all of the histological follow-ups to our work, we were never able to identify instances of specific neuronal sprouting mediating the behavioral recovery that we observed. More recent evidence from other laboratories (Fisher et al., 1987; Hefti, 1986; Hefti, Dravid, & Hartikka, 1984) does suggest, however, that NGF treatments enhance AChE levels and promote survival of cholinergic septal neurons. This finding has been taken as rather good, indirect evidence that the protein enhances synaptic proliferation (sprouting) in response to neural injury.

The key issue here is that recovery can be induced, not just by neuronal replacement, as is thought to be the case with transplants, but by enhancing the levels of neurotrophic activity in the damaged brain. Despite the fact that NGF has beneficial effects, its potential as a clinical treatment itself suffers from several handicaps. First, it must be extracted from animal tissue (it has not yet been synthesized), and it is only available in very small quantities. Second, it is a relatively large molecule that apparently does not cross the blood–brain barrier, and therefore it has to be given intracerebrally or intraventricularly. Thus, a complex and more dangerous surgical maneuver than simple intramuscular injection is required for clinical practice.

Under the circumstances it seemed appropriate to ask if other substances could be administered by systemic injection to induce recovery from brain damage. One such class of substances that we have been recently using are the gangliosides. Gangliosides are glycosphingolipids that come in many different species and are important constituents of cell membranes. High levels of gangliosides are found in the brain, particularly during development. These substances appear to play an important role in neuronal membrane function and repair, and disorders in ganglioside storage and utilization can result in very severe mental retardation (e.g., Tay-Sachs disease).

Gangliosides have been shown to play a synergistic role in enhancing neuronal growth in vitro when they are combined with neurotrophic factors such as NGF (Leon et al., 1984; Roisen, Bartfeld, Nagel, & York, 1981). We became interested in the use of gangliosides after learning that they had been successfully employed to encourage recovery from lesions of the nigrostriatal pathway in adult rats (Toffano et al., 1984). In addition, Karpiak (1983) was able to show that repeated injections of mixed gangliosides could improve learning ability after unilateral lesions of the entorhinal cortex. In addition, Karpiak and Mahadik (1984) and Karpiak (1986) found that ganglioside treatments could significantly reduce postischemic mortality by as much as 50% in gerbils that had middle cerebral artery occlusions.

For these reasons, we began to examine whether treatment with GM1 ganglioside could enhance recovery of function following bilateral injury to CNS structures implicated in complex spatial learning and motor performance. Because we had previously shown that intracerebral injections of NGF could enhance recovery from spatial reversal learning in rats with lesions of the caudate nucleus, we decided to employ the same testing situation in caudate-damaged animals given two weeks of daily, intraperitoneal injections (i.p.) of GM1 ganglioside (Sabel, Slavin, & Stein, 1984).

As Figure 11 shows, rats with bilateral caudate lesions given repeated doses of GM1 were able to learn the spatial reversal task more rapidly than lesion counterparts given only i.p. injections of saline; however the GM1-treated rats did not perform as well as the completely intact controls. When the rats were retested about 50 days after reaching criterion, the animals given GM1 still retained the learned reversals significantly better than saline-treated control animals with similar lesions. The finding that recovery from very severe brain damage could be facilitated by GM1 corroborated Karpiak's earlier work. In addition,

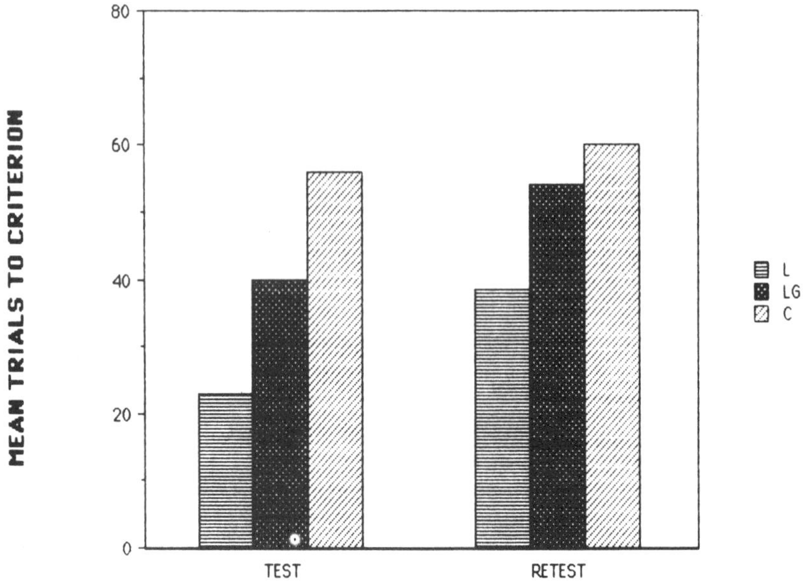

Figure 11. Spatial reversal performance in adult rats with bilateral lesions of the caudate nucleus given repeated, systemic injections of GM1 ganglioside or saline solution. The figure on the right shows retention performance 50 days after reaching the initial learning criterion. L is the lesions alone group, LG is the group with lesions followed by chronic injections of GM1 gangliosides, and C is the control group—no lesions, no injections. Adapted from Sabel, Slavin, and Stein (1984) by permission.

it showed that the recovery itself was long-lasting and not just due to temporary "intoxication" caused by the repeated administration of the substance.

In subsequent research, we partially transected the nigrostriatal pathway on one side of the brain of adult rats and used this preparation to study stereotyped rotation in response to amphetamine injections (Sabel, Dunbar, & Stein, 1984). Animals with this type of lesion show an initial, ipsiversive rotation which gradually disappears, but which can be reinstated by an injection of amphetamine. The underlying model assumes that the rotation is due to an imbalance in dopamine caused by deafferentation of the caudate nucleus following transection of the nigrostriatal pathway. It is further assumed that if GM1 could enhance neuronal regeneration or even spare damaged neurons from further destruction or death, the dopamine imbalance (between intact and damaged side of the brain) would be lessened and there would be less stereotyped rotation in response to amphetamine (see Feeney & Sutton, 1987, for more detailed review).

Our behavioral experiments (Sabel, Dunbar, et al., 1984) supported the hypothesis that GM1 could improve recovery following nigrostriatal lesions. Rats given GM1 showed significantly less rotations to amphetamine intoxication within two days after the treatments were initiated. Apomorphine-induced rotations by GM1 treatments could be reduced as late as 42 days after the hemitransections.

What do these data imply? First, that the treatments with GM1 can facilitate recovery from brain damage early after the damage has been inflicted and at later times as well. Second, pharmacological treatment can be effective in recovery without additional surgical manipulations such as transplants or intracerebral administration of a neurotrophic substance.

Although the behavioral recovery was evident, the underlying anatomical or physiological mechanisms remained to be clarified. Some workers had thought that gangliosides could prevent retrograde degeneration of dopaminergic fibers that project to the striatum (Agnati et al., 1983), whereas others argued that injury-induced cell loss was due to gangliosides' ability to reduce brain edema or loss of sodium-potassium-ATPase (Karpiak, 1986; Karpiak & Mahadik, 1984). In general, the thought was that the treatments somehow spare neurons that would ordinarily die following the primary or secondary consequences of the CNS trauma.

We tested this notion directly in rats with nigrostriatal lesions by using the HRP enzyme to label neurons projecting from the substantia nigra to the caudate nucleus. HRP is transported retrogradely from neuron terminals to the cell body so we reasoned that if GM1 supported the survival of injured nigral neurons, more of them would be labelled by the HRP than animals treated with saline. By 5–7 days after treatment, rats given GM1 gangliosides showed more HRP-labelling of nigral neurons than saline-treated counterparts. Our results demonstrated that although there is considerable neuronal loss following these massive lesions, GM1 does appear to spare neurons that might ordinarily die as a result of the injury. The enhanced neuronal sparing might then play a role in reducing the asymmetry in catecholamine levels responsible for the ipsiversive rotation typically observed after this type of lesion.

In this case, survival of neurons, rather than new sprouting, may have been the mechanism involved in mediating the behavioral recovery. Indeed, we cannot always assume that sprouting is necessary or beneficial to the recovery process. For example, in a recent series of studies, Fass and Ramirez (1984) gave GM1 to rats with bilateral entorhinal cortex lesions (EC) and then studied unlearned hyperactivity responses in an open-field situation. The treatments reduced the hyperactivity and enabled the rats to habituate to novelty more readily than saline-treated control rats. Fass and Ramirez also employed histochemical techniques to examine whether cholinergic fibers from the septum to hippocampus had sprouted into the deafferented dentate gyrus of the hippocampus (the primary afferents come from the EC, which had been damaged by the lesions).

Instead of observing enhanced sprouting, these workers found that the enzyme markers for ACh were significantly reduced. This was taken to mean that the ganglioside treatments enhanced behavioral recovery by reducing septodentate sprouting (refer to Earle, 1987, for a discussion of this question).

These findings should not be discouraging to those concerned with promoting functional recovery from brain injury. The data from Fass and Ramirez and our own work simply show that there may be a variety of neural mechanisms underlying recovery from brain damage. Indeed, in some (or all) areas of the brain, biochemical alterations following CNS injury may be more critical for recovery than the sprouting of new fiber paths or the survival of neurons that would ordinarily die. For example, Feeney and his students have shown dramatic instances of almost immediate behavioral recovery in rats and cats with cortical lesions of the visual or motor areas following i.p. injections of amphetamine (see Feeney & Sutton, 1987, for detailed review). Here, the recovery is too rapid to be accounted for in terms of regenerative phenomena and instead may be due to the increased levels of neurotransmitters (DA) caused by the amphetamine intoxication. Recovery is also maintained long after treatments have terminated—if the animals are given appropriate behavioral experience (e.g., visual stimulation, permitted to move about, etc.).

In conclusion, the main point I wish to stress here is that although intensive research on pharmacologically induced recovery from brain injury is really in its infancy and more needs to be accomplished, it now seems likely that we may soon have effective clinical treatments available to patients with brain and spinal injuries. The data and experiments that I have reviewed in this chapter also can be taken to demonstrate that recovery itself is, by no means, a monolithic process. Instead, we researchers will have to recognize that there are many different mechanisms involved and that no one approach to the problem, no matter how elegant, may be sufficient to define how the processes occur.

It is becoming increasingly clear, however, that contextual and organismic factors must be appreciated in defining or describing what the outcome of brain injury will be. It is simply no longer sufficient to assume that damage to a given structure will always result in the same set of symptoms from one organism to the other, or that one treatment approach will be the best for all types of injury or when different areas are damaged. To proceed with our understanding of recovery mechanisms and to make more progress in developing treatments for brain and spinal cord injuries, a new paradigm will be required. For real progress to be made, we must begin to recognize that the context (organismic and environmental) in which the injury or trauma occurs will be a critical factor in determining the severity of the deficit as well as the prognosis for recovery and the appropriate treatments to be applied.

Those of us concerned with therapy and rehabilitation of the brain injured cannot expect to find a single, "magic bullet" that will "cure" brain damage. However, we can expect that combinations of biochemical, pharmacological, and environmental manipulations may lead us to discover new and long-lasting treatments for CNS trauma.

In the final analysis, I believe that both molecular and behavioral approaches to the study of functional recovery can make significant contributions to our understanding of brain organization. At the present time, emphasis is on the molecular techniques as being more "scientific" and more worthy of study, but this view will change as we begin to recognize that functional evaluation of organisms is critical to our understanding of how the brain repairs itself in a way that is both beneficial and adaptive to the organism.

References

Adametz, J. (1959). Rate of recovery of functioning in cats with rostral reticular lesions. *Journal of Neurosurgery*, *16*, 85–98.

Ades, H. W. (1946). Effects of extirpation of parastriate cortex in learned visual discrimination in monkeys. *Journal of Neuropathology and Experimental Neurology*, *5*, 60–66.

Agnati, L. G., Fuxe, K., Calza, L., Benfenati, F., Cavicchioli, L., Toffano, G., & Goldstein, M. (1983). Gangliosides increase the survival of lesioned nigral dopamine neurons and favor the recovery of dopaminergic synaptic function in stratum of rats by collateral sprouting. *Acta Physiologica Scandinavica*, *119*, 347–363.

Alstermark, B., Lundberg., A., Pettersson, L. G., Tantisira, A., & Walkowska, M. (1987). Recovery after serial lesions of defined pathways in cats. *Neuroscience*, *22* (Suppl. 54), Abstract.

Attella, M., Nattinville, A., & Stein, D. G. (1987). Hormonal state affects recovery from frontal cortex lesions in adult female rats. *Behavioral and Neural Biology*, *48*, 352–367.

Azmitia, E. C., & Bjorklund, A. (Eds.). (1987). Cell and tissue transplantation into the adult brain. *Annals of the New York Academy of Science*, *495*.

Barbas, H., & Spear, P. (1976). Effects of serial unilateral and serial bilateral visual cortex lesions on brightness discrimination relearning in rats. *Journal of Comparative and Physiological Psychology*, *90*, 279–292.

Barde, Y. A., Lindsay, R. M., Monard, D., & Thonen, H. (1978). New factor released by cultured glioma cells supporting survival and growth of sensory neurons. *Nature* (London), *274*, 818.

Behan, P., & Geschwind, N. (1985). Dyslexia, congenital anomalies, and immune disorders: The role of the fetal environment. *Annals of the New York Academy of Science*, *457*, 13–18.

Bjorklund, A., & Stenevi, U. (1972). Nerve growth factor: Stimulation of regenerative growth of central noradrenergic neurons. *Science*, *175*, 1251–1253.

Bjorklund, A., & Stenevi, U. (Eds.). (1985). *Neural grafting in the mammalian CNS*. Amsterdam: Elsevier.

Broverman, D. E., Klaiber, E., Kobiash, Y., & Vogel, W. (1968). Roles of activation and inhibition in sex differences in cognitive abilities. *Psychological Review, 75*, 23–50.

Butters, N., Rosen, J. J., & Stein, D. G. (1974). Recovery of behavioral functions after sequential ablation of the frontal lobes of monkeys. In D. G. Stein, J. J. Rosen, & N. Butters (Eds.), *Plasticity and recovery of function in the central nervous system* (pp. 429–466). New York: Academic Press.

Dalyrimple-Alford, J. D., & Kelche, C. (1985). Behavioral effects of pre-operative–post-operative differential housing in rats with brain lesions: A review. In B. E. Will, P. Schmitt, & J. D. Dalyrimple-Alford (Eds.), Brain plasticity, learning, and memory. *Advances in Behavioral Biology, 28*, 441–458.

Dunnett, S. B., Low, W. C., Iversen, S. D., Stenevi, U., & Bjorklund, A. (1982). Septal transplants restore maze learning in rats with fornix-fimbria lesions. *Brain Research, 251*, 335–348.

Earle, E. (1987). Lesion size and recovery of function: Some new perspectives. *Brain Research Reviews, 12*, 307–320.

Eclancher, F., Ramirez, J. J., & Stein, D. G. (1985). Neonatal brain damage and recovery: Intraventricular injection of NGF at time of injury alters performance of active avoidance. *Developmental Brain Research, 19*, 227–235.

Fass, B., & Ramirez, J. J. (1984). Effects of ganglioside treatments on lesion-induced behavioral impairment and sprouting in the CNS. *Journal of Neuroscience Research, 12*, 445–458.

Feeney, D. M., & Sutton, R. L. (1987). Pharmacotherapy for recovery of functions after brain injury. *CRC Critical Reviews in Neurobiology, 3*, 135–197.

Finger, S., Marshak, R. A., Cohen, M., Scheff, S., Trace, R., & Neimand, D. (1971). Effects of successive and simultaneous lesions of somatosensory cortex on tactile discrimination in the rat. *Journal of Comparative and Physiological Psychology, 77*, 221–227.

Finger, S., & Stein, D. G. (1982). *Brain damage and recovery: Research and clinical perspectives*. New York: Academic Press.

Finger, S., Walbran, B., & Stein, D. G. (1973). Brain damage and behavioral recovery: Serial lesion phenomena. *Brain Research, 63*, 1–18.

Fisher, W., Wictorin, K., Bjorklund, A., Williams, L. R., Varon, S., & Gage, F. H. (1987). Amelioration of cholinergic neuron atrophy and spatial memory impairment in aged rats by nerve growth factor. *Nature, 329*, 65–68.

Gash, D., & Sladek, J. (Eds.). (in press). *Transplantation into the CNS*. New York: Elsevier.

Gentile, A. M., Green, S., Nieburgs, A., Schmeltzer, W., & Stein, D. G. (1978). Disruption and recovery of locomotor and manipulatory behavior following cortical lesions in rats. *Behavioral Biology, 22*, 417–455.

Geschwind, N. (1985). Mechanisms of change after brain lesions. *Annals of the New York Academy of Science, 457*, 1–12.

Geschwind, N., & Behan, P. O. (1982). Left-handedness: Association with immune disease, migraine and developmental learning disorders. *Proceedings of the National Academy of Science*, (USA), *79*, 5097–5100.

Gilad, G. M., Gorio, A., & Kreutzberg, G. W. (Eds.). (1986). Processes of recovery from neural trauma. *Experimental Brain Research, Suppl. 13*. Berlin: Springer-Verlag.

Goldman, P. (1975). Age, sex and experience as related to the neural basis of cognitive development. In N. A. Buchwald & M. A. B. Brazier (Eds.), *Brain mechanisms in mental retardation* (pp. 379–392). New York: Academic Press.

Hart, T., Chaimas, N., Moore, R., & Stein, D. G. (1978). Effects of nerve growth factor on behavioral recovery following caudate nucleus lesions in rats. *Brain Research Bulletin, 3*, 245–250.

Hebb, D. O., & Williams, K. A. (1946). A method of rating animal intelligence. *Journal of General Psychology, 34*, 59–65.

Hefti, F. J. (1986). Nerve growth factor (NGF) promotes survival of septal cholinergic neurons after fimbrial transections. *Journal of Neuroscience, 6*, 2155–2162.

Hefti, F., Dravid, A., & Hartikka, J. (1984). Chronic intraventricular injections of nerve growth factor elevate hippocampal choline acetyltransferase activity in adult rats with partial septohippocampal lesions. *Brain Research, 293*, 305–311.

Jackson, J. H. (1879). On affection of speech from disease of the brain. *Brain, 2*, 323–356.

John, E. R., Tang, Y., Brill, A. B., Young, R., & Ono, K. (1986). Double-labelled metabolic maps of memory. *Science, 233*, 1167–1175.

Jorgenson, O. S., Labbe, R., & Stein, D. G. (1988). *Neuronal antigens as markers for a transplant medicated trophic effect on recovery from damage.* Manuscript submitted for publication.

Juraska, J. M. (1986). Sex differences in developmental plasticity of behavior and the brain. In W. T. Greenough & J. M. Juraska (Eds.), *Developmental neuropsychobiology* (pp. 409–422). Orlando: Academic Press.

Kandel, E., & Schwartz, J. H. (Eds.). (1981). *Principles of neuroscience.* New York: Elsevier.

Karpiak, S. E. (1983). Ganglioside treatment improves recovery of alternation behavior after unilateral entorhinal cortex lesion. *Experimental Neurology, 81*, 330–339.

Karpiak, S. E. (1986). Acute effects of gangliosides on CNS injury. In G. Tettamanti, R. W. Ledeen, K. Sandhoff, Y. Nagai, & G. Toffano (Eds.), *Gangliosides and neuronal plasticity* (pp. 407–414). Padova, Italy: Livinia Press.

Karpiak, S. E., & Mahadik, S. P. (1984). Reduction of cerebral edema with GM1 ganglioside. *Journal of Neuroscience Research, 12*, 485–492.

Kelche, C. R., & Will, B. (1978). Effets de l'environnement sur la restauration fonctionelle apres lesion hippocampiques chez des rats adultes. *Physiology and Behavior, 21*, 935–941.

Kesner, R. P., Fiedler, P., & Thomas, G. J. (1967). Function of the midbrain reticular formation in regulating level of activity and learning in rats. *Journal of Comparative and Physiological Psychology, 63*, 452–457.

Kesslak, J. P., Nieto-Sampedro, M., Globus, J., & Cotman, C. W. (1986). Transplants of purified astrocytes promote behavioral recovery after frontal cortex ablation. *Experimental Neurology, 92*, 377–390.

Kuhn, T. (1970). *The structure of scientific revolutions* (2nd ed.). Chicago: University of Chicago Press.

Labbe, R., Firl, A., Mufson, E., & Stein, D. G. (1983). Fetal brain transplants: Reduction of cognitive deficits in rats with frontal cortex lesions. *Science, 221*, 470–472.

Leon, A., Benugnu, D., Dal Toso, R., Presta, D., Facci, L., Giorgi, O., & Toffano, G. (1984). Dorsal root ganglia and nerve growth factor: A model for understanding the mechanism of GM1 effects on neuronal repair. *Journal of Neuroscience Research, 12*, 277–287.

Levi-Montalcini, R., & Callissano, P. (1979). The nerve growth factor. *Scientific American, 240*, 68–78.

Lindsay, R. M. (1979). Adult rat brain astrocytes support survival of both NGF-dependent and NGF-insensitive neurons. *Nature* (London), *282*, 80–82.

Markowitsch, H. J. (1984). Can amnesia be caused by damage of a single brain structure? *Cortex, 20*, 27–46.

Marshall, J. F. (1984). Brain function: Neural adaptations and recovery from injury. *Annual Review of Psychology, 35*, 277–308.

McGlone, J. (1978). Sex difference in functional brain asymmetry. *Cortex, 14*, 122–128.

Morris, R. (1981). Spatial localization does not require the presence of local cues. *Learning and Motivation, 12*, 239–260.

Nieto-Sampedro, M., & Cotman, C. W. (1985). Growth factor induction and temporal order in CNS repair. In C. W. Cotman (Ed.), *Synaptic plasticity* (pp. 407–455). New York: Guilford Press.

Ounstead, C., & Taylor, D. C. (Eds.). (1972). *Gender differences: Their ontogeny and significance.* London: Churchill.

Patrissi, G., & Stein, D.G. (1975). Temporal factors in recovery of function after brain damage. *Experimental Neurology, 47*, 470–480.

Riese, W. (1950). *Principles of neurology in the light of history and their present use.* New York: Nervous and Mental Disease Monographs.

Riese, W. (1977). Selected papers on the history of aphasia. *Neurolinguistics, 7*, 11.

Roisen, F. J., Bartfeld, H., Nagel, R., & York, G. (1981). Ganglioside stimulation of axonal sprouting in vitro. *Science, 214*, 577–578.

Rokeach, M. (1960). *The open and closed mind* (pp. 31–70). New York: Basic Books.

Sabel, B. A., Dunbar, G. L., & Stein, D. G. (1984). Gangliosides minimize behavioral deficits and enhance structural repair after brain injury. *Journal of Neuroscience Research, 12*, 429–443.

Sabel, B. A., Slavin, M., & Stein, D. G. (1984). GM1 ganglioside treatment facilitates behavioral recovery from bilateral brain damage. *Science, 225*, 340–342.

Scheff, S., Bernardo, L., & Cotman, C. W. (1977). Progressive brain damage accelerates axon sprouting in the adult rat. *Science, 197*, 795–797.

Schoenfeld, T. A., & Hamilton, L. W. (1977). Secondary brain changes following lesions: A new paradigm for lesion experimentation. *Physiology and Behavior, 18*, 951–967.

Schultze, M., & Stein, D. G. (1975). Recovery of function in the albino rat following either simultaneous or seriatum lesions of the caudate nucleus. *Experimental Neurology, 46*, 291–301.

Seil, F. J., Herbert, E., & Carlson, B. M. (Eds.). (1987). Neural regeneration. *Progress in Brain Research, 71*. Amsterdam: Elsevier.

Sherrington, C. S. (1906). *The integrative action of the nervous system.* New Haven: Yale University Press.

Squire, L. R. (1982). The neuropsychology of human memory. *Annual Review of Neuroscience, 5*, 242–273.

Squire, L. R. (1987). *Memory and brain* (134–148, 175–198). New York: Oxford University Press.

Stein, D. G. (1974). Some variables influencing recovery of function after central nervous system lesions in the rat. In D. G. Stein, J. J. Rosen, & N. Butters (Eds.), *Plasticity and recovery of function in the central nervous system* (pp. 373–428). New York: Academic Press.

Stein, D. G. (1981). Functional recovery from brain damage following treatment with nerve growth factor. In M. W. Van Hof & G. Mohn (Eds.), *Functional recovery from brain damage* (pp. 423–443). Amsterdam: Elsevier/North Holland Biomedical Press.

Stein, D. G., Labbe, R., Attella, M., & Rakowsky, H. (1985). Fetal brain transplants reduce visual deficits in adult rats with bilateral lesions of the occipital cortex. *Behavioral and Neural Biology*, *44*, 266–277.

Stein, D. G., Labbe, R., Firl, A., & Mufson, E. J. (1985). Behavioral recovery following implantation of neural tissue into mature rats with bilateral cortical lesions. In A. Bjorklund & U. Stenevi (Eds.), *Neural grafting in the CNS* (pp. 605–614). Amsterdam: Elsevier.

Stein, D. G., & Mufson, E. J. (1987). Morphological and behavioral characteristics of embryonic brain-tissue transplants in adult, brain-damaged subjects. In E. C. Azmitia & A. Bjorklund (Eds.), Cell and tissue transplantation into the adult brain. *Annals of the New York Academy of Science*, *495*, 444–472.

Stein, D. G., Palatucci, C., Kahn, D., & Labbe, R. (1988). Temporal factors influence recovery of function after embryonic tissue transplants in adult rats with frontal cortex lesions. *Behavioral Neuroscience*, *102*, 260–267.

Stein, D. G., Rosen, J. J., Graziadei, J., Mishkin, D., & Brink, J. J. (1969). Central nervous system: Recovery of function. *Science*, *166*, 528–530.

Stein, D. G., & Sabel, B. A. (Eds.). (in press). *Pharmacological approaches to the treatment of brain and spinal cord injury*. New York: Plenum Press.

Taylor, J. (Ed.). (1958). *Selected writings of J. H. Jackson* (422–443). New York: Basic Books. (Reprinted from Jackson, J. H. *Relations of difference divisions of the central nervous system to one another and to parts of the body*, 1898)

Thompson, R. F. (1986). The neurobiology of learning and memory. *Science*, *233*, 941–947.

Thompson, W. G. (1890). Successful brain grafting. *New York Medical Journal*, *51*, 701–702.

Toffano, G., Agnati, L. F., Fuxe, K., Aldino, C., Consolazione, A., Valenti, G., & Savoini, G. (1984). Effect of GM1 ganglioside treatment on the recovery of dopaminergic nigro-striatal neurons after different types of lesion. *Acta Physiologica Scandinavica*, *122*, 313–321.

Ulrich, R. (1984). View through a window may influence recovery from surgery. *Science*, *224*, 420–421.

Whitaker-Azmitia, P. M., Ramirez, A., Noreika, L., Gannon, P. J., & Azmitia, E. C. (1987). Onset and duration of astrocytic response to cells transplanted into the adult mammalian brain. In E. C. Azmitia & A. Bjorklund (Eds.), Cell and tissue transplantation into the adult brain. *Annals of the New York Academy of Science*, *495*, 10–23.

Will, B., & Stein, D. G. (1981). La recuperation apres lesion cerebrales. *Pour la recherche*, *43*, 66–77.

Zangwill, O. L. (1963). The cerebral localization of psychological function. *Advancement of Science*, *20*, 335–344.

RICHARD F. THOMPSON

BRAIN SUBSTRATES OF LEARNING AND MEMORY

Richard F. Thompson is Keck Professor of Psychology and Biological Sciences at the University of Southern California. Prior to this he was Bing Professor of Human Biology and professor of psychology at Stanford University, where he served as Chair of the Human Biology Program from 1980 to 1985. Previous positions include professor of psychobiology in the School of Biological Sciences at the University of California at Irvine, professor of psychology (Karl Lashley's chair) at Harvard University and professor of medical psychology and psychiatry at the University of Oregon Medical School. He received his BA degree at Reed College, his PhD in psychobiology at the University of Wisconsin, and did postdoctoral research in the Laboratory of Neurophysiology at the University of Wisconsin and in the Laboratory of Neurophysiology at the University of Goteborg in Sweden.

His area of research and scholarly interest is the broad field of psychobiology with a focus on the neurobiological substrates of learning and memory. He has written several texts, edited several books, and published over 200 research papers. Honors include the Distinguished Scientific Contribution Award of the American Psychological Association and a Research Scientist Career Award from the National Institute of Mental Health. He is a member of the Society of Experimental Psychologists and the National Academy of Sciences, Councillor of the Society for Neuroscience, Chair of the Psychonomic Society, and President of Division 6 of the American Psychological Association.

He has been involved in a wide range of scientific–administrative activities at the national level, including activities at the Assembly of Behavioral and Social Sciences of the National Research Council and at a Presidential Task Panel on Research in Mental Health, being Chair of the Board of Scientific Affairs of the American Psychological Association, Chair of the Committee on Animal Research and Experimentation of the American Psychological Association, Chair of the Psychology Section of the American Association for the Advancement of Science, and Chair of the Psychology Section of the National Academy of Sciences. He was previously Chief Editor of the journals *Physiological Psychology* and the *Journal of Comparative and Physiological Psychology*. He is currently Chief Editor of the journal *Behavioral Neuroscience*, Regional Editor of the journals *Physiology and Behavior* and *Behavioural Brain Research*, Associate Editor of the *Annual Review of Neuroscience*, and is on the editorial board of a number of other scientific journals. Thompson also has served on several research and training grant panels for the National Science Foundation and the National Institutes of Health, and served on committees of the National Research Council/National Academy of Sciences. He has also been involved in a number of local administrative activities at the University of Oregon, the University of California at Irvine, Harvard University, and Stanford University. He has an active and productive laboratory and is most fortunate to have an outstanding group of postdoctoral fellows, visiting professors, and graduate and undergraduate students working with him on basic neuronal mechanisms of learning and memory. His laboratory has received continuous federal research grant support since 1959 and is currently funded through 1992.

RICHARD F. THOMPSON

BRAIN SUBSTRATES OF LEARNING AND MEMORY

Perhaps the ultimate goal of research in the area of brain function and behavior is an understanding of the human mind. A key aspect of the mind is the nature of thoughts or cognitions—how are they assembled and maintained? Simply put, how do people learn and how do they remember? Without memory, there can be no mind.

How it is that the brain codes, stores, and retrieves memories is among the most important and baffling questions in science. At the cellular level, there are two fundamental types of information coding. One of these is the familiar genetic code, shared by organisms from viruses to humans. In higher organisms, literally millions of bits of information are coded in the DNA of the cell nucleus. Over the course of evolution, a quite different kind of information coding has developed—the cellular encoding of acquired information in the brain. This coding is no less remarkable than the genetic code. It has been estimated that a well-educated adult human has millions of bits of acquired information stored in the brain.

The generic term for acquired information coding in the brain is the *memory trace* or *engram*. The fundamental difference between the

The research in this paper was supported by grants from the National Science Foundation (BNS 8117115), the Office of Naval Research (N00014-83), the McKnight Foundation, and the Sloan Foundation.

genetic code and the engram code is, of course, that each individual human's engram store is acquired through experience and learning. It is the biological substrate for the growth of knowledge and civilization. The individual uniqueness of each human being is due largely to the engram store—the biological residue of memory from a lifetime of experience.

The development, elaboration, and growth in size of the human brain over the past three million years is unprecedented in evolution. Indeed, some biologists now feel that a new principle or mechanism of evolution may have come into play, a mechanism that involved the rapidly growing ability to learn, with its consequent development of culture and transmitted knowledge. The learning that occurred in each individual created a more complex environment that required still better learning, and hence a larger brain to survive and be fit. The cellular roots of this ability to learn can be traced to simpler organisms. It is best developed in mammals, where basic phenomena of learning (e.g., Pavlovian and instrumental conditioning) exhibit the same fundamental properties from rat and rabbit to human. The complexity of information processing and learning increases in an orderly fashion in classes above mammals.

In the past generation, the understanding of the biological basis of learning and memory has undergone a revolution. The earlier notion that memory is diffusely distributed in the brain has been largely discounted. It is now clear that various forms and aspects of learning and memory involve particular systems and circuits in the brain. This realization means that it is now both theoretically and technically possible to define these circuits, localize the sites of memory storage, and analyze the cellular and molecular mechanisms of memory.

The roots of this new understanding lie in several different disciplines. From psychology has come a clear characterization of the behavioral properties of learning (e.g., what learning and memory are) and a developing theoretical analysis of the nature of the associative processes that form the basis of learning and memory. The term *associative*, incidentally, describes the basic property of learning, the fact that stimulus or event becomes associated with another stimulus, event, or response, as in learning a foreign language.

From the broad field of psychobiology or behavioral neuroscience has come the recognition that identifiable neural memory systems and circuits in the brain can be characterized and analyzed. From the field of neurobiology, we scientists learn about the cellular, biophysical, and molecular mechanisms that underlie elementary forms of associative learning in simple neural circuits.

The success of this collective approach has been the source of great optimism in the field; fundamental insights into the physical basis of memory will continue to be achieved over the next few years. Indeed, many people feel that the field is now in the critical "breakthrough" stage—the present would seem to be the most exciting phase in the history of the field.

Human Memory

A several-stage model of the workings of human memory is suggested by basic research in cognitive psychology. Sensory information is held very briefly in a photographic-like memory. Some of this sensory memory is held for a few seconds in a short-term memory system. Part of this memory, in turn, is stored in long-term or permanent memory. Most people really think only of this third stage when they speak of memory, but all these different time-course events occur in human information processing and memory formation. Learning and memory are two sides of the same coin—learning is the process of acquiring and storing information, and memory is the stored information that may be retrieved.

You have probably heard of people with a "photographic" memory, although such individuals are exceedingly rare. One of the few known cases was studied by the Soviet psychologist, A. R. Luria. His book, *The Mind of a Mnemonist* (1968), makes fascinating reading. Mr. S., the subject of Luria's book, was of below-average intelligence, but he possessed an extraordinary memory. After looking briefly at a complicated diagram or a long list of numbers, Mr. S. could remember and exactly reproduce the diagram or numbers much later. He made his living traveling about the Soviet Union giving shows as a memory wizard.

Actually, everyone has a photographic memory. The problem is that it works for only about 1/10 of a second. Some years ago, Sperling (1960) developed a way of testing the immediate memory of a person. He presented an array of letters very briefly (i.e., 50 milliseconds) using a special device called a tachistoscope. He then immediately presented a blank screen with a dot where one of the letters had been. If the dot was given less than 1/10 of a second after the array, the person would almost always identify the letter correctly, no matter which letter the dot indicated. However, the longer the time between seeing the array and seeing the dot, the worse this immediate memory became—it decayed. This immediate photographic memory has been termed *iconic memory* from the Greek word *icon*, meaning image. It is often called *sensory memory*. A normal person can hold the complete array of numbers correctly in iconic or sensory memory for this brief period of about 1/10 of a second.

It appears that many young children have such persisting iconic or photographic memory. However, it is lost at about the time they begin to learn to read. Some anthropologists suggest that persisting iconic memory is much more common among adults in preliterate cultures—societies where people do not learn to read and write. Learning to read may somehow interfere with photographic memory ability.

If one looks up a telephone number and does not repeat the number several times, the number fades from the short-term memory. The decay time for short-term memory is a few seconds. The capacity of short-term memory is quite limited. In most people, it ranges from about 5 to 9 items of new information, although a few individuals have a larger capacity. This capacity was once described by psychologist George Miller (1956) as "the magic number seven, plus or minus two." This very limited capacity is the case only for new items. If one is already familiar with the items, especially if they can be grouped in categories (e.g., vegetables, flowers, or meaningful phrases), then the person will remember more of them, because they are already in the long-term memory store.

Short-term memory is another way of describing consciousness or awareness, as psychologist William James noted many years ago. Short-term memory is what one is aware of at a given point in time, and includes some part of the permanent memory store as well. To put it another way, what one is aware of at a given moment is the content of his or her short-term memory.

If one practices a new telephone number, he or she will manage to remember it more or less permanently; it will be placed in long-term or permanent memory. The memory capacity of the average person seems almost without limit. There is a story about the first president of Stanford University, a distinguished biologist and an expert on fish. As he became older, he stopped learning the names of new students because he said that every time he learned a new student's name he forgot the name of a fish. Although he may have thought this was so, it is in fact not necessarily true that learning new things requires that a person forget old items. Learning French does not make one forget English.

Estimates of the number of items or bits of information stored in the brain of a well-educated adult are very high, ranging at least in the millions. Consider the size of a person's vocabulary. Each word contains several bits of information. Furthermore, consider all the faces someone has seen in his or her life. If the person sees the face again, he or she will recognize many of them. A student at a larger university will learn to recognize literally hundreds of fellow students' faces over a period of four years. This visual memory ability to remember and recognize faces may be unique to people, or at least primates.

It seems that some visual information, such as faces and scenes, may pass rather directly from iconic to permanent memory. Haber (1970), in his studies at Cornell University, indicated the remarkable storage capacity of human visual memory. In one class session, he showed students over 2,000 slides, one after the other. The slides were obtained from pictures of people and scenes. The next day the students were shown all the slides again, but two slides were shown each time. Each slide they had seen the day before was paired with a new slide they had not seen before. For each pair, the students were asked to indicate which slide they had seen before. They scored an amazing 90% correct. (Note that all they had to do was recognize the picture, not describe it from memory; recognition memory is much better than recall memory.)

Brain Substrates of Memory

The several-stage model of memory just described is supported by studies of the brain substrates of learning and memory. One of the most dramatic examples comes from the clinical literature on the effects of brain surgery on memory: the case of HM, who had brain surgery to correct seizures associated with his serious epileptic condition. The surgery was successful in treating his epilepsy, but its other consequences were so tragic that this type of surgery has not been repeated.

The surgery performed on HM removed a portion of each temporal lobe, including portions of the two major limbic forebrain structures, the hippocampus and the amygdala, on both sides. HM lost the ability to remember his own experience. In contrast to normal people, he cannot hold new information in memory for more than a few seconds if he is distracted. Surprisingly, there are other aspects of HM's current memory that are quite normal. He has a normal short-term memory (e.g., he can remember a new telephone number). If someone is asked to memorize a new telephone number, he or she can do so by repeating it and perhaps developing a trick association (e.g., a mnemonic device) to remind him or her of it. HM cannot do this. He is very good at developing trick associations to help him remember things, and this works as long as he is able to repeat it to himself. The trouble is that as soon as he is distracted, he forgets both the number and the trick association. It is never stored in long-term permanent memory.

HM has a normal memory for motor skills. He can learn a complex motor skill (e.g., playing tennis) about as well as most other people. But imagine being HM's tennis instructor—you would have to reintroduce yourself at each lesson. Suppose HM had learned a slice serve from you and did not know how to do it or what it was called before his operation. At each lesson you would have to again describe a slice serve. But you would not have to teach him the motions—how to do it. He would learn the actual skill—his slice serve would improve with practice and remain with him as well as it would for other pupils. He just cannot remember what it is called, anything you said about it, or, for that matter, who you are. To HM, you are a stranger in a new setting each time he takes his tennis lesson.

Studies of patients such as HM suggest that there may be at least two kinds of long-term memory systems in the brain. You remember what you had for breakfast, a conversation you had with a friend last week, and the lovely restaurant to which you went on your last birthday. Every person has a vast memory store of his or her own past experiences (i.e., experiential memory). This memory store is time-tagged. A person remembers roughly when the experiences happened in the past and their approximate sequence in time. In addition, people have a vast store of general knowledge that is not time-tagged (e.g., one's vocabulary). These aspects of long-term verbal–experiential memory are often called *declarative* or *reference memory*. Motor-skill learning seems very different from these aspects of memory. Learning the movement in a difficult sport such as tennis or golf requires much practice. Thinking about it is not good enough—the movements and strokes must be practiced until they become automatic.

Squire (1987) has termed motor-skill learning *procedural* to distinguish it from declarative memory. He has worked extensively with a number of amnesia (memory loss) patients, including HM. Squire believes the distinction between declarative and procedural memory systems in the brain is fundamental. Procedural learning is not limited to motor skills and can extend to complex cognitive learning as well. As an example, Squire and his associates use the task of learning to read text in a mirror. If you hold this text up to a mirror and attempt to read it, you will find it is not an easy task. With much practice, however, people can learn to read mirror text well. Squire classifies learning to mirror read as procedural memory. Declarative memory is the memory for the actual text that the person reads in the mirror. Humans with amnesia can learn to mirror read as can normal people—they improve with practice to the point that they can read quite well. However, unlike normal people, they cannot remember what they have read. In amnesia victims, procedural learning and memory are normal, but declarative learning and memory are markedly impaired.

It is only in the past few years that scientists have succeeded in developing animal models of the more complex aspects of human memory (e.g., the declarative memory system that was so severely impaired in HM). Mishkin (1982), at the National Institute of Mental Health in Bethesda, Maryland, did so by removing both the hippocampus and amygdala on both sides in monkeys. Before the operation, Mishkin trained his monkeys on a simple short-term visual-recognition memory task. A tray was first presented with a single small block or toy object covering a food well that contained a peanut. The monkey reached out, moved the object, and got the peanut. The tray was removed so the monkey could not see it and another tray presented with the old object and a new object, each covering a food well. But only the well under the new object had a peanut. The monkey must remember and recognize the old object to choose the new object and get the peanut. The monkey must learn the principle of always selecting the new object and, of course, remembering which was the old object—*delayed non-matching-to-sample*, as the task is called. They learned this task very rapidly, and as Mishkin noted, it is one to which the naturally inquisitive monkey is already predisposed.

After bilateral removal of both the hippocampus and the amygdala, the animals had great difficulty in such recent visual memory tasks. In other work, it was shown that damage to an association area of the cerebral cortex, called area TE, impaired memory for visual patterns and forms in monkeys. Where the memories are actually stored is not yet known.

Memory Consolidation

One of the more striking facts about memory is it seems very easy to influence memories when they are being formed (i.e., when learning is occurring) but it is extremely difficult to influence older, well-established memories. A simple example is surgical anesthesia. The surgical level of anesthesia damps down the electrical and chemical activity of the brain markedly and produces profound unconsciousness. When the patient awakens from the anesthetic, the memory system is intact except that memories may be a little vague for the last few minutes before the anesthetic took hold.

Well-established memories are extremely tough. Nothing short of major brain damage can permanently destroy them, a fact supporting the possibility that permanent memory is coded by structural–anatomical changes among neurons in the brain.

A vivid example is provided in a pioneering study by Duncan (1949) at Northwestern University. Rats were placed in one of the two compartments with a small barrier they could jump over. A light came on for 10 seconds followed by shock on the side where the rats were located. If they jumped over the barrier before the light went off, they could avoid the shock. The animals received one trial per day. Rats in various groups received an electroconvulsive shock (ECS) after each day's trial; the trial–ECS interval ranged from 20 seconds to 14 hours. The results of this experiment were striking: The closer the ECS followed the learning trial in time, the more deleterious effect it had on performance. If the two were separated by more than an hour, there appeared to be no effect of the ECS on learning. ECS is used as a treatment for certain forms of depression in humans and produces the same effect on recent memory in humans as it does in rats (i.e., a profound amnesia for experience and memories formed before the ECS treatment). The amnesia can last from minutes to weeks, depending on the nature of the ECS treatment.

Increased forgetting is not a very useful thing. It was earlier thought that ECS helped depressed patients because it interfered with memories and thoughts that were depressing them, but this is now thought not to be the case. Why it helps certain forms of depression is still not known.

The other and more useful side of the coin would be treatments that facilitate formation of memories. McGaugh (1983) and his associates at the University of California at Irvine have demonstrated that certain drugs produce a marked facilitation of memory performance in animals. Two such drugs are strychnine and amphetamine. Strychnine is a convulsant poison; it blocks certain forms of neuronal inhibition and causes death from convulsions in higher doses. Amphetamine is a very dangerous and much-abused stimulant drug.

Many of the drugs that facilitate memory performance may actually be acting peripherally on the endocrine system, particularly the adrenal gland. Indeed, prior removal of the adrenal gland can prevent the facilitating effects of drugs on memory and even lessen the impairing effects of ECS on subsequent memory performance in animals. The adrenal gland is the "emotional" gland, par excellence, of the endocrine system. When people experience even moderate emotion, particularly associated with stress, the sympathetic (emergency) part of the autonomic nervous system is activated. This results in increased heart rate, dry mouth, and other effects, one of the most important being activation of a part of the adrenal gland (medulla) to release epinephrine (adrenalin) and norepinephrine into the bloodstream. In animal studies, norepinephrine is one of the most powerful memory-enhancing agents. At the same time, the brain causes the pituitary gland to release adrenocorticotrophic hormone (ACTH), which acts on another part of the adrenal gland (cortex), causing it to release cortisol, the "stress" hormone, into the bloodstream. Cortisol can also have powerful effects on memory performance. It has been known for a long time that events occurring at a time when emotion or stress is also experienced are well remembered. For example, many of us remember where we were and what we were doing when President Kennedy was assassinated.

Among the more impressive drug effects that have been found to improve memory performance in humans are those that enhance the neurotransmitter Acetylcholine (ACh), a chemical used by certain neurons in the brain to transmit information to other neurons. Several well-controlled studies on normal adults show that drugs that result in higher brain levels of ACh, such as physostigmine, can improve learning and memory performance above "normal" levels. However, most of these drugs have rather serious side effects and are neither recommended nor legally available. On the other hand, choline itself (the part of the acetylcholine molecule that must be obtained from the diet) is safely available in health food stores in the form of lecithin and is also present in egg yolks. Of course, if you eat more lecithin, you will increase your intake of fatty acids. There is as yet no good evidence that increased dietary choline does enhance memory performance in normal people.

The Search for the Memory Trace

The idea that memory traces can be localized to particular circuits in the brain is not new. Karl Lashley began the search for the memory trace early in the century. He trained rats to learn mazes and then removed portions of the "highest" region of their brains, the cerebral cortex. But he was unable to find any one region of the cortex that seemed to be particularly involved in the memories for the maze habit. Because of his (and others') inability to find localized memory traces in the cerebral cortex, Lashley drew the following rather pessimistic conclusion at the end of his career:

> This series of experiments has yielded a good bit of information about what and where the memory trace is not. It has discovered nothing directly of the real nature of the engram. I sometimes feel, in reviewing the evidence on the localization of the memory trace, that the necessary conclusion is that learning just is not possible. It is difficult to conceive of a mechanism which can satisfy the conditions set for it. Nevertheless, in spite of such evidence against it, learning does sometimes occur. (Lashley, 1950, pp. 447–478).

With the advantage of hindsight it now appears that certain brain structures below the level of the cerebral cortex play a more important role in maze learning in the rat. One such structure is the hippocampus, discussed earlier, that seems to be involved in amnesia in humans.

As Lashley recognized early on, the overriding problem for analysis of memory traces in the mammalian brain is localization. In order to analyze neuronal and synaptic mechanisms of memory storage and retrieval, it is first necessary to identify and localize the brain circuits, structures, and regions that are critically involved. The general approach to localization of memory traces that has proved most productive is to use what are termed *model biological systems*—to utilize a form of basic associative learning in an animal preparation where the memory circuits can be identified and analyzed.

A Pavlovian Approach

Ivan Pavlov was perhaps the first to develop and use the model biological system approach to learning and memory. From the time he discovered the conditioned reflex, he saw it as a tool to investigate higher functions of the brain. Lashley, influenced by Pavlov, Bechterev, and Watson, was the first Western scientist to state explicitly the model system approach, namely to use simply conditioned reflexes as models of associative learning and to localize memory traces by tracking the essential conditioned response (CR) circuitry through the brain.

In the Western world, discrete behavioral responses (e.g., leg flexion or eyelid closure) have been more widely used than autonomic responses (e.g., salivation) to study the properties of associative learning. But they all show the same basic properties and phenomena of Pavlovian learning in all mammals, including humans, and in invertebrate preparations as well. The major breakthroughs that have occurred in the past few years in terms of identifying critical memory trace circuits and processes in both invertebrates and vertebrates have used Pavlovian conditioning procedures. These basic procedures, completely under the control of the experimenter, are an important part of the model system approach.

Some years ago, a particularly clear cut and robust form of asso ciative learning in the intact mammal was adopted as a model system: Pavlovian conditioning of the rabbit eyelid response to an acoustic or visual conditioned stimulus (CS) using a corneal airpuff unconditioned stimulus (US). Thus, a tone CS is sounded and about a quarter of a second later a puff of air is delivered to the cornea of the eye. Initially, the tone does not evoke any response of the eye and the airpuff US evokes eyelid closure, a simple defensive reflex of the eye. By repeating such pairings, the tone comes to elicit a full-blown closure of the eye, a conditioned response (CR), that closely resembles the reflex eyeblink initially elicited by the airpuff. It is a highly adaptive learned response. Over a wide range of time intervals from tone onset to airpuff onset (e.g., from 1/10 second to more than a second), the animal (and human) learns to close the eye maximally at the time the airpuff to the cornea occurs, thus providing maximal protection of the eye.

Classical conditioning of the eyelid response was first done in humans. Hilgard, now emeritus professor of psychology at Stanford, was the first to study eyelid conditioning in infrahuman animals in his classical work with Marquis on dogs and monkeys (Hilgard & Marquis, 1936). They recognized immediately that eyelid conditioning provided an excellent model system for analysis of brain substrates of memory and they undertook a series of lesion studies with the assistance of Fulton. They used a visual CS and showed that the visual cortex was not essential. Their results pointed to a subcortical memory trace. Gormezano (1972) was the first to publish reports of studies using eyelid conditioning in the rabbit, an animal that is docile and tolerates restraint well. The conditioned eyelid response in the rabbit has been used to very good effect in analysis of basic theoretical issues in learning (Rescorla & Wagner, 1972; Wagner, 1981).

Classical conditioning of the rabbit eyelid response has a number of advantages for analysis of brain substrates of learning and memory. A particular advantage of the conditioned eyelid response is the fact that eyelid conditioning has become perhaps the most widely used paradigm for the study of basic properties of classical or Pavlovian conditioning of striated muscle responses in both humans and infrahuman subjects. It displays the same basic laws of learning in other animals and humans. Consequently, it seems highly likely that neuronal mechanisms found to underlie conditioning of the eyelid response in rabbits will hold for all mammals, including humans. The conditioned eyelid response can be viewed as an instance of the general class of discrete, adaptive behavioral responses learned to deal with aversive stimuli. Therefore, one can adopt the working assumption that neuronal mechanisms underlying associative learning of the eyelid response will in fact be general for all such learning.

The Search for the Locus of the Memory Trace

In science, it is generally easier to rule out possibilities rather than rule them in, as Sherlock Holmes was fond of pointing out. My colleagues and I completed a long series of studies ruling out various brain structures and circuits as a part of the essential memory trace circuit or locus of the essential memory trace itself. In brief, our results and work from other laboratories argued against essential participation of such higher brain structures as the cerebral cortex and hippocampus. Interestingly, memory traces do develop in the hippocampus as a result of such basic associative learning, but this hippocampal memory trace circuit is not essential for learning. The development of such higher order memory systems in basic associative learning, incidentally, may provide simplified models for the study of neuronal substrates of the more complex or cognitive functions of higher regions of the brain (e.g., declarative memory).

We also ruled out certain circuits in the brain stem as the locus of the memory trace (e.g., the primary auditory nuclei that relay information from the ear about the tone CS to other brain structures and the motor nuclei that generate the behavioral response), although portions of them are, of course, a part of the memory trace circuit. But we were still left with much of the brain stem, midbrain, and cerebellum as possible sites. Because there was no a priori way of determining which of these regions and structures are involved in the memory trace, we undertook, beginning some years ago, to map these structures by systematically recording neuronal unit activity in already-trained animals. For this purpose we developed a chronic micromanipulator system that permits recording of nerve cell activity in a substantial number of neural loci per animal. Increases in unit activity that form a temporal model within a trial of the learned behavioral response were prominent in certain highly localized regions of the cerebellum, in the cortex, and in the interpositus nucleus (Thompson, 1986). The results of the mapping studies pointed to substantial engagement of the cerebellar system in the generation of the CR. An example is shown in Figure 1 with unit recordings from the cerebellar interpositus nucleus on the same side

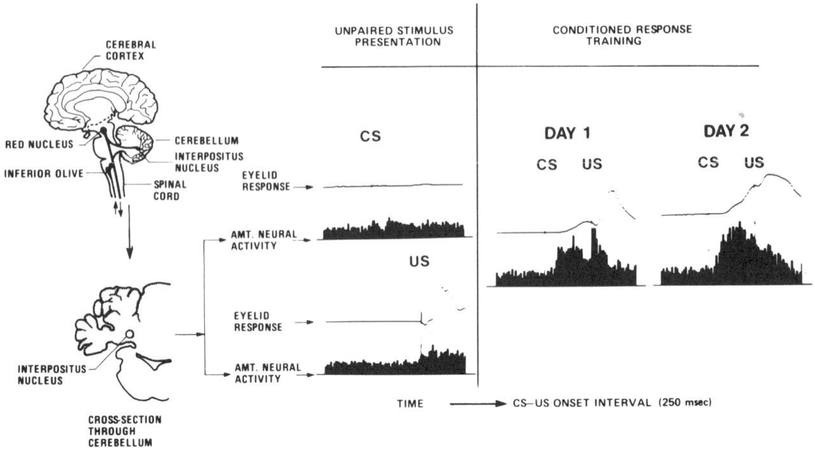

Figure 1. Histograms of unit recordings obtained from a chronic electrode implanted at the lateral border of the interpositus nucleus. The animal was first given random, unpaired presentations of the tone and airpuff (104 trials of each stimulus) and then trained with two days of paired training (117 trials each day). Each histogram is an average over the entire day of training indicated. The upper trace represents movement of the nictitating membrane (NM). The first vertical line represents the onset of the tone conditioned stimulus (CS), and the second line represents the onset of the corneal airpuff unconditioned stimulus (US). Each histogram bar is 9 milliseconds in duration. Notice that these neurons develop a model of the conditioned but not unconditioned response during learning, and that this neuronal model precedes the learned behavioral response substantially in time. Reprinted from McCormick and Thompson (1984) by permission.

as the trained eye (McCormick & Thompson, 1984). This animal was given unpaired training before acquisition began. Average histograms revealed that the unit activity showed only minimal responses to the tone and airpuff during the unpaired day of the training. However, during acquisition, as the animal learned, the unit activity developed a "model" of the CR but no clear model of the unconditioned response (UR). The cerebellar neuronal unit model of the learned response precedes the behavioral response significantly in time and predicts the actual amplitude-time course of the learned behavioral CR. The course of development of the conditioned behavioral response and the concomitant growth in the neuronal unit model of the CR in the interpositus nuclear region show very high correlations (e.g., $r = .90$). The neural unit recordings displayed in Figure 1 are from small groups of clusters of neurons, so-called multiple unit recording. In current work in which we record the action potentials from single neurons, we find two patterns of activity in neurons that respond in relation to the behavioral learned response: (a) those that show increases in frequency of discharge that precede and predict the form of the learned behavioral response, as in Figure 1, and (b) those that show mirror images of such responding (inhibition) but are equally predictive of the learned response. Neurons showing these positive or negative models of the learned response are found in very localized regions of the interpositus nucleus and in very localized regions of the cerebellar cortex, where the neurons have been identified as Purkinje cells, the only neurons that send information out from the cerebellar cortex, in this case to the interpositus nucleus.

We have found that lesions on the same side as the trained eye in the cerebellum (see Figure 2) permanently abolish the CR but have no effect on the UR and do not prevent subsequent learning by the other eye. If the lesion is made before training, no learning occurs. The critical region is the lateral interpositus nucleus. Perhaps most dramatic is a recent study involving kainic acid (it destroys nerve cell bodies but not nerve fibers or terminals): Destruction of neuron cell bodies in a region as small as a cubic millimeter in the lateral portion of the interpositus causes complete and permanent loss of the learned eyelid response (Lavond, Hembree, & Thompson, 1985).

Electrical stimulation through recording microelectrodes in the critical lateral interpositus nuclear region of the cerebellum elicits a discrete eyelid closure response prior to training. In fact, a wide range of discrete behavioral responses (e.g., eyelid closure, leg flexion, and head turning) can be elicited by microstimulation of the interpositus, the type of response depending on the exact location of the stimulating electrode.

The results indicate that the essential memory trace circuits for these learned responses are extremely localized in the brain. How general is this finding? Most of our work has been on the learned eyelid response, but we have shown that a different part of the interpositus is essential for hindlimb flexion conditioning. We and our associated laboratories are now exploring the generality of our results across learning procedures and species.

At this point, we feel we can generalize our essential cerebellar circuit to discrete, adaptive responses learned to deal with aversive stimuli in both classical and instrumental avoidance learning paradigms in mammals.

In other work, we have identified much of the efferent or output pathways from the interpositus nucleus to motor nuclei (see Figure 3). Our results indicate that it courses out the superior cerebellar peduncle, crosses to the contralateral side in the peduncle, relays in the magnocellular division of the red nucleus, crosses back to the ipsilateral side and projects to the lower brain stem as a part of the descending rubral pathway (Thompson, 1986). The essential CR circuit we have so far defined could be called the "efferent" limb, in that destruction of any part of the circuit abolishes the CR to any CS (e.g., light or tone),

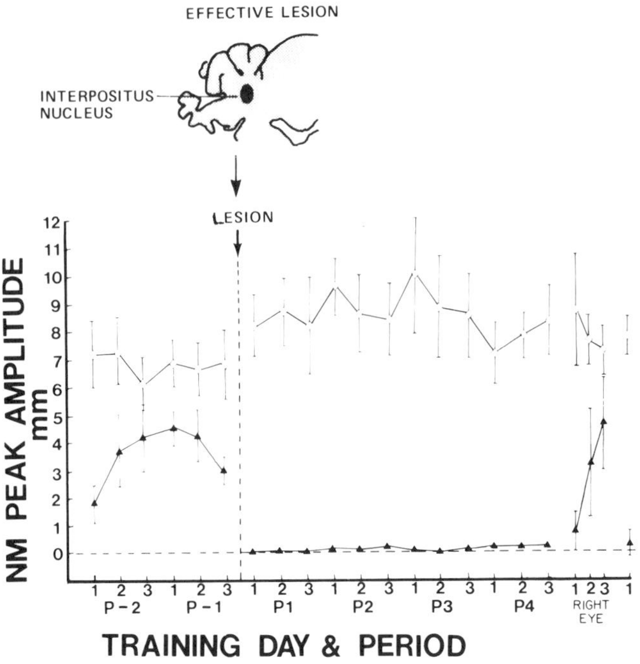

Figure 2. Effects of lesions of the left lateral interpositus nucleus of the cerebellum on the learned NM/eyelid response for six animals. Solid triangles represent the amplitude of the conditioned response (CR); open diamonds represent the amplitude of the unconditioned response (UR). All training was to the left eye (ipsilateral to lesion) except where labeled right eye. The cerebellar lesion completely and permanently abolished the CR of the ipsilateral eye but had no effect on the UR. P-2 and P-1 indicate initial learning on the two days prior to the lesion. P1-P4 are four days of postoperative training to the left eye. The right eye was then trained and learned rapidly, thus controlling for nonspecific lesion effects. The left eye was again trained and showed no learning. Numbers on abscissa indicate 40 trial periods except for those labeled right eye, which are 24 trial periods. Reprinted from McCormick, Clark, Lavond, and Thompson (1982) by permission.

but the association between CS and US/UR appears to be formed in the cerebellum, as will be seen in the next section.

A Hypothetical Model

In late 1983, we developed a hypothetical schema or model of how the cerebellar memory trace circuit might work, based on the well-known anatomy of the system, on our results described earlier, and on theories

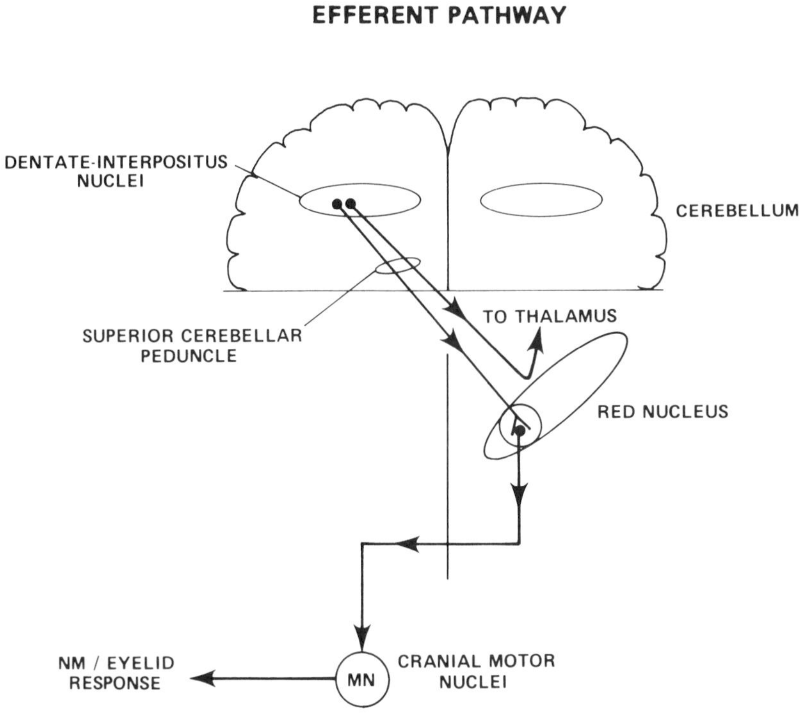

Figure 3. The efferent (output) pathway from the cerebellar memory trace system to motor nuclei.

of how the cerebellum might function as a learning machine (see Figure 4). The cerebellar cortex has great appeal to theoreticians and modelers because of its elegant uniformity and simplicity and because of the striking fact of two quite different inputs to each Purkinje cell—a mossy fiber-granule cell-parallel fiber input that is widely distributed and a climbing fiber input that is highly localized. All models, both verbal–logical and computational, have stressed this point, and researchers who focus on learning and memory have universally hypothesized that the mossy fiber-granule cell-parallel fiber system is the learning input, and the climbing fiber input is the "teaching" input (Albus, 1971; Eccles, 1977; Ito, 1974; Marr, 1969).

The details of our schema are not elaborated here (see Figure 4). In brief, it is assumed that the locus of the memory trace is at the Purkinje cells in cerebellar cortex (or in analogous cells in the interpositus nucleus). A given CS (tone or light) is assumed to activate a subset of mossy fibers-granule cells-parallel fibers that in turn weakly activate a number of Purkinje cells. The US (corneal airpuff) is assumed

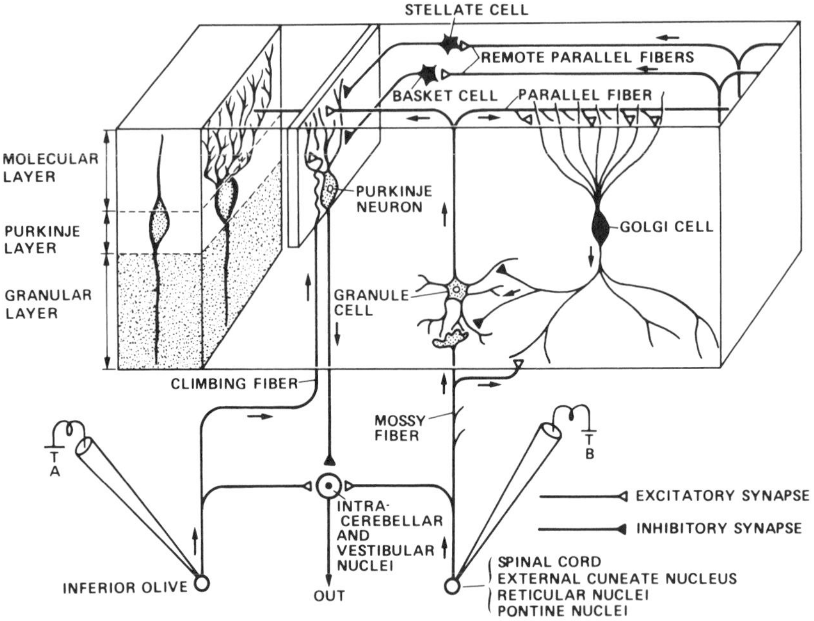

Figure 4. Synaptic organization of the cerebellar cortex. Purkinje cells are excited directly by climbing fibers and indirectly (via parallel fibers from the granule cells) by the mossy fibers. Stellate and basket cells, which are excited by parallel fibers, act as inhibitory interneurons. The Golgi cells act on the granule cells with feedback inhibition (when excited by parallel fibers) and feedforward inhibition (when excited by climbing and mossy fiber collaterals). The output of the Purkinje cell is inhibitory upon the cells of the intracerebellar and vestibular nuclei.

In normal behavioral training, a tone is used as the conditioned stimulus (CS) and a corneal airpuff, which elicits an eyeblink, is used as the unconditioned stimulus (US). However, electrical microstimulation of a portion of the inferior olive (IO)-climbing fiber projection to the cerebellum (microeloctrode A in IO) can also elicit an eyeblink response and serves as a very effective US in place of a corneal airpuff. Similarly, electrical microstimulation of the mossy fiber projection to the cerebellum (microeloctrode B in pontine nuclei) can serve as a very effective CS in place of tone or light. Finally, joint stimulation of climbing fibers as the US and mossy fibers as the CS produces normal learning of discrete behavioral responses.

to activate a limited number of climbing fibers from the inferior olive (IO) that in turn strongly activate only a few of the Purkinje cells also activated by the CS, the few that result in activation of the appropriate motor program via the interpositus nucleus (e.g., eyelid closure for a corneal airpuff or leg flexion for a paw shock). When parallel fiber activation occurs at the appropriate time just prior to climbing fiber activation, the connections of the parallel fibers to the Purkinje cells activated by the particular US are altered. The schema accounts for stimulus specificity. For example, the fact that CRs show a stimulus generalization gradient (if a different stimulus is used as a test CS, the learned response will be weaker or nonexistent), the more different the CS is from the training CS. It also accounts for response specificity of learned responses and is consistent with all our evidence to date. Although much of this circuit was hypothetical, insofar as it's being a substrate for the formation of memories is concerned, each aspect and assumption is testable. Indeed, current work in our laboratory is providing strong new evidence favoring such a schema.

The role of the inferior olive. A major system that projects information to the cerebellum is the IO-climbing fiber system (see Figure 4). In recent work, we have found that lesions of the appropriate region of the IO (rostromedial dorsal accessory olive) do not abolish the CR but instead lead to relatively normal extinction with continued paired CS–US training. Lesions of all other regions of the IO do not affect the CR. The dorsal accessory olive (DAO) appears to be the essential afferent limb for the reinforcing or teaching input from the US. The fact that lesions of the DAO do not immediately abolish the CR but instead lead to its eventual extinction means that the essential memory trace cannot be there (McCormick, Steinmetz, & Thompson, 1985).

In current work, we find that electrical microstimulation of the DAO (see Figure 4) can elicit a variety of behavioral responses including eyelid closure, the nature of the threshold response being determined by the exact location of the stimulating electrode. If this is now used as the US/UR and paired with a tone CS, the exact response elicited by DAO stimulation is learned to the tone as a CR rapidly and with all the properties of a normal CR. Lesion of the critical interpositus region abolishes this IO-established CR, and abolishes the response elicited by IO stimulation. Control stimulation 1–2 mm dorsal to the DAO in the reticular formation can also elicit movements, presumably by activation of descending pathways, but these elicited movements cannot be trained to a CS (Mauk, Steinmetz, & Thompson, 1986).

These IO results strengthen the argument that the IO and its climbing fiber input to the cerebellum is the essential US teaching input and that the trace is localized to the cerebellum (see Figure 5). This is also the first clear empirical evidence supporting the pioneering hypothesis and network models of Albus, Eccles, Ito, Marr, and others (see previous discussion) that the IO-climbing fiber system is the "teaching" input for behavioral learning in the cerebellum. (Ito has developed analogous findings in the context of plasticity of the vestibulo-ocular reflex; Ito, 1984.)

The use of mossy fiber projections as a CS pathway. We have succeeded in creating a known CS pathway by using electrical microstimulation of mossy fiber projections to the cerebellum as the CS (see

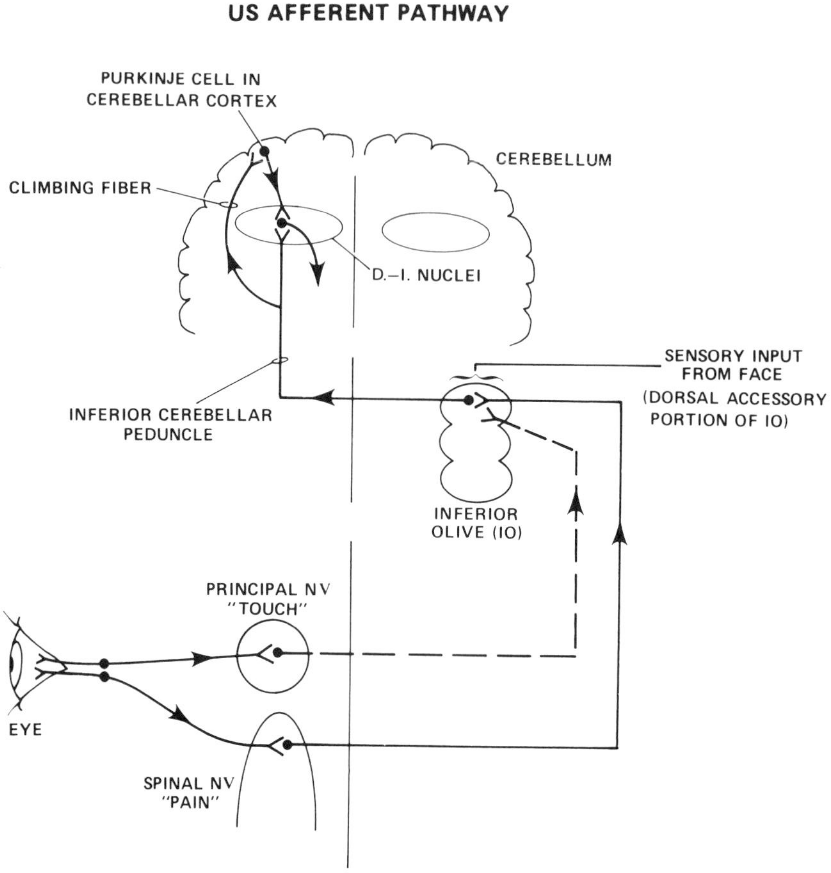

Figure 5. A hypothesis of the effective US reinforcing or teaching input circuit from the cornea of the eye to the cerebellum. The critical region of the inferior olive is the dorsal accessory olive. The D.-I. nuclei is the dentate-interpositus nuclei and the NV is the fifth cranial nerve.

Figure 4). Animals rapidly learn normal behavioral CRs to this CS (e.g., eyeblink CR with corneal airpuff US). To date we have successfully used stimulation of mossy fibers from the dorsolateral pontine nucleus, the lateral reticular nucleus, and the mossy fibers themselves as CSs.

Finally, in current pilot work we find that normal behavioral CRs are learned with electrical stimulation of mossy fibers as the CS and of DAO-climbing fibers as the US, thus creating a "reduced" preparation within the intact, behaving animal (see Figure 4). This preparation promises much in terms of fine-grained localization of the memory traces and analysis of mechanisms.

In the more general terms, our results have demonstrated quite clearly that the essential memory trace circuits in the brain for the basic category of associative learning we have studied are highly localized; and all our evidence to date points to discrete regions of the cerebellum as the locus of memory storage for discrete, adaptive behavioral responses learned associatively to deal with aversive events.

The effects of cerebellar damage in humans are to impair movements, particularly skilled movements. Most movements that humans make are to a significant degree learned (i.e., skilled). In this context, Eccles has proposed the following:

> We can say that normally our most complex muscle movements are carried out subconsciously and with consummate skill. The more subconscious you are in a golf stroke, the better it is, and the same with tennis, skiing, skating, or any other skill. In all these performances we do not have any appreciation of the complexity of muscle contractions and joint movements. All that we are conscious of is a general directive given by what we may call our voluntary command system. It is my thesis that the cerebellum is concerned in this enormously complex organization and control of movement, and that throughout life, particularly in the earlier years, we are engaged in an incessant teaching program for the cerebellum. As a consequence, it can carry out all of these remarkable tasks that we set it to do in the whole repertoire of our skilled movements in games, in techniques, in musical performances, in speech, dance, song, and so on. (Eccles, 1977, p. 328).[1]

One of the most striking features of the cerebellum is the high degree of regularity in the anatomical organization of the cortex over its extent and over species. It is highly and regularly organized; indeed, it is hardwired. If a major function of this structure is to code the associative learning of discrete, adaptive movements and more generally skilled movements, then the basic neural circuitry for such learning preexists. No new pathways are formed. Instead, the memory traces must involve changes in the excitability of preexisting circuits. In this sense, at least, our results are closely consistent with studies of invertebrate preparations that exhibit learning, where the circuits are hardwired and the mechanisms appear to involve changes in membrane properties.

The general possibility that learning circuits are hardwired in the mammalian brain is consistent with all we know about the high degree of anatomical organization of the brain and not inconsistent with all we know about learning and memory. Even the most complex form of human learning and memory, language, appears to have differentiated anatomical substrates in the cerebral cortex and uniformities in the "deep

[1]Reprinted from Eccles (1977) by permission.

structure" of language itself across all languages. In terms of mechanisms, the possibility that memory circuits are hardwired does not exclude anatomical substrates for memories in terms of the growth or alteration of the microstructure (i.e., changes in the size and properties of synapses or even the development of new synapses).

The work that has been discussed in this chapter provides a particularly clear example where theoretical computational models derived from such fields as artificial intelligence and cognitive psychology can interact with and guide empirical neurobiological research. When my colleagues and I set out to find the essential US teaching pathway, we had two major choices. Information about the corneal airpuff and other face skin sensations is conducted into the brain by the 5th cranial nerve to the 5th nucleus. From here there are two major ways this information can get to the cerebellum: directly by way of mossy fibers and indirectly by way of the inferior olive and climbing fiber. The computational theories of cerebellar learning pointed to the climbing fiber system as the teaching input because of its unique anatomical organization, one climbing fiber to one Purkinje cell, as opposed to the distributed projections of the mossy fiber-granule cell-parallel fiber system to many Purkinje cells (see previous discussion). Following these models, we focused on the climbing fiber system and found that it was indeed the necessary and sufficient teaching input for the learning of discrete, adaptive behavioral responses.

The distributed nature of the mossy fiber-granule cell-parallel fiber system, on the other hand, makes it ideally suited as the "learning" input, a point also stressed by the computational models. Again, following the models, we have shown that activation of mossy fibers is indeed a very effective CS learning pathway.

As we define the essential cerebellar memory trace circuit in more detail, it will permit us to develop more precise and powerful computational models that could well have more general and practical applicability (i.e., perhaps for control and guidance systems and for robotics). In terms of this last possibility, the manner in which our animals learned to make very precise and discrete movements to a "command" (tone CS) when electrical microstimulation of the IO is used as the teaching US input is strikingly machine-like. As noted earlier, animals learn to make the exact movement evoked by the electrical stimulus and show no sign of emotion or affect when doing so. The cerebellum does indeed appear to be an extremely efficient biological machine for the learning of precise movements. Perhaps when we understand in sufficient detail how it accomplishes this, we can make use of the same principles in nonbiological machines.

In general terms, it seems clear that as the neuronal circuits in the brain are defined that are essential for learning and other aspects of behavior, it will be necessary to develop theoretical computational models of these circuits. Even with very simple circuits, it is not possible to predict with any precision what in fact the circuit does or is capable of doing without quantitative modeling of the circuit.

Cellular Mechanisms of Memory

There are hints in current research that suggest that certain chemical and anatomical processes and changes might serve as the physical basis of memory in nerve cells of the brain. One of the clues comes from studies on invertebrates with very simple nervous systems in which experience-induced changes in neuron activity can occur at a single synapse (the junction between two neurons). For example, Kandel and Schwartz (1982) and Alkon (1980), working on different species, have found long-lasting changes in the ability of the nerve cell to conduct certain small ions (e.g., potassium or calcium) across the cell membrane.

Another intriguing clue comes from the "rich rat" studies, in which animals were raised in groups in large "penthouse" cages with many objects and toys. Rosenzweig (1970) and Greenough (1984) have shown that the neurons in the cerebral cortex of the "rich" rats develop more branching of their fibers and more synaptic contact zones (spines) than is true for rats raised separately in standard laboratory cages. There is even some evidence of such brain "growth" in adult animals when they are placed in enriched environments. Although such findings are provocative, it is not yet known how they relate to learning and memory storage in the mammalian brain. But the search for memory traces is progressing rapidly, and it seems likely they will be found soon, at least for basic forms of learning such as classical conditioning.

The ability to learn is an emergent property of cellular tissue. The ability as such, has a clear genetic base; it is dependent on the structural and functional organization of the brain and on the elaboration of cellular storage processes. It would not be surprising if the genetic material itself plays a role in the process of learning. We will someday understand the genetic basis of the ability of the brain to store memory. But only from the study of the brain and behavior can we know the actual memories that are stored in the brain.

References

Albus, J. S. (1971). A theory of cerebellar function. *Mathematical Bioscience, 10*, 25–61.

Alkon, D. L. (1980). Cellular analysis of a gastropod (hermissenda crassicornis) model of associative learning. *The Biological Bulletin, 159*, 505–506.

Duncan, C. P. (1949). The retroactive effect of electroshock on learning. *Journal of Comparative and Physiological Psychology, 42*, 34–44.

Eccles, J. C. (1977). An instruction-selection theory of learning in the cerebellar cortex. *Brain Research, 127*, 327–352.

Gormezano, I. (1972). Investigations of defense and reward conditioning in the rabbit. In A. H. Black & W. F. Prokasy (Eds.), *Classical conditioning II: Current research and theory* (pp. 151–181). New York: Appleton-Century-Crofts.

Greenough, W. T. (1984). Structural correlates of information storage in the mammalian brain: A review and hypothesis. *Trends in Neuroscience, 7*, 229–233.

Haber, R. N. (1970). How we remember what we see. *Scientific American, 222*(5), 104–112.

Hilgard, E. R., & Marquis, D. G. (1936). Conditioned eyelid responses in monkeys, with a comparison of dog, monkey, and man. *Psychology Monographs*, 47:212, 185–198.

Ito, M. (1974). The control mechanism of cerebellar motor systems. In E. 0. Schmitt (Ed.), *Neuroscience: Third study program* (pp. 293–303). Cambridge, MA: MIT Press.

Ito, M. (1984). *The cerebellum and neural control.* New York: Raven Press.

Kandel, E. R., & Schwartz, J. H. (1982). Molecular biology of learning: Modulation of transmitter release. *Science, 218*, 433–443.

Lashley, K. S. (1950). In search of the engram. *Society of Experimental Biology, Symposium 4*, 454–482.

Lavond, D. G., Hembree, T. L., & Thompson, R. F. (1985). Effect of kainic acid lesions of the cerebellar interpositus nucleus on eyelid conditioning in the rabbit. *Brain Research, 326*, 179–183.

Luria, A. R. (1968). *The mind of a mnemonist.* New York: Basic Books.

Marr, D. (1969). A theory of cerebellar cortex. *Journal of Physiology* (London), *202*, 437–470.

Mauk, M. D., & Steinmetz, J. E., & Thompson, R. F. (1986). Classical conditioning using stimulation of the inferior olive as the unconditioned stimulus. *Proceedings of the National Academy of Sciences*, USA, *83*, 5349–5353.

McCormick, D. A., Clark, G. A., Lavond, D. G., & Thompson, R. F. (1982). Initial localization of the memory trace for a basic form of learning. *Proceedings of the National Academy of Sciences, 79*(8), 2731–2742.

McCormick, D. A., & Steinmetz, J. E., & Thompson, R. F. (1985). Lesions of the inferior olivary complex cause extinction of the classically conditioned eyeblink response. *Brain Research, 359*, 120–130.

McCormick, D. A., & Thompson, R. F. (1984). Neuronal responses of the rabbit cerebellum during acquisition and performance of a classically conditioned nictitating membrane-eyelid response. *Journal of Neuroscience, 4*(11), 2811–2822.

McGaugh, J. L. (1983). Preserving the presence of the past: Hormonal influences on memory storage. *American Psychologist, 38*(2), 161–174.

Miller, G. A. (1956). The magical number seven, plus or minus two: Some limits on our capacity for processing information. *Psychological Review, 63*, 81–97.

Mishkin, M. (1982). A memory system in the monkey. *Philosophical Transactions of the Royal Society of London B, 298*, 85–95.

Rescorla, R. A., & Wagner, A. R. (1972). A theory of Pavlovian conditioning: Variations in the effectiveness of reinforcement and nonreinforcement. In A. H. Black & W. A. Prokasy (Eds.), *Classical conditioning II: Current theory and research* (pp. 64–99). New York: Appleton-Century-Crofts.

Rosenzweig, M. R. (1970). Evidence for anatomical and chemical changes in the brain during primary learning. In K. H. Pribram & D. F. Broadbent (Eds.), *Biology of memory* (pp. 69–85). New York: Academic Press.

Sperling, G. (1960). The information available in brief visual presentation. *Psychological Monographs, 74* (Whole No. 498).

Squire, L. R. (1987). *Memory and brain.* London: Oxford University Press.

Thompson, F. R. (1986). The neurobiology of learning and memory. *Science, 233,* 941–947.

Wagner, A. R. (1981). SPO: A model of automatic memory processing in animal behavior. In N. E. Spear & R. R. Miller (Eds.), *Information processing in animals: Memory mechanisms* (pp. 5–47). Hillsdale, NJ: Erlbaum.

MAUREEN DENNIS

LANGUAGE AND THE YOUNG DAMAGED BRAIN

Maureen Dennis came to child neuropsychology from a background in both animal physiological and child clinical psychology. Currently the recipient of a Research Associateship from the Ontario Mental Health Foundation, she is a member of the Research Institute of the Hospital for Sick Children in Toronto and holds a cross-appointment as an associate professor in the Department of Behavioural Science within the Faculty of Medicine of the University of Toronto.

Dennis has researched how early damage to the brain affects the development of later cognitive abilities, and has published this research in edited books and in neuropsychology and developmental psychology journals. Asking empirical questions of clinical data, she uses the procedures of psycholinguistics and cognitive psychology to analyze the language of children with various forms of developmental brain damage. In her professional practice as a pediatric neuropsychologist, she is consulted by legal firms in Canada and the United States about the effects on cognitive functions of head injury and other trauma in children involved in personal injury litigation.

Dennis has been supported in her research and writing by the Ontario Mental Health Foundation and the Ontario Ministry of Community and Social Services. She has served on the Board of Governors of the International Neuropsychological Society, and on the editorial boards of several neuropsychology journals. In recognition of her mid-career research achievements, she was the recipient in 1986 of the first Benton Award of the International Neuropsychological Society.

MAUREEN DENNIS

LANGUAGE AND THE YOUNG DAMAGED BRAIN

A *good problem* is one that is ripe for solving, one that lies on the boundary between problems already solved and those that seem unsolvable. An *important problem*, in contrast, is one whose solution would affect people's ideas about themselves or their lives. As Miller (1984) noted when proposing the distinction, important problems are not always good problems.

How injury to the young brain affects the state of existing language function and the course of future language development has always been an important problem. The answers to it influence ideas about the time frames of language acquisition, the internal organization of the language domain, and the way such time frames and organization are represented in the growing brain. They also affect attempts to remediate the language-based cognitive disorders arising from early brain injury.

But it was not always a good problem. For many years it was even a bad problem, one that permitted many different answers, none of which could easily be dismissed. Only recently has it emerged as a good problem that, if not yet solved, is nonetheless poised for solution. How did the always-important question about language and the young dam-

Personal and project support for the work described in this chapter has long been provided by the Ontario Mental Health Foundation. The author wishes to thank her colleagues, Bruno Kohn and Jack Fletcher, for their thoughtful and knowledgeable comments on the earlier manuscript draft.

aged brain cease being a bad problem and become a good one? Certain traditional assumptions about language and early brain damage caused unsolvable problems to be posed. When these assumptions were reconsidered and revised, the problems become better defined and more solvable, and this made it possible for recent studies to explore, not only how language varies with certain aspects of early brain damage, but also to begin validating hypothetical language constructs.

Old Assumptions About Early Brain Damage and Language

Any exploration of language and the brain is conducted within the framework established by a particular set of assumptions about language, brain, and how they might be related. The core assumptions about language and early brain damage in the period from, roughly, 1870 to 1970, not only established just which research questions would be posed, but also determined the kind of data that would be invoked to answer them.

Language is a Unitary Behavioral Function

Interest in the effects of early brain damage on language dates as least as far back as 1868, with an analysis of the incidence of language loss after congenital injury to one or other of the cerebral hemispheres (Cotard, 1868). As the pace of research into the behavioral effects of adult brain damage increased in the latter part of the 19th century, more and more functional distinctions within the language system came to be made. But treatment of language as a unitary function persisted longer in studies of children than in studies involving adults, perhaps because the study of early brain damage was pursued less vigorously than the analysis of brain damage sustained later in life. And even in studies of language loss after adult brain damage, the distinctions about language involved the kinds of operations brain-damaged patients could or could not perform—for example, expressing, comprehending, or repeating—rather than the use of particular constituents of language in expression, comprehension, or repetition. That is to say, the functional distinctions within the language system concerned what brain-damaged individuals might do with a particular language constituent rather than the constituent itself.

Child Language is a Simplified Version of Adult Language

Early in its history, the field of developmental psycholinguistics promised to explain how children induct the language rules of their adult community from their exposure to ambient speech. Child language was assumed to be adult language in simplified, less elaborated, or smaller form (and we might note in passing that the null hypothesis in developmental psychology still asserts that the cognitive mechanisms of children and adults are identical; see Macnamara, 1982). Maintaining this assumption causes research questions about language and early brain damage to focus on the distal end point of language acquisition, adult language, rather than on the proximal levels of language development and the course of movement from one level to the next. It means, further, that research questions will concern the quantity of future adult language the child might lose after brain injury rather than the changes in the child's language system existing at the time the brain was damaged.

Adult Aphasia is the Framework for Analyzing Child Language Loss

If adult language were the appropriate reference point for child language, then the loss of speech and language from brain damage in adulthood (termed *adult aphasia*) would be the correct framework for analyzing how children lose language after brain damage. This assumption has been quite pervasive in research even until now, with assertions that it does not matter whether brain-damaged children have age-inappropriate language, only whether they show adult aphasia (Bishop, 1981). But perhaps the most unfortunate result of this focus on comparing brain-damaged children and brain-damaged adults is that it has caused attention to be deflected from the far more important comparison, which is that between brain-damaged children and their normally developing age peers.

It was long assumed that the adult pattern of language representation in the brain was achieved by linear increments; that is, that each extra portion of chronological age brought with it one extra portion of whichever brain construct mediated language (e.g., Lenneberg, 1967). This assumption entailed some presuppositions about the immature nervous system that are demonstrably incorrect (see Isaacson, 1975, for a discussion); for example, that the child brain is like the adult brain, only in weaker form, and that the brain systems important for acquiring a skill are the same as those that sustain the skill, once it is acquired. By focusing on quantitative differences in brain organization between child and adult, this assumption serves to deflect attention away from qualitative differences, which are of equal, or even greater, importance.

Caused Unsolvable Problems to be Posed

Do Brain-Damaged Children Show Adult Aphasia?

Adult aphasia is predicated on an adult language system, and only when one's language approximates that of the adult can one become an adult aphasic. So the strict answer to the question, Do brain-damaged children show adult aphasia? is "No": Lacking the adult language system on which adult aphasia is predicated, brain-damaged children, of course, cannot sustain an adult aphasia. But the question is the wrong one to ask. And by distracting from the possibility that brain-damaged children do in fact lose age-appropriate language even though they do not show adult aphasia, it has often lead to the incorrect inference that an absence of adult aphasia means an absence of language impairment.

When is the Critical Development Period for the Onset of Adult Aphasia?

Researchers thought that a time during development when brain damage would produce adult aphasia could be pinpointed. Although it is certainly true that child language eventually becomes adult language, it is not meaningful to ask when brain damage produces aphasia in children, because the language behavior on which the idea of aphasia is predicated does not emerge until childhood is ending.

When Does Cerebral Dominance Develop?

Cerebral dominance, which refers to the relative importance of one side of the brain over the other for a particular aspect of cognitive functioning, is a construct inferred from behavioral maturation, or from the behavioral effects of brain damage: It is not independently verifiable with reference to specific features or loci of the brain.

The developmental course of cerebral dominance is inferred by studying certain behaviors in children who are normal or brain-damaged. Depending on which behaviors are considered, cerebral dominance will seem to occur either earlier or later. Assuming that cerebral dominance would begin at the exact time when left-sided brain injury produced adult aphasia, Lenneberg (1967) noted that left-sided brain damage in children produced adult aphasia only at puberty. Now what he used to infer the onset of dominance—adult aphasia—could not have occurred earlier than puberty. Clearly, what is meant by cerebral dominance is highly task-dependent. The question, When does cerebral dominance develop? is unanswerable, or, perhaps more accurately, it has any number of answers (depending on how we measure it) none of which can readily be dismissed.

These unanswerable questions about language and early brain damage share two problems, somewhat interrelated. They view child language, not in its own, developmental, terms, but solely in relation to the end-point of development, adult language. And in an area critically concerned with development, they fail to pose developmental questions.

Revised Assumptions About Child Language

Recent research has provided new factual information about early brain damage and language, information that was uncovered when new research questions were posed. The new questions resulted from rethinking old assumptions. I will describe some of the changed ideas about language and early brain damage so that it may be better understood how they enabled new, different—and more answerable—research questions to be posed.

Child Language is More Than a Simpler Version of Adult Language

Children are active contributors to the process of language learning and language acquisition: They develop their own grammar and rule systems; they adopt strategies and form hypotheses that are confirmed or denied on the basis of language input and experience (de Villiers & de Villiers, 1978). Child language is increasingly viewed as a system internally consistent with the rules and hypotheses of the children that generate it, and not simply as a weaker or simpler version of adult language. Even the replacement of the term *language acquisition* with the term child language (Pinker, 1984) attests to an alteration in the core assumption about the nature of just what is being developed.

Child Language Involves Functional Inhibition as Well as Acquisition

From one perspective, language development is the gradual mastery of a mature communication system. But from another viewpoint, this is incomplete. Although some language functions are added with age, others gradually disappear. The wide range of language sounds produced by the child early in life, for example, becomes narrowed with age as those sounds not part of the native tongue are lost. A similar principle operates in the developing brain. As the sensory–motor system matures, new skills are acquired at the same time as certain types of motor output disappear. Just as the child's brain is not just a schematic of what it will later become, so is child language not merely a simpler version of adult language. In each instance, it is not so much the acquisition of new functions as the loss of irrelevant old functions that enhances the child's behavioral repertoire, that permits skilled production of speech sounds, or allows increasingly fine-tuned sensation and movement. And even theories that stress the learnability of language and the continuity between child and adult language allow for the existence, during development, of ad hoc child grammars that do not resemble adult grammars and that are expunged during the course of neural maturation (e.g., Pinker, 1984).

Once the idea is accepted that development involves not only the imposition of new functions, but also the inhibition or loss of the irrelevant components of existing functions, different kinds of questions about language and early brain damage will be asked. For example, psychologists will become concerned with discovering the role that early brain damage might play in preventing the emergence of time-dependent inhibitory changes such that speech sounds not part of the native tongue would continue to be produced beyond the age when they would normally be lost.

Functional Distinctions Within the Language System

Language is not a unified cognitive function; instead, it comprises various domains (Slobin, 1979; Smith & Wilson, 1979; Wardhaugh, 1977). Theoretical linguistics, developmental psycholinguistics, cognitive science, and experimental psychology have each fractioned language. Current research with brain-damaged populations (e.g., Kean, 1985) involves four broad areas of analysis: phonology, grammar, semantics, and pragmatics.

Phonology, which concerns sounds, is a cover term for both phonetics and phonemics. *Phonetics* is the study of the production, transmission, and reception of speech sounds. A *phonetic feature* is a minimal phonetic characteristic, such as the use of the lips, or of the top teeth, or of low tongue position, or of the nasal cavity. *Phonemics* refers to the procedures for establishing the phonemes of a language, and, also, to the system that results. A *phone* is a discriminable speech sound, a sound considered as an articulatory–acoustic target. A *phoneme* is a minimal significant contrastive unit in the phonological system of a language, a group of sounds functioning as a single contrastive unit. A theory of phonology has two tasks: to provide a means of representing the pronunciation of words and sentences, and to describe the form and function of the phonological rules that relate words and their phonetic representations, or pronunciations. The study of phonology in brain-damaged individuals involves issues such as producing the sounds of English, analyzing missed articulatory targets, and specifying the acoustic elements on which improperly produced or understood speech sounds differ.

Grammar, or language structure, is what intervenes between the speech sounds people hear or say and the meanings they connect with them. Broadly, grammar is that which must be known beyond individual word meanings in order to interpret a sentence. Grammar encodes relational concepts that hold between words—concepts of agency, location, causality, temporal sequence, and the like, and it does so by means of word order and markers. *Word order* contributes to understanding the subject–object relation by revealing who is doing what to, or with, whom. The two types of *markers* are function words and inflections. *Function words* do not make direct reference, but serve instead to mark words grammatically or to mark grammatical relations between words. Examples of function words are articles (*a*, *the*), prepositions (*by*, *with*), and conjunctions (*and*, *but*). *Inflections* are particles attached to words (for example, prefixes or suffixes) that encode grammatical relations such as number (plural *-s*), tense (past *-ed*) and case (accusative inflections occur in some languages). These various grammatical devices serve to identify grammatical class (for example, *the* identifies a noun), specify subject–object relations, and signal meanings (*-ing* signals ongoing activity, *-s* signals plurality).

Grammar involves the formation of words as well as sentences; that is to say, it comprises both morphology and syntax. *Morphology* is the analysis of how words are formed. Morphological structure is the permissable combinations of prefixes, roots, and suffixes that go to make up a word, and the grammar must specify the rules governing the combination: for example, that *-dom* is a suffix turning a noun into a noun, that *-ly* is a suffix turning an adjective into an adverb, or that - *en* is a suffix turning an adjective into a verb. *Syntax* involves how words and parts of words are put together to form sentences. The study of morphology and syntax in brain-damaged individuals involves questions about the omission of grammatical markers; the production of word-order errors, the conditions of success or failure in understanding syntactically complex sentences; and the way in which lexical information memorized with grammatical morphemes is used or misused.

Semantics is the study of the structures of meaning underlying words and sentences, or, more particularly, how words relate to their referents. A *semantic feature* is a distinguishable element of meaning in a word, such as *animate*, *human*, or *female*. The *lexicon* is the vocabulary, or total stock of words, of a language or of a language user. The lexicon codes information about a word's pronunciation, morphology, and grammar, as well as its semantic properties. The study of semantics in brain-damaged populations is concerned with such issues as the referential basis of words as they are used or misused; the way in which semantic features are successfully or unsuccessfully identified and produced; the nature of lexical access; the processes underlying semantic categorization; and the types of semantic propositions that are most easily identified or recalled.

In addition to communicating meaning compactly and efficiently, people must also communicate socially appropriate messages. Utterances perform pragmatic functions, that is, they not only convey meaning through various grammatical devices, but they are used in social settings to fulfill a variety of social functions. Knowledge of language must therefore include pragmatic rules. *Pragmatics* is the study of the social and interpersonal uses and effects of language, including not only the analysis of the social variation of language use, but also how conversations and narratives serve interpersonal communication and discourse functions. The study of pragmatics in brain-damaged subjects is concerned with such issues as the use and misuse of various linguistic elements to form a cohesive text; how the meaning of a text is understood both at a local and at a global level; and how pragmatic and real-world knowledge is used or misused in the understanding of utterances.

As soon as it is assumed that language comprises different constituents, the questions that can be posed about language and the young damaged brain will be significantly altered. We researchers will ask how to measure the various language domains, in addition to considering whether or not language is globally intact. We will wonder whether different language constituents might be differentially affected by early brain damage, and whether a loss of one constituent might occur without a correlative loss in another. We will think about how the language constituents are related to each other in the normal course of development, and how well such interrelations will be maintained in the face of brain injury.

A New Heuristic for Studying How Brain Damage Affects Emerging, Developing, and Established Skills

Half a century ago, Kennard (1936, 1938) reported that motor cortical lesions early in life disrupted motor skill less than lesions sustained later in development. It seemed that early lesions were less debilitating of function than comparable later lesions. Now there is some reason to doubt whether Kennard's early and late lesions were comparable (Isaacson, 1975, suggests that the later lesions involved more tissue damage), but what should be highlighted are three of Kennard's other observations that have been generally ignored: first, that behavioral impairments occurring immediately after early lesions are different from those that appear immediately after late lesions; second, that certain behavioral impairments do not occur immediately after early brain damage, but emerge only later in development, at a time when the relevant behavior would normally appear; and third, that the magnitude of any behavioral difference between early and late lesions is variable, being much greater for some behaviors than for others (Kennard, 1940, 1942). What Kennard proposed, in essence, was that lesions in infancy produce relatively few immediate problems but that, during ensuing development, young brain-damaged organisms "fail to acquire" (1940, p. 388) their expected complement of skills. It is these failures to acquire skill after early brain damage that have been generally ignored.

I want to propose a heuristic for describing the possible effects of early brain damage on a behavioral skill that begins with Kennard's neglected ideas and that draws on some of the learning disability research of Rourke (1976) and Satz, Fletcher, Clark, and Morris (1981). This is shown in Figure 1.

The heuristic depicts how brain damage at various points in the evolution of a behavioral skill might influence how successfully or unsuccessfully that skill can become functional. Three degrees of skill maturation are distinguished: emerging, developing, and established. An *emerging skill* is one that is not yet functional or in the preliminary stages of acquisition. A *developing skill* has been partially acquired, and it is functional, albeit incompletely so. An *established skill* is one that has been fully acquired. Five aspects of skill function are distinguished: onset, order, rate, strategy, mastery, control, and upkeep. The *onset* of a skill is that time in development when it would normally begin to be behaviorally evident. The *order* in which a skill is acquired refers to its temporal emergence relative to the child's other behavioral and cognitive capacities. The *rate* of skill acquisition is the speed of its developmental course. *Skill strategy* refers to the behavioral and cognitive tactics used to put it into effect. *Skill mastery* is the final level of competence attained. The *control* of a skill is the ability to use or effect it when required. The *upkeep* of a skill refers to its long-term maintenance and deployment.

What might happen to a skill were brain damage to be sustained at each of three different points in development—infancy, childhood, and adulthood? How would the consequences for that skill differ according to the developing timing of the brain damage?

Brain damage in utero or in infancy has widespread potential consequences, in that it places at some degree of risk the entire course of skill development. The most obvious questions to ask of a skill after brain damage in infancy, however, concern its onset and its order. The onset of a skill may be normal or delayed, a *delay* involving a deferral in its expected time of onset. The order in which a skill develops may be normal or garbled, a *garble* referring to a jumble in the expected order of skill emergence vis-à-vis other skills.

Brain damage in childhood has important functional consequences, most particularly for the rate, strategy, and mastery of that large com-

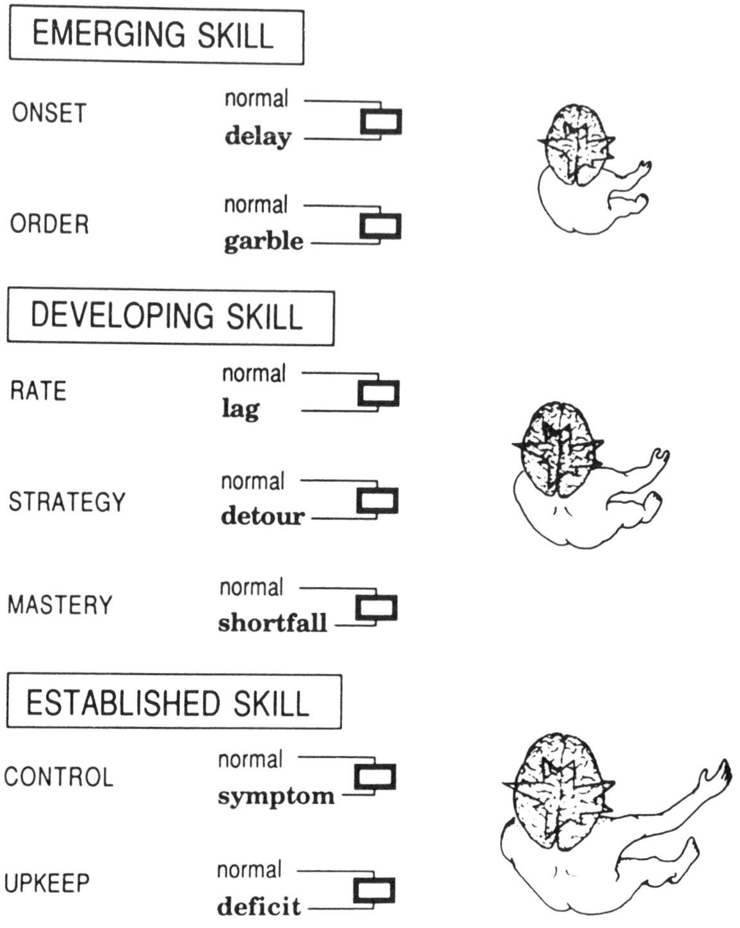

Figure 1. Heuristic framework for describing how brain damage affects emerging, developing, and established skills.

plement of childhood abilities that are in various stages of maturation. The rate at which a skill develops may be normal or lagging, a *lag* referring to a slowed progression, or even an arrest, through the projected developmental course. The strategic mode for skill acquisition may be normal or detoured, a *detour* being an atypical tactic that achieves the normal endstate of the skill through a circuitous or time-consuming manoeuvre. The mastery of a skill may be normal or shortfalled, a *shortfall* involving a final level of skill competence that is less than would normally have been projected.

Brain damage in adulthood affects primarily established skills. The control of a skill may be normal or symptomatic, a *symptom* being a loss of the ability to use or effect the skill, when required. The upkeep of a skill may be normal or defective, a *deficit* involving a loss of long-term skill maintenance.

The heuristic emphasizes that the extent of functional impairment after brain damage in infancy or childhood cannot be assessed for a considerable time after the onset of the damage; not, in fact, until that point in development when the function would normally have developed (for animal models relevant to this principle, see Goldman, 1972). Clearly, the intactness of a skill cannot be judged without making reference to the elapsed time since the onset of brain injury. The model also forces us researchers to consider future or unacquired skills as well as skills functional or semifunctional at the time of brain damage. In showing that brain damage has possible consequences for the functioning of any subsequent skill, the model suggests (in contrast to earlier assumptions of fewer and weaker effects of brain damage in children than in adults) that the earlier the brain damage, the more extensive the potential functional consequences: Brain damage in utero, for instance, places in potential jeopardy the onset, order, rate, strategy, mastery, control, and upkeep of each and every cognitive skill developed during the life span. The model thus underscores the fact that early brain damage actually may have more long-lasting and more widespread potential consequences than brain injury sustained later in life.

The various elements in Figure 1 are presented as existing as fully independent. In practice, insufficient information exists about some possible consequences of early brain damage (for example, how a delay in the onset of one skill affects the order in which related skills can be acquired) to decide whether the assumption of independence is justified. As empirical data on these issues are gradually accumulated, certain contingencies may become apparent (for instance, that delayed skill onset occurs commonly with garbled skill order) that would necessitate modifications in the heuristic.

The spatial juxtaposition of the three human brain-damaged manikins with the three skill levels in Figure 1 would imply that brain damage in infancy influences emerging skill, brain damage in childhood influences developing skill, and brain damage in adulthood affects established skill. Although this is broadly true, it is far from being absolute. A new skill may emerge and develop after brain damage at any age. Any new skill acquired by an adult with brain damage sustained in adulthood would be at risk for delayed onset or garbled order of acquisition. Although many childhood skills are in the process of development, others are fully developed, so these latter skills may show symptoms and deficits after brain damage in childhood.

New Investigations of Language and Early Brain Damage

As a result of changes in the assumptions guiding the study of language after early brain injury (in particular, a greater appreciation of the cognitive differences between child and adult; an awareness of the diverse nature of language itself; and the use of developmental frameworks like the one I have just discussed), the new questions that are being asked about early brain damage and language are different in several respects from the old ones. In essence, current research investigations have been guided by questions that are better defined, more specific, and developmental in nature.

Which aspects of early brain damage affect existing language function and later language acquisition, and which do not? Which language impairments, in existing function and later acquisition, are associated with the various aspects of early brain damage? These are the kinds of questions posed in current research investigations, questions concerned with identifying those features of early brain damage that place a child at risk for present or future language deficit, and with predicting particular patterns of language deficit from knowledge of specific features of early brain damage. In order to answer such questions, it is necessary to understand how the functional consequences of early brain damage vary, not only with the degree of skill evolution (see Figure 1), but also with the developmental timing and particular characteristics of the brain lesions.

The Effect of Developmental Timing of the Brain Lesion on Language

The developmental timing of a brain lesion is relevant to language outcome. But developmental timing involves at least three dimensions—age at lesion, age of lesion, and age at test—and it is important to distinguish among them in terms of their effects on language outcome after brain damage. What must also be considered is the extent to which the subject's age at test may validly be invoked as a variable of direct explanatory significance for the later language function of brain-damaged children.

Age at Lesion

Congenital and perinatal lesions have been shown to produce problems involving the onset and rate of language. Early damage to the left hemisphere delays the acquisition of syntactic awareness (Dennis & Whitaker, 1976). Hydrocephalus is a disturbance of pressure in the brain that arises from an imbalance in the production and absorption of cerebrospinal fluid, and that leads to engorgement of the cerebral ventricles and loss of brain volume. Congenital hydrocephalus produces changes in the developmental rate of language such that, with advancing age, hydrocephalics become increasingly less competent in a variety of language skills than their age peers (Dennis, Hendrick, Hoffman, & Humphreys, 1987).

Similar brain damage produces different effects on language at different developmental periods. Early vascular malformations of the left hemisphere produce selective problems in the rate, mastery, and strategy of discrete language functions (Dennis, 1980a, 1980b; Dennis & Kohn, 1975; Dennis & Whitaker, 1976), whereas later cerebrovascular accidents produce more widespread language symptoms and deficits that correspond in some measure to those seen in adult aphasia (Dennis, 1980c). Even during the later stages of development, similar forms of brain damage may produce effects on language function that differ in magnitude depending on the age at lesion onset. The diffuse damage associated with closed head injury produces deficits in written language skills more in middle childhood than in adolescence (Ewing-Cobbs, Fletcher, Landry, & Levin, 1985). Generally speaking, congenital and perinatal lesions cause problems of delayed onset, strategic detour, and lagging rate of acquisition. Later lesions produce symptoms and deficits.

Age of Lesion

It has long been known that some aspects of behavioral outcome after adult brain damage are related to the age of the lesion. In the acute phase of adult brain injury, the patterning of IQ test results is related to the side of the lesion; after the lesion has become chronic, it is not (Fitzhugh, Fitzhugh, & Reitan, 1962). In contrast, IQ results are not related to lesion duration after early brain lesions (Dennis, 1985a).

How lesion age affects language function in individuals with early brain damage has not been systematically studied, with the result that the acute and chronic effects on language of early lesions are not well understood. In studies of early brain damage and language the age of the lesion and the age of the child should be kept separate, and the length of time a brain lesion has existed must not be confounded with the point in development when it was sustained (see Dennis & Whitaker, 1977, for a discussion).

Age at Test

That children of different chronological ages vary in their ability to perform cognitive tasks is no less true for brain-damaged children than for their normal age peers. For example, success in finding names in response to a semantic description (being able to answer "elephant" in response to the question, "what lives in the jungle, and has big floppy ears and a trunk?") depends on being older at the time of testing for both hydrocephalic and control children (Dennis, Hendrick, Hoffman, & Humphreys, 1987). But the subject's age at testing may affect language differently in normal and brain-damaged states. For example, the speed of semantic access to the lexicon (how rapidly the response "elephant" can be given to the question, "what lives in the jungle, and has big floppy ears and a trunk?") depends on an interaction between the presence of early hydrocephalus and being older at the time of testing (Dennis, Hendrick, Hoffman, & Humphreys, 1987). These and other examples show that the age of the child at behavioral testing is an important determinant of language function, both in its own right and in interaction with other variables.

The subject's age at behavioral testing must certainly be included in any discussion of the effects of early brain damage on language. But age per se is neither a mechanism of recovery after early brain damage (Fletcher, Miner, & Ewing-Cobbs, 1987), nor a variable with direct explanatory significance (Fletcher, Levin, & Landry, 1984; Fletcher & Satz, 1983). Age is better considered as an independent variable that marks the temporal course of development, demarcates periods of developmental change, and delineates different developmental phases (Siegel, Bisanz, & Bisanz, 1983; Wohlwill, 1973) than as an explanation, either necessary or sufficient, for the varying effects of early brain damage on language.

How Language Varies with Particular Dimensions of Early Brain Damage

The brain has many facets to its structure and function, so it cannot be characterized by a single dimension. Recent neuropsychological studies have shown that several different dimensions of brain structure and function (involving facts about lesion site, pathology, associated symptoms, and so on) are of demonstrated importance for a child's intellectual function subsequent to early brain injury (e.g., Dennis, 1985a). Similarly, several different brain dimensions are proving to be important for a developmental neuropsychology of language (e.g., Dennis, 1987c). Let us consider the impact of some of these dimensions of early brain damage on later language function.

Pathological Substrate

Brain damage comes about in consequence of some pathological process, quite aside from where, and how extensively, such a process might occur in the brain. Three types of investigations are useful in attempting to understand the role of pathology in later language function after early brain damage: comparisons of children and adults who have been selected for study on the basis of similar language symptoms and deficits, but who differ in pathology; comparisons of language symptoms and deficits in children and adults with similar pathological processes underlying their brain damage; and comparisons of different pathologies within a broad category of childhood brain damage.

Neither the frequency nor the type of pathological brain processes in children are identical to those in adults: For instance, there is a lower prevalence of unilateral vascular disease in children (Satz & Bullard-Bates, 1981). Childhood language symptoms and deficits will most often occur because of brain trauma, whereas adult language symptoms and deficits will characteristically be caused by cerebrovascular accidents. Children and adults selected for study on the basis of language symptoms and deficits will almost certainly have different pathological substrates for their causative brain damage, as well as differing in age at lesion onset. When pathology is held constant, language symptoms in children and adults show more similarity: For example, studies of language deficit secondary to vascular disease in children show a fair parallel with the adult pattern (e.g., Aram, Rose, Rekate, & Whitaker, 1983; Dennis, 1980c). To ignore the pathological substrate of the brain damage in any comparison of children and adults is to risk an improper inference, to interpret differences in language function as due to age or maturation when in fact they may arise in equal measure from pathology.

Even in studies comparing language after brain damage in children of different ages, pathology has been either ignored or confounded with other factors (see Dennis, 1980c; Satz & Bullard-Bates, 1981, for a discussion). For example, both the Hecaen (1976) and the Alajouanine and Lhermitte (1965) papers sum over trauma, tumor, meningitis, and arteriopathy cases in attempting to calculate the incidence of language disorder in brain-damaged children, thereby making the results impossible to evaluate. Woods and Teuber (1978) found that poor language recovery in brain-damaged children was related to cerebrovascular pathology and later lesion onset, their confound between pathology and age obscuring just which factor actually predicted language recovery.

Within one set of congenital brain malformations, the pathological substrate of the early brain damage is a determinant of language outcome. The child with hydrocephalus caused by perinatal disturbances is more likely to maintain an age-appropriate rate of language acquisition in later childhood and adolescence than one whose hydrocephalus stems from anomalies of the ventricular system originating in the early months of gestation (Dennis, Hendrick, Hoffman, & Humphreys, 1987). Different types of pathology sustained in later childhood produce contrasting effects on language. In middle childhood, cerebrovascular accidents to the left hemisphere produce symptoms and deficits in phonology, semantics, morphology, and pragmatics (Dennis, 1980c), whereas diffuse brain damage from closed head injury incurred at the same age results in nonspecific and subclinical changes in language function (Ewing-Cobbs, Fletcher, Landry, & Levin, 1985). Pathology is also one determinant of how fully language recovers after early brain damage. Children with traumatically acquired aphasia show better recovery from language symptoms than those with acquired vascular abnormalities (Guttmann, 1942; van Dongen & Loonen, 1977).

To be sure, understanding the role of early pathological brain processes in later language function is far from complete. We researchers do not know how each form of pathology is related to the extent of tissue damage. Is it always the case, for instance, that brain trauma from head injuries produces more extensive tissue damage than vascular lesions? It is well documented that certain pathologies have an affinity for particular brain sites (for example, the brain tumor, craniopharyngioma, characteristically occurs around the optic chiasm), but we do not know how reliably each of the many pathological processes occurs in specific brain locations. We have little information about the comparative importance for language of the various congenital brain pathologies. Although epileptogenic lesions in childhood contribute to intellectual impairments (Dennis, Fitz, et al., 1981) as well as to selective language disorders (Kohn, 1980), it is not known how debilitating epileptogenic lesions are in comparison to other pathologies. As yet, we are unable to answer questions such as the following: Of three brain lesions occurring in middle childhood (a tumor in the left temporal lobe, an epileptogenic focus in the left temporal lobe, and a tumor in the left frontal lobe), which two produce the most similar language impairments?

Despite these gaps in our understanding of the functional consequences of the various early brain pathologies, the emerging evidence does indicate that comparative studies of brain-damaged children and adults cannot simply assume them to have comparable pathologies (see also St. James-Roberts, 1979), and also that pathology cannot be ignored in any account of language in the young damaged brain. Pathological substrate is a dimension of early brain damage that, if not fully understood, is at least being explored.

Epilepsy, Signs, and Symptoms

In some forms of early brain damage, the predictors of later language function are the symptoms associated with the brain insult, rather than the insult itself. A progressive loss of existing language in children can occur in consequence of epileptic seizures (Gascon, Victor, Lombroso, & Goodglass, 1973; Worster-Drought, 1964). Epilepsy in the left side of the brain curtails syntactic development in an atypical, right hemisphere substrate (Kohn, 1980). The presence of an epileptic disorder signals that recovery from childhood acquired aphasia is likely to be poor (van Dongen & Loonen, 1977). Whether and how language is altered by other signs and symptoms associated with damage to the immature brain remains to be studied.

Focal, Multifocal, and Diffuse Damage

Our knowledge of this dimension of brain damage exists only in broad outline. However, the emerging evidence is consistent with the idea that diffuse and multifocal brain disorders, so prevalent in children, are associated with significant later cognitive impairments.

In children with head injury, it is the severity of diffuse brain injury, as opposed to the presence or lateralization of a focal lesion, that determines language function (Ewing-Cobbs, Fletcher, Landry, & Levin, 1985). And within a group of head-injured children, the younger ones are at greater risk for widespread cognitive deficits after diffuse head injury (Levin, Eisenberg, Wiig, & Kobayashi, 1982).

Several forms of brain injury occurring in children rather than adults (for example, intraventricular hemorrhage, congenital hydrocephalus, dysraphic conditions of the spine and skull, and cerebral palsy) involve pathological processes that are diffuse or multifocal, rather than being localized in one region of the brain. Only recently has attention been directed toward studying such brain perturbations of childhood (perhaps because there are few neurological conditions in adults to which they can be compared). These early brain insults produce significant developmental impairments (Fletcher, Levin, & Landry, 1984) although, as yet, we are uncertain as to the range and type of the resulting cognitive disorders.

Laterality, Length, and Depth of Lesion Localization

We should first distinguish between lateralization and localization, because the two terms are sometimes used, incorrectly, as synonyms. *Lateralization* refers to whether a function is deemed to be represented, or whether a lesion has occurred, on the right or the left side of the brain. *Localization* refers to regional brain geography for putative representation of a function or occurrence of a lesion. Localization is the more general term, which includes lateralization as one of its dimensions.

The three dimensions along which brain lesions may be localized are the laterality or right–left dimension; the length or front–back dimension; and the depth, or up–down dimension (Dennis, 1977). Each of these will be discussed in turn.

Laterality or right–left dimension. Language appears to be functionally lateralized to the left hemisphere in children, just as it has been shown to be in adults. At each point in development, lesions of the left hemisphere are more likely than comparable right-sided lesions to compromise language.

Prenatal vascular malformations of the left hemisphere with subsequent removal of the diseased brain half cause delayed onset of syntactic understanding, relative to comparable right hemisphere lesions (Dennis & Whitaker, 1976). Later in development, left hemidecorticate infantile hemiplegics show incomplete mastery of syntax (Dennis & Kohn, 1975); and such mastery as they do attain appears to be effected by strategic detours (Dennis, 1980a). Some consequences of these impairments include problems in integrating information across sentences (Dennis, Lovett, & Wiegel-Crump, 1981) and an inability to produce extended units of cohesive narrative discourse (Lovett, Dennis, & Newman, 1986; Newman, Lovett, & Dennis, 1986).

Similar results appear to hold for children with very early lateralized brain lesions who have not had surgical removal of one entire brain half. Children with infantile hemiplegia from left hemisphere lesions at birth show poorer syntactic understanding than either their siblings or infantile hemiplegics with right hemisphere birth lesions (Kiessling, Denckla, & Carlton, 1983; Rankin, Aram, & Horwitz, 1981). Children with hemiplegia from early left hemisphere lesions are delayed in the onset of word combinations relative to chidren with right-sided lesions (Bishop, 1967; Rankin, Aram, & Horwitz, 1981). Early left-sided brain lesions disrupt the acquisition of spoken syntax more than do early right-sided lesions (Aram, Ekelman, & Whitaker, 1986). Children with left-sided brain lesions are slower and less accurate at word-finding than right-lesioned age mates, regardless of when in childhood the lesions began (Aram, Ekelman, & Whitaker, 1987).

All of these results point to the vulnerability of the young left hemisphere to language deficits. They suggest, further, that some language components are significantly more vulnerable than others to early left-sided lesions.

Length or front–back dimension. This aspect of lesion localization has been studied much more extensively in adults than in children. Nevertheless, the evidence in children shows it to have important functional consequences.

Thinning or stretching of the cortex and underlying white matter at birth or in the first months of life (based on the extent of dilation of the brain ventricles relative to overall brain size, a procedure that equates for age differences) is related to later cognitive function—but in a manner that depends on the front–back dimension of the young brain. In hydrocephalic children, a selective thinning and stretching of the posterior brain relative to the anterior brain is predictive of relatively poor nonverbal intelligence (Dennis, Fitz, et al., 1981).

The anterior regions of the brain, both right and left, are important for sustaining access to the lexicon in young brain-damaged individuals, whereas the posterior brain regions in either hemisphere appear to play no comparable role (Dennis, 1987c). In children with deficits in previously acquired language, disorders of auditory–verbal comprehension occur principally after lesions within the temporal lobe, rather than as a result of either anterior or posterior lesions (Hecaen, 1976).

Depth or up–down dimension. Although this dimension has not been studied extensively in brain-damaged children, it appears to have enormous importance for later cognitive and language functioning. What the emerging evidence shows is that some lesions within the up–down dimension of the brain have similar effects in children and in adults, whereas others have different functional consequences depending on age.

Some lesions in deep parts of the brain have somewhat similar consequences in children and adults. The language symptoms that follow focal left subcortical vascular lesions in adulthood also arise from acute focal left subcortical vascular lesions in middle childhood (Aram, Rose, Rekate, & Whitaker, 1983). Other subcortical lesions have different effects in children and adults. Impairments in nonverbal intelligence occur after acute right hemisphere cortical lesions in adulthood (e.g., Fitzhugh, Fitzhugh, & Reitan, 1962) but in consequence of acute or chronic right hemisphere subcortical lesions in children and adolescents (Dennis, 1985a).

It is not surprising that disturbances in the brain's subcortex and white matter should affect the acquisition of cognitive skills. Many forms of early brain perturbation involve subcortical and white matter lesions. The loss of brain volume in congenital hydrocephalus especially involves the white matter (Harwood-Nash & Fitz, 1976). Neuropathological findings in individuals dying from perinatal cerebral palsy demonstrate primarily subcortical lesions involving sclerosis and degeneration of the white matter (Painter & Low, 1986).

The Functional Importance of These Three Dimensions and Age

Although some functional consequences of lesion localization appear similar after early and later brain injury, it is also apparent that the importance of a particular dimensions of lesion localization may change—or even reverse—during the course of development. In consequence, not only may there be differences between early- and late-lesioned individuals in the characteristic pattern of functional brain localization at maturity, but the importance of particular brain regions for behavioral functions such as language may alter significantly during the course of development.

It was proposed long ago that the brain systems required to acquire a behavior might differ from those needed to sustain the behavior, once acquired (e.g., Hebb, 1942). Later research has supported this principle. In nonhuman primates, damage to one part of the prefrontal cortex produces a behavioral deficit that later resolves, whereas damage to a different prefrontal region delays or prevents the future acquisition of another behavior (Goldman, 1972). In humans, Rourke (1987) has suggested that what the brain's subcortex and white matter contribute to the acquisition of functional systems within the cortex is different from what they add to the maintenance of these systems once they are acquired. And recent research with brain-damaged children suggests that skill acquisition and skill maintenance may call upon different localizations within each hemisphere of the brain, or even upon different hemispheres.

Within the right hemisphere, there appears to be a depth shift during development, such that the functions underlying nonverbal intelligence become progressively more encephalized: Nonverbal intelligence is most disrupted by subcortical lesions in childhood (Dennis, 1985a, 1985b), but by acute cortical lesions in adulthood. Within the left hemisphere, also, there are suggestions of a functional depth shift in certain language skills: Access to the lexicon through the sound structure of words is typically impaired by left cortical lesions in adulthood (e.g., Lecours, Lhermitte, & Bryans, 1983); but, although left cortical lesions also impair this skill in early-damaged individuals, left subcortical lesions are relatively more disruptive (Dennis, 1987c).

Perhaps one aspect of these developmental shifts in brain localization involves a switch in functional control from one hemisphere to the other. The development of nonverbal skills after early brain injury involves a left hemisphere mediation of skills that are characteristically maintained by a right hemisphere in adulthood (Kohn & Dennis, 1974). Pragmatic discourse competence is usually held to be impaired by right hemisphere lesions in adulthood (e.g., Gardner, 1983) but early left hemisphere damage and removal impairs these functions in children and adolescents (Newman, Lovett, & Dennis, 1986).

This idea—that the functional dimensions of the brain that acquire a behavioral skill are different from those that sustain it at maturity—is yet to be fully specified. It is not clear whether variables other than lesion localization contribute to the apparent differences between children and adults; nor have direct comparisons been made of early- and late-lesioned individuals performing the identical cognitive tasks. But it is clear that the idea has considerable import for how we view the functioning of the immature brain and its ongoing developmental course.

Validation of Hypothetical Language Constructs

I have discussed a variety of facts about early brain damage and its effects on language. Focusing on different features of the brain, I have asked of each one, "Does it affect language?" Now it is time to change the viewpoint. Focusing on one component of the language system, the lexicon, I will discuss whether—and how—different forms of lexical access might exist in the young damaged brain.

Validating Constructs About the Lexicon

Access to the lexicon has been studied by three methods: the analyses of single cases; the dissociation of language skills within and between groups; and the pattern and factor structure of individual difference data. Each approach, explicitly or implicitly, attempts to validate constructs about the lexicon. Construct validation, part of a set of scientific procedures for developing and confirming theories (Cronbach & Meehl, 1955), is a way of explicating how a test operates as a measure of some feature that is not operationally defined.

Most, if not all, of the single case studies in neuropsychology journals have been concerned with some form of cognitive component analysis. Proponents of such case histories aim to provide a functional decomposition of the lexicon within a single individual (e.g., Caramazza, 1985). In this approach, each case involves a separate decomposition and permits an extra kink in the theoretical position that evolves from the additive effects of the successive decompositions. Studies of brain-damaged groups, in contrast, have generally been concerned with describing average performance differences in one task between two or more groups and average differences in two or more task performances within one group.

What the case history and the group study have in common is that they approach questions about the lexicon in terms of construct representation, a form of validation that focuses on task variability rather than subject variability, and that attempts to decompose the underlying mechanisms of task performance (Embretson, 1983). For the case history advocate, individual differences are simply ignored; for proponents of the group study, individual differences mess up group means.

But individual differences in the way brain-damaged children and adolescents perform language tests should not be ignored or suffered; actually, they represent an important source of validation for language constructs. The formal analysis of individual differences conducted within a nomothetic span framework (Embretson, 1983), that is, one emphasizing the degree to which individual differences reveal theoretically relevant constructs, can provide a new approach to the question of how the lexicon might be represented in the young damaged brain.

Individual Differences in Language Test Performances Reveal Language Factors

The following investigation (Dennis, 1987c) was concerned with validating various language constructs in a population of children with early brain damage. What prompted the study was the idea that functional distinctions within the language domain, including those concerned with the lexicon, might be used to parse the young damaged brain. To *parse* is to resolve something into its component parts and describe them (Fowler & Fowler, 1958); to parse the young damaged brain with language is to group certain characteristics of brain injury according to how they sustain or disrupt language performance.

A large group of brain-damaged children, adolescents, and young adults was given a set of language tests. The pathology in the subjects covered most forms of early brain damage; in every instance, overt brain injury had been sustained in utero, at birth, in infancy, or during childhood. (The subject sample is described in Dennis, 1987c.) Testing of language was performed at varying times after the onset of brain insult. The data core involved 55 test measures described in various sources (Denckla & Rudel, 1974; Dennis, 1983; Dennis, Hendrick, Hoffman, & Humphreys, 1987; Dennis & Kohn, 1975, 1985; Dennis, Lovett, & Wiegel-Crump, 1981; Dennis, Sugar, & Whitaker, 1982; Dennis & Whitaker, 1976; Wiegel-Crump & Dennis, 1986). The following language skills, tapping the operation of the phonological system, grammar and syntax, semantics and the lexicon, and pragmatic use and understanding, were assessed: the accurate phonetic production of the sounds and blends of English; the ability to name common objects when confronted with them; the speed and accuracy of naming using three different types of lexical access (semantic information, rhyming forms, and pictures); the speed and accuracy of automatized lexical production; the prototypicality of lexical choices (the extent to which the lexical items produced to fill a semantic category are semantic "signatures" of their category, e.g., robins are prototypical birds, whereas kiwis, being flightless, are not); semantic fluency in response to letter cues; the recall and repetition of semantically and syntactically complex sentences; the speed and accuracy of understanding different syntactic forms; the detection and correction of semantic anomalies in sentences; the detection and correction of syntactic errors in sentences; the construction of sentences from target words; comprehension of single lexical items represented visually; comprehension of semantically complex oral commands; the production of surface morphological and syntactic features in tag questions; and the understanding of pragmatic sentence features involving premises, presuppositions (real-world conditions that must be met if a sentence is to be interpreted in the intended manner), and entailments or implications.

These language data were analyzed by means of factor analysis. Two parallel analyses were conducted, a principal components analysis and a form of common factor analysis (Hunter, 1980). These analyses reduced the 55 test measures to the following 13 factors (see Table 1).

Factor 1 was concerned with semantic competence; tests loading on this factor involved the ability to produce target names, to access

Table 1
Language Factors

Factor	Description
1	Semantic competence
2	Surface structure syntax production
3	Rapid identification of syntactic form
4	Accurate identification of syntactic form
5	Speed of visual lexical access
6	Sentence recall and repetition
7	Identification of entailment and presupposition
8	Articulation of speech sounds and blends
9	Identification of premises
10	Prototypicality of later category instances
11	Speed of phonological lexical access
12	Prototypicality of initial category instances
13	Mechanics of speech pacing

Note. Adapted from Dennis (1987c) by permission.

the lexicon, in response to semantic information ("What is an animal that lives in the jungle, walks on four feet, has a mane, and roars?"), the ability to make discriminations among different lexical items, and the ability to understand oral commands. Speed of retrieving names for objects seen, speed of visual lexical access, was tapped by Factor 5, which contrasted with speed of access to the lexicon through phonological form (Factor 11), the latter tested by the ability to retrieve names within a semantic category in response to a rhyming form. Factor 12 and Factor 10 were concerned with the hierarchical structure within semantic categories, and they were indexed by the degree of prototypicality for semantic category instances in the initial (Factor 12) or later (Factor 10) stages of producing names. Factor 2 involved the phonetic realization of surface structure syntax, and it was measured by the ability to produce tag questions that reflected specific grammatical and morphological features of their declarative prompts. Factors 3 and 4 were concerned with understanding how the grammatical structure of a sentence reflected its logical form, and here there was a clear differentiation between syntactic speed (Factor 3) and syntactic accuracy (Factor 4). Factor 8 was concerned with phonetics, with the articulation of speech sounds, and it was measured by the ability to produce accurately the sounds and blends of English. Echoic sentence recall and repetition were involved in Factor 6, with the measures of this factor all concerning the ability to repeat sentences without lexical or grammatical error. Factor 13 tapped a mechanical aspect of phonetics, and involved fluent language production, the avoidance of pacing errors. A pragmatic interface between language form and content and the real world was involved in judging the truth values of statements in which propositional negation either did or did not interact with different types of matrix verbs: In Factor 9, the judgments concerned the premises of implicative verbs; in Factor 7, the truth value judgments involved the presuppositions of factive verbs and the entailments of implicative verbs.

The patterning of the factors is revealed more clearly by grouping them. Five factors were concerned with conceptualizing experience, of which three involved symbolizing (Factors 1, 5, and 11) and two involved categorizing (Factors 10 and 12). Symbolizing experience tapped such skills as naming and understanding names, and accessing the lexicon rapidly and easily. Categorizing experience involved the internal organization of the lexicon with respect to such issues as its prototypicality. Three factors (Factors 2, 3, and 4) concerned how language was computed and formally specified, that is, they tapped linguistic form as opposed to language content. Two (Factors 7 and 9) addressed pragmatic considerations, the interface between the form of what was said and real world considerations involving what an utterance presupposed and entailed. Three (Factors 6, 8, and 13) tapped certain mechanical aspects of phonetic production.

Language factors are constructs that are hypothetical but still closely tied to language test performance. The factors were established by examining the pattern of individual differences in the performance of brain-damaged individuals on language tests. At the same time, the factors are also presumed to be what gave rise to those performances.

Language Factors and Features of Early Brain Damage

Having established the set of language factors, the next step in the investigation was to discover how each one was related to the brain damage the children and adolescents had sustained. Some 100 facts about each subject's brain damage were coded, in order to survey how the injury arose, its pathological type, where it was localized, the symptoms associated with it, and how it was treated. The variables were selected so as to signal events, symptoms, signs, or findings from the period of gestation to the time of the language testing. Such a range of facts was necessary because I did not know in advance which facts would be relevant to language.

How can the language factors be used to discriminate among different features of the young damaged brain in such a way as to determine which constellations are most important for particular language constructs? I will describe which of all the facts coded about early brain damage were predictive of each of three factors concerned with access to the lexicon (Factor 1, semantic competence; Factor 5, visual lexical access; and Factor 11, phonological lexical access). By comparing and contrasting the features of early brain damage to which each factor is most closely related, some hypotheses will emerge about the nature of the young brain's representation of the lexicon.

The statistical approach used to address this issue involved multiple regression (Dillon & Goldstein, 1984). In regression analysis, scores on outcome variables can be predicted from constellations of variables in another domain. Multiple regression was used here to predict the three language factor scores from the cumulative effects of sets of medical variables, in which each medical variable was considered in concert with the effects of the others.

The output of a multiple regression for a particular factor identifies three types of variables: those that disrupt the function, those that sustain it, and those to which it is not relevant. A variable disrupts a function when it causes it to operate at a lower level than it would without the variable being present. A variable that sustains a function is not necessarily something that would enhance language in the normal population; it is, rather, an aspect of brain damage whose presence will cause a function to be maintained at a level higher than that expected in the rest of the brain-damaged sample (see Dennis, 1985a, for a discussion). A variable that is not relevant to a function will neither disrupt nor sustain it.

Each of the three lexical access factors was associated with a different constellation of brain damage features. These features involved lesion localization; pathological substrate; seizures, signs, and symptoms; and demographic features. In relation to semantic competence and phonological lexical access, visual lexical access depended on peripheral neurological processes more than on the integrity of particular brain loci.

Semantic competence was impaired by lateralized damage to the left hemisphere, in an even manner from cortical into deeper subcortical regions. It was sensitive to disruption by pathological conditions such as anoxia or coma that involved diffuse perturbations of deep and central regions of the brain. It was unaffected by symptom patterns.

Sustenance and impairment of phonological lexical access were lateralized to the left hemisphere, although impairment was localized more strongly in deeper subcortical brain regions. It was unaffected by pathological condition, symptoms, and demographic features.

Visual lexical access had no identifiable lesion localization for either impairment or sustenance, but could be predicted from the level of associated symptoms. It was disrupted by cortical sensory loss, fine motor problems, and tonic-adversive seizures, but sustained in the face of generalized seizures.

Using Individual Differences in Early Brain Damage Data to Validate Constructs About Lexical Access

On the basis of the evidence just presented, how might researchers go about deciding about the validity of constructs about lexical access?

What would it mean to say that different types of lexical access had been selectively impaired by early brain injury? What would convince us that a given lexical access system had a singular brain representation, and what types of evidence would lead us to reject such an idea? First we might operationalize the question along something like the following lines:

1. A lexical access factor would be discrete if it remained isolable from other lexical access factors within the same brain-damaged population; that is, if they did not rise and fall together in a group of brain-damaged individuals. A discrete lexical access, then, would emerge as a separate factor from an analysis of a large number of language test scores in a large brain-damaged sample.

2. A lexical access factor would be distinct if it could be shown to have a characteristic pattern of brain damage parameters that disrupted or sustained it. A distinct lexical access factor would be one whose status could be predicted by a different constellation of brain damage features from others. Distinctness is something that is judged by comparing the similarities and differences between the features of brain damage associated with different lexical access factors. A lexical access factor might be distinct with respect to certain dimensions of brain damage but not to others: The more a lexical access factor depended on peripheral neurological processes and the less it required the integrity of core features of the central nervous system, the less would it be brain-distinct.

3. A lexical access factor would be autonomous to the extent that it maintained its boundaries in the face of brain damage, that is, if brain damage-induced changes in its level were not accompanied by compensatory changes in the levels of other lexical access factors. Decisions about functional autonomy are complex, and require a set of procedures for specifying the structure of factor interrelations.

In reviewing the status of the three lexical access factors as discrete, distinct, and autonomous, one might consider them as orderable according to something such as the following hierarchy: All distinct factors are discrete, but not every discrete factor is distinct; and all autonomous factors are both distinct and discrete, but not every distinct factor will be autonomous.

Each lexical access factor is functionally discrete in that it rises or falls with considerable independence in an early brain-damaged population. A different constellation of brain damage variables was associated with each factor, indicating that each is to some extent distinct. But although they were distinct in different ways, the factors intersected along certain dimensions of brain damage. To answer the question of whether the factors have autonomous brain representations, it would be necessary to compare and contrast normal and brain-damaged populations, not only in terms of the language factors themselves, but also in terms of the structure of the factor interrelations. Procedures like confirmatory factor analysis (e.g., Joreskog & Sorbom, 1979) are required to incorporate substantively meaningful constraints in comparing the transitivity of factor structures across populations.

This study has provided one methodological basis for asking neuropsychological questions about access to the lexicon, and for using information derived from brain-damaged children to answer them. It is clear that constructs about lexical access can be validated, not just by postulates about their internal representation or by functional decompositions, but also by studies that reveal their place within the broader framework of linguistic function in young brain-damaged language users.

Implications for Viewing Brain Damage in Children and Adults

Adult brain damage and child brain damage are different in important ways. Neither the prevalence of certain types of brain pathology nor the behavioral consequences of particular lesions are the same in children as in adults.

It is not that the child is more resilient to brain damage than the adult—on the contrary, youth does not confer immunity from brain damage-induced language disorders, and even malformation of the brain in the first months of gestation have consequences for later anomalies of language development (Dennis, Hendrick, Hoffman, & Humphreys, 1987)—but, rather, that the kind of brain damage that prevents the development of a skill appears to be different from the damage that disrupts the maintenance of that skill, once acquired. All of this makes it incorrect to use the adult damaged brain as the sole reference point or framework within which to understand brain damage in children.

The view of early brain damage that I have outlined is one that sits squarely in the context of developmental psychology. Brain damage in children must be cast in a developmental perspective if we are to understand its behavioral effects (Dennis, 1987b). Early brain damage poses developmental problems that must be solved by asking developmental questions of the kind I have outlined, not by an appeal to buzzwords (*plasticity*, *equipotentiality*, and the like) that, purporting to address development, actually impose adult-based analogies that obscure the varied effects of early brain injury, some associated with preserved functional competence, others with long-term failures to acquire or maintain a skill (e.g., Buchtel, 1978; Isaacson, 1975). It is critical that we study early brain damage within a developmental context.

Implications for the Diagnostic Assessment of Brain-Damaged Children

In many of the research studies I have discussed, the level of particular language skills was shown to be related to specific aspects of early brain damage at the same time as traditional psychometric measures such as IQ were not related. The implication of these findings is not that psychometric measures are of no value—it is, after all, important to know whether brain injury has compromised a child's intellectual ability—but rather that standard psychological assessment of brain-injured children will not necessarily reveal the presence of significant and long-term language deficits.

Mainstream research into the psychology of language has considerably advanced our understanding of these cognitive processes. Research neuropsychology has exploited these developments and has applied test instruments based on this research to the elucidation of cognitive impairment in brain-damaged children (Dennis, 1987a). Examples are studies of reading within the framework of cognitive analyses of automaticity and text processing (Dennis, Lovett, & Wiegel-Crump, 1981), and studies of language processes, such as the understanding of grammar, the production of surface structure syntactic forms, and the mechanisms of word finding, all within a framework of developmental psycholinguistics (Dennis & Kohn, 1985; Dennis, Sugar, & Whitaker, 1982; Wiegel-Crump & Dennis, 1986). Perhaps it is time for some of these research techniques to be incorporated into the standard neuropsychological assessment of brain-injured children.

Implications for Remediation of the Cognitive Effects of Brain Injury

Early brain damage was found to be highly selective in its effects on language. This has implications for the cognitive and educational remediation of brain-injured children.

The slow-learning child, the child with developmental language impairments, and the child with discrete losses within the language domain as a result of particular types of brain injury may each benefit from a program of general language remediation. But it is not clear that each child would benefit equally from nonspecific language remediation, nor that this would be the best approach to ameliorating language problems for those brain-damaged children with discrete functional losses in language, for whom, perhaps, an attempt at targeting specific areas of language loss would be a more efficient and more economical remedial technique.

Early brain damage was shown to affect language throughout a protracted developmental course. In some instances, the type and extent of language disorders were not apparent for some years postinjury. This has important implications for remediation. The usual assumption, and one that certainly seems appropriate to adults, is that the most energetic remediation of cognitive deficits induced by brain damage should occur at a point in time close to the brain injury. But in children, as we have seen, pronounced cognitive difficulties may occur well after the acute phase, at a point in time quite removed from the onset of brain injury.

It is important to understand the nature of the educational skills that would typically be acquired at the time of maximum projected cognitive deficit. If a particular form of early brain damage were known to produce difficulties with reading comprehension and inferencing five years postinjury, then it would be these skills that would require educational attention, even if the brain damage itself occurred many years earlier, when a quite different set of cognitive skills were being acquired.

The research described in this chapter has implications for the relative effectiveness of different language remediation approaches for the amelioration of particular types of language disorders, but ultimately, of course, these implications must be evaluated by appropriate empirical studies. But what is clear, even now, is that an understanding of the natural evolution of language deficits after early brain damage should help guide strategies for remediation. If remedial efforts are to be optimally geared to the time scale of neuropsychological recovery, we must begin to understand how deficits in brain-damaged children can emerge and evolve as their contingent functional skills develop.

Implications for the Psychological Reality of Linguistic Constituents

The issue here is whether the constituent processes of language assumed to be separate on the basis of linguistic or psycholinguistic theory are also separately affected by early brain damage, that is, whether damage to the developing brain produces effects on language that are discrete and selective, rather than global. By and large, recent research has supported the notion of neurologically separable language functions in the young damaged brain. Different types of brain damage sustained at similarly early points in development cause losses in distinct language functions. For example, some forms of congenital absence of the midline commissures may produce a loss of awareness of the form of language, although it does not affect speech fluency (Dennis, 1981); congenital dysraphism of the spine with resulting hydrocephalus within the midline ventricular system generally preserves syntax better than fluency (Dennis, Hendrick, Hoffman, & Humphreys, 1987). Deficits in syntax after early removal of the left, but not right, hemisphere are not associated with disturbances in speech articulation or lexical semantics (Dennis, 1980b). In a large brain-damaged sample, syntax is separate from other aspects of language, with some subcomponents of syntax being separate from one another (Dennis, 1987c).

To be sure, evidence does not exist that each and every constituent proposed on the basis of linguistic theory has a discrete brain representation. In that event, linguistic theory would be fully constrained on the basis of developmental neuropsychological language data, which is not the case. Nonetheless, recent research does support the idea that the breakdown of language in the young brain occurs along lines that bear a relation to certain distinctions drawn in linguistic and psycholinguistic theories. What is yet to be fully understood are the limits of this parallel between linguistic theory and neuropsychological data and, also, the extent to which particular linguistic constituents can be predicted from particular attributes of the early brain injury.

Implications for Psychological Theories of Language and Cognition

Whether neuropsychological studies of language and brain damage are deemed relevant to theories of language and cognition in mainstream psychology depends on the acceptance of the basic idea that the way language breaks down after discrete brain lesions reflects how it is normally organized in the brain (e.g., Zurif, 1980). The idea itself is not unreasonable, but I think there are difficulties with its application. Interpreted in the broadest sense, the idea would license us to accept any dissociation among the behavioral skills of brain-damaged individuals as grist for the mill of some theory about language (and see Dunn & Kirsner, 1988). And the idea itself does not specify how normal and aberrant function are related in brain-damaged individuals. In the study of brain damage and lexical access described earlier, these problems were at least addressed: Analysis was made of both deficit and intact function within the same brain-damaged individuals, and specification was made about how information from the language skills of brain-damaged children may confirm or disconfirm theories about language (Dennis, 1987c).

Conclusion

It would be false to assert that we fully understand how early brain damage influences the state of existing language function and the course of future language acquisition. Several categories of relevant information are missing (e.g., how early brain damage affects the order in which skills are acquired), and important longitudinal studies that assess language in the same brain-damaged children at regular intervals from infancy through adulthood have not yet been carried out.

But even if we have not completed the picture, we have surely sketched a good working diagram. We now have a framework within which to pose research questions about early brain damage and language, a framework that respects something of the complexity of both the young brain and child language.

And so the questions we are starting to ask are real ones, that is, they are not questions that permit many different answers, none of which can be shown to be incorrect. If false, the new answers about early brain damage and language will be shown to be such in the ongoing course of clinical research. With a shared agenda that generates real, developmental, research questions, we can at last begin to discover how present and future language is affected by early brain damage. The problem has finally reached the point where it is both important and good. If not yet solved, it is surely ripe for solution.

References

Alajouanine, T., & Lhermitte, F. (1965). Acquired aphasia in children. *Brain, 88*, 653–662.

Aram, D. M., Ekelman, B. L., & Whitaker, H. A. (1986). Spoken syntax in children with acquired unilateral hemisphere lesions. *Brain and Language, 27*, 75–100.

Aram, D. M., Ekelman, B. L., & Whitaker, H. A. (1987). Lexical retrieval in left and right brain lesioned children. *Brain and Language, 31*, 61–87.

Aram, D. M., Rose, D. F., Rekate, H. L., & Whitaker, H. A. (1983). Acquired capsular/striatal aphasia in childhood. *Archives of Neurology, 40*, 614–617.

Bishop, D. V. M. (1981). Plasticity and specificity of language localization in the developing brain. *Developmental Medicine and Child Neurology, 23*, 545–546.

Bishop, N. (1967). Speech in the hemiplegic child. In *Proceedings of the 8th Medical and Educational Conference of the Australian Cerebral Palsy Association* (pp. 141–153). Melbourne, Victoria: Tooronga Press.

Buchtel, H. A. (1978). On defining neural plasticity. *Archives Italiennes de Biologie, 116*, 241–247.

Caramazza, A. (1985). Some aspects of language processing revealed through the analysis of acquired aphasia: The lexical system. *Reports of the Cognitive Neuropsychology Laboratory*. Baltimore, MD: The Johns Hopkins University.

Cotard, J. (1868). *Etude sur l'atrophie cerebrale. Thèse pour le Doctorat en Médecine*. Paris: A Parent.

Cronbach, L. J., & Meehl, P. E. (1955). Construct validity in psychological tests. *Psychological Bulletin, 52*, 281–302.

Denckla, M. B., & Rudel, R. (1974). Rapid "automatized" naming of pictured objects, colors, letters and numbers by normal children. *Cortex, 10*, 186–202.

Dennis, M. (1977, August 1–4). Gradients of function in the developing brain. *Symposium on Developmental Psychology*. International Neuropsychology Society Meeting. Oxford University, England.

Dennis, M. (1980a). Capacity and strategy for syntactic comprehension after left or right hemidecortication. *Brain and Language, 10*, 287–317.

Dennis, M. (1980b). Language acquisition in a single hemisphere: Semantic organization. In D. Caplan (Ed.), *Biological studies of mental processes* (pp. 159–185). Cambridge, MA: MIT Press.

Dennis, M. (1980c). Strokes in childhood I: Communicative intent, expression and comprehension after left hemisphere arteriopathy in a right-handed nine-year-old. In R. Rieber (Ed.), *Language development and aphasia in children* (pp. 45–67). New York: Academic Press.

Dennis, M. (1981). Language in a congenitally acallosal brain. *Brain and Language. 12*, 33–53.

Dennis, M. (1983). The developmentally dyslexic brain and the written language skills of children with one hemisphere. In U. Kirk (Ed.), *Neuropsychology of language, reading, and spelling* (pp. 185–208). New York: Academic Press.

Dennis, M. (1985a). Intelligence after early brain injury I: Predicting IQ scores from medical variables. *Journal of Clinical and Experimental Neuropsychology, 7*, 526–554.

Dennis, M. (1985b). Intelligence after early brain injury II: IQ scores of subjects classified on the basis of medical history variables. *Journal of Clinical and Experimental Neuropsychology, 7*, 555–576.

Dennis, M. (1987a). Advances in neuropsychological assessment. In J. D. Call, R. L. Cohen, S. I. Harrison, I. N. Berlin, & L. E. Stone (Eds.), *Basic handbook of child psychiatry: Advances and new directions* (pp. 164–169). New York: Basic Books.

Dennis, M. (1987b). Language after damage to the immature brain. *Encyclopedia of Neuroscience* (pp. 559–561). Boston, MA: Birkhauser.

Dennis, M. (1987c). Using language to parse the young damaged brain. *Journal of Clinical and Experimental Neuropsychology, 9*, 723–753.

Dennis, M., Fitz, C. R., Netley, C. T., Sugar, J., Harwood-Nash, D. C. F., Hendrick, E. B., Hoffman, H. J., & Humphreys, R. P. (1981). The intelligence of hydrocephalic children. *Archives of Neurology, 38*, 607–615.

Dennis, M., Hendrick, E. B., Hoffman, H. J., & Humphreys, R. P. (1987). The language of hydrocephalic children and adolescents. *Journal of Clinical and Experimental Neuropsychology, 9*, 593–621.

Dennis, M., & Kohn, B. (1975). Comprehension of syntax in infantile hemiplegics after cerebral hemidecortication: Left hemisphere superiority. *Brain and Language, 2*, 472–482.

Dennis, M., & Kohn, B. (1985). The Active–Passive Test: An age-referenced clinical test of syntactic discrimination. *Developmental Neuropsychology, 1*, 113–137.

Dennis, M., Lovett, M. W., & Wiegel-Crump, C. A. (1981). Written language acquisition after left or right hemidecortication in infancy. *Brain and Language, 12*, 54–91.

Dennis, M., Sugar, J., & Whitaker, H. A. (1982). The acquisition of tag questions. *Child Development, 53*, 1254–1257.

Dennis, M., & Whitaker, H. A. (1976). Language acquisition following hemidecortication: Linguistic superiority of the left over the right hemisphere. *Brain and Language, 3*, 404–433.

Dennis, M., & Whitaker, H. A. (1977). Hemispheric equipotentiality and language acquisition. In S. J. Segalowitz & F. A. Gruber (Eds.), *Language acquisition and neurological theory* (pp. 93–106). New York: Academic Press.

de Villiers, J. G., & de Villiers, P. A. (1978). *Language acquisition*. Cambridge, MA: Harvard University Press.

Dillon, W. R., & Goldstein, M. (1984). *Multivariate analysis: Methods and applications*. New York: Wiley.

Dunn, J. C., & Kirsner, K. (1988). Discovering functionally independent mental processes: The principle of reversed association. *Psychological Bulletin, 95*, 91–101.

Embretson, S. (1983). Construct validity: Construct representation versus nomothetic span. *Psychological Bulletin, 93*, 179–197.

Ewing-Cobbs, L., Fletcher, J. M., Landry, S. H., & Levin, H. S. (1985). Language disorders after pediatric closed head injury. In J. K. Darby (Ed.), *Speech and language evaluation in neurology: Childhood disorders* (pp. 97–111). New York: Academic Press.

Fitzhugh, K. B., Fitzhugh, L. C., & Reitan, R. M. (1962). Wechsler-Bellevue comparisons in groups with "chronic" and "current" lateralized and diffuse brain lesions. *Journal of Consulting Psychology, 26*, 306–310.

Fletcher, J. M., Levin, H. S., & Landry, S. H. (1984). Behavioral consequences of cerebral insult in infancy. In C. R. Almi & S. Finger (Eds.), *Early brain damage: Research orientations and clinical observations* (pp. 189–213). New York: Academic Press.

Fletcher, J. M., Miner, M. E., & Ewing-Cobbs, L. (1987). Developmental issues and recovery from head injury in children. In H. S. Levin, J. Grafman, & H. Eisenberg (Eds.), *Neurobehavioral recovery after head injury* (pp. 279–291). New York: Oxford University Press.

Fletcher, J. M., & Satz, P. (1983). Age, plasticity, and equipotentiality: A reply to Smith. *Journal of Consulting and Clinical Psychology, 51*, 763–767.

Fowler, H. W., & Fowler, F. G. (1958). *The concise Oxford dictionary of current English* (4th rev. ed.). Oxford: Oxford University Press.

Gardner, H. (1983). *Frames of mind*. New York: Basic Books.

Gascon, G., Victor, D., Lombroso, C. T., & Goodglass, H. (1973). Language disorder, convulsive disorder, and electroencephalographic abnormalities. *Archives of Neurology, 28*, 156–162.

Goldman, P. S. (1972). Developmental determinants of cortical plasticity. *Acta Neurobiologica Experimentalis, 32*, 495–511.

Guttmann, E. (1942). Aphasia in children. *Brain, 65*, 205–219.

Harwood-Nash, D. C. F., & Fitz, C. R. (1976). *Neuroradiology in infants and children*. Vol. 2 (pp. 609–667). St. Louis, MO: Mosby.

Hebb, D. O. (1942). The effect of early and late brain injury upon test scores, and the nature of normal adult intelligence. *Proceedings of the American Philosophical Society, 85*, 275–292.

Hecaen, H. (1976). Acquired aphasia in children and the ontogenesis of hemispheric functional specialization. *Brain and Language, 3*, 114–134.

Hunter, J. E. (1980). Factor analysis. In P. R. Monge & J. N. Cappella (Eds.), *Multivariate techniques in human communication research* (pp. 229–257). New York: Academic Press.

Isaacson, R. L. (1975). The myth of recovery from early brain damage. In N. R. Ellis (Ed.), *Aberrant development in infancy* (pp. 1–25). Hillsdale, NJ: Erlbaum.

Joreskog, K. G., & Sorbom, D. (1979). *Advances in factor analysis and structural equation models*. Cambridge, MA: Abt Books.

Kean, M.-L. (Ed.). (1985). *Agrammatism*. New York: Academic Press.

Kennard, M. A. (1936). Age and other factors in motor recovery from precentral lesions in monkeys. *American Journal of Physiology, 115*, 138–146.

Kennard, M. A. (1938). Reorganization of motor function in the cerebral cortex of monkeys deprived of motor and premotor areas in infancy. *Journal of Neurophysiology*, *1*, 477–496.

Kennard, M. A. (1940). Relation of age to motor impairment in man and in subhuman primates. *Archives of Neurology and Psychiatry*, *44*, 377–397.

Kennard, M. A. (1942). Cortical reorganization of motor function: Studies on series of monkeys of various ages from infancy to maturity. *Archives of Neurology and Psychiatry*, *47*, 227–240.

Kiessling, L. S., Denckla, M. B., & Carlton, M. (1983). Evidence for differential hemispheric function in children with hemiplegic cerebral palsy. *Developmental Medicine and Child Neurology*, *25*, 727–734.

Kohn, B. (1980). Right hemisphere speech representation and comprehension of syntax after left cerebral injury. *Brain and Language*, *9*, 350–361.

Kohn, B., & Dennis, M. (1974). Patterns of hemispheric specialization after hemidecortication for infantile hemiplegia. In M. Kinsbourne & W. L. Smith (Eds.), *Hemispheric disconnection and cerebral function* (pp. 34–47). Springfield, IL: Charles C. Thomas.

Lecours, A.-R., Lhermitte, F., & Bryans, B. (1983). *Aphasiology*. London: Bailliere Tindall.

Lenneberg, E. H. (1967). *Biological foundations of language*. New York: Wiley.

Levin, H. S., Eisenberg, H. M., Wiig, E. R., & Kobayashi, K. (1982). Memory and intellectual ability after head injury in children and adolescents. *Neurosurgery*, *11*, 668–673.

Lovett, M. W., Dennis, M., & Newman, J. E. (1986). Making reference: The cohesive use of pronouns in the narrative discourse of hemidecorticate adolescents. *Brain and Language*, *29*, 224–251.

Macnamara, J. (1982). *Names for things: A study of child language*. Cambridge, MA: Bradford/MIT Press.

Miller, G. A. (1984, August). When we think, what thinks? [Review of The wonder of being human: Our brain and our mind] *New York Times Book Review*, p. 22.

Newman, J. E., Lovett, M. W., & Dennis, M. (1986). The use of discourse analysis in neurolinguistics: Some findings from the narratives of hemidecorticate adolescents. *Topics in Language Disorders*, *7*, 31–44.

Painter, M. J., & Low, N. L. (1986). Cerebral palsy. In V. C. Kelly (Ed.), *Practice of pediatrics* (Ch. 36). Philadelphia: Harper & Row.

Pinker, S. (1984). *Language learnability and language development*. Cambridge, MA: Harvard University Press.

Rankin, J. M., Aram, D. M., & Horwitz, S. J. (1981). Language ability in right and left hemiplegic children. *Brain and Language*, *14*, 292–306.

Rourke, B. P. (1976). Reading retardation in children: Developmental lag or deficit? In R. Knights & D. Bakker (Eds.), *The neuropsychology of learning disorders: Theoretical approaches* (pp. 125–137). Baltimore, MD: University Park Press.

Rourke, B. P. (1987). Syndrome of nonverbal learning disabilities: The final common pathway of white matter disease/dysfunction? *The Clinical Neuropsychologist*, *1*, 209–234.

Satz, P., & Bullard-Bates, C. (1981). Acquired aphasia in children. In M. T. Sarno (Ed.), *Acquired aphasia* (pp. 399–426). New York: Academic Press.

Satz, P., Fletcher, J., Clark, W., & Morris, R. (1981). Lag, deficit, rate and delay constructs in specific learning disabilities: A re-examination. In A. Ansara,

N. Geschwind, A. Galaburda, M. Albert, & N. Gartrell (Eds.), *Sex differences in dyslexia* (pp. 129–150). Towson, MD: The Orton Dyslexia Society.

Siegel, A. W., Bisanz, J., & Bisanz, G. L. (1983). Developmental analysis: A strategy for the study of psychological change. *Contributions to Human Development, 8*, 53–80.

Slobin, D. E. (1979). *Psycholinguistics* (2nd ed.). Glenview, IL: Scott, Foresman.

Smith, N., & Wilson, D. (1979). *Modern linguistics: The results of Chomsky's revolution*. Harmondsworth: Penguin Books.

St. James-Roberts, I. (1979). Neurological plasticity and recovery from brain insult. In H. W. Reese & L. P. Lipsitt (Eds.), *Advances in child development and behavior* (Vol. 5, pp. 253–319). New York: Academic Press.

van Dongen, H. R., & Loonen, M. C. B. (1977). Factors related to prognosis of acquired aphasia in children. *Cortex, 13*, 131–136.

Wardhaugh, R. (1977). *Introduction to linguistics* (2nd ed.). New York: McGraw-Hill.

Wiegel-Crump, C. A., & Dennis, M. (1986). Development of word finding. *Brain and Language, 27*, 1–23.

Wohlwill, J. (1973). *The study of behavioral change*. New York: Academic Press.

Woods, B. T., & Teuber, H.-L. (1978). Changing patterns of childhood aphasia. *Annals of Neurology, 3*, 273–280.

Worster-Drought, C. (1964). An unusual form of acquired aphasia in children. *Folia Phoniatria, 16*, 223–227.

Zurif, E. B. (1980). Language mechanisms: A neuropsychological perspective. *American Scientist, 68*, 305–311.

EDITH KAPLAN

A PROCESS APPROACH TO NEUROPSYCHOLOGICAL ASSESSMENT

Edith Kaplan is an associate professor of neurology and psychiatry and a core faculty member in the recently established PhD Behavioral Neuroscience Program at the Boston University School of Medicine, and an affiliate professor of psychology at Clark University. She has been the Director of Clinical Neuropsychological Services at the Boston Veterans Administration Medical Center for the past eleven years where she was responsible for the development of an internationally renowned pre- and postdoctoral clinical neuropsychological internship training program.

Kaplan's major contributions to the field of clinical neuropsychology have been in the areas of teaching, training, and test development. She is best known for her process-oriented approach to clinical neuropsychological assessment. She is co-author of *The Assessment of Aphasia and Related Disorders*, *The Boston Naming Test*, *The California Verbal Learning Test*, *The WAIS-R as a Neuropsychological Instrument*, as well as numerous research and clinical publications.

Kaplan has served as a member of the governing board of the Academy of Aphasia from 1974 to 1977, as the President of the International Neuropsychological Society from 1979 to 1980, as the President of Division 40 of the American Psychological Association from 1986 to 1987, and is currently President of the Boston Neuropsychological Foundation, which she founded with Dean Delis in 1983. She is also one of the founders of the American Board of Clinical Neuropsychology and was among the first psychologists to be awarded the Diplomate in Clinical Neuropsychology.

EDITH KAPLAN

A PROCESS APPROACH TO NEUROPSYCHOLOGICAL ASSESSMENT

Clinical neuropsychologists typically rely on either a fixed (Boll, 1981) or flexible (Lezak, 1983) battery of relatively well-normed standardized tests (for a current review of standardized and flexible battery approaches, see Kane, in press). For the most part, these tests, designed to assess cognitive functioning, are predicated on the idea that the final solution to a problem, arrived at within a given time, is an objective measure of an underlying unitary mechanism. Test items are for the most part scored right or wrong and summed to yield an overall score. This focus on global achievement does not address the nature and effectiveness of the strategies that an individual may employ enroute to either an incorrect or correct solution.

Werner (1937) expressed his great concern about conclusions drawn from results based only on achievement scores. Borrowing the concept of analogous function from biology and anatomy (i.e., that a given function may be subserved by organs distinctly different in structure), Werner demonstrated that a given final solution may be arrived at via diverse processes which themselves may reflect the activity of distinctly different structures in the central nervous system (CNS).

For Werner (1956) every cognitive act involves "microgenesis," (i.e., an "unfolding process over time"). Thus close observation and careful monitoring of behavior enroute to a solution (process) is more likely to provide more useful information than can be obtained from right or wrong scoring of final products (achievement).

A process orientation to neuropsychological assessment is a clinical approach, akin to Luria (1980), and Christensen (1975a; 1975b), in that it is patient centered. It is sensitive to a variety of patient variables such as age; sex; handedness; familial history of handedness; educational and occupational background; premorbid talents; patient's and family's medical, neurologic, and psychiatric history; etiology of the CNS dysfunction; and laterality and locus of the lesion. Most of these variables obviously contributed greatly to the patient's premorbid level of cognitive functioning. Together with the nature of the posed task, the stimulus parameters, and the modality of input and output, they will determine the expression of both spared and impaired abilities, and not infrequently provide new insights into brain and behavior relations. Furthermore, they will have significant impact on the strategies that the patient will employ to compensate for his or her impairment(s). The careful documentation and quantification of these strategies, be they adaptive or maladaptive, more effectively inform rehabilitation workers than global scores obtained from an achievement approach. The process-oriented approach also best captures the quality of the patient's performance by a finer analysis of the patient's problem-solving behavior (Kaplan, 1983; Milberg, Hebben, & Kaplan, 1986). This in turn is more useful for monitoring the recovery course and the effectiveness of a given intervention, be it surgical, pharmacological, or behavioral. Obviously, expanded scores based on a finer analysis are less likely to result in a type 2-like error (i.e., indicating no change when in fact there has been significant improvement).

Another source of error in interpreting test findings resides in the multifactorial aspect of most standardized tests. To permit a better understanding of how it is that the underlying process has been affected (or not affected), it may be necessary to modify the test administration or introduce additional tests so that one can parse out the factors that may be involved in a particular task.

In general then, the process approach to neuropsychological assessment differs from the fixed and flexible battery approaches in that the standardized and experimental tests are not scored in the standardized binary fashion (right or wrong), and in many cases are not administered in the standardized manner. It differs from the clinical investigative approach in that qualitative aspects of behavior are quantified and subjected to statistical analyses rather than just described, and that testing of clinical limits is operationally defined, repeatable, and quantifiable, as opposed to particularized for a given patient.

The advantages of the process approach for diagnosis, monitoring the course of functioning, making recommendations for therapeutic interventions, understanding brain and behavior relations, and research are best illustrated by examples of different patient's performances on a variety of standardized and experimental tests. The examples presented in this chapter illustrate the richness of the approach as well as the rationale for the scoring and modification of test procedures.

Block Design

Block Design is a timed visuospatial subtest of the Wechsler Adult Intelligence Scale-Revised (WAIS-R) that contributes to the global Performance IQ (Wechsler, 1981). Scoring is absolute, with full credit given only if the design totally corresponds to the model and is completed within a specified time (bonus credits are given for more rapid completion). Performance on this subtest is naively considered to be mediated by the right hemisphere (i.e., a poor block design performance is thought to signal a dysfunctional right hemisphere, particularly involving the right parietal lobe). The clearest evidence that this is not the case comes from two pathological sources: patients with cerebral dysconnection (Geschwind, 1965, 1979; Geschwind & Kaplan, 1962) and patients with focal lateralized vascular lesions (Kaplan, 1983; Kaplan, Palmer, Weinstein, & Baker, 1981).

Commissurotomized patients, serving as their own controls, provide the most dramatic demonstration that both cerebral hemispheres play an important role in visuospatial processing. These patients, suffering from intractable seizures, had undergone a radical surgical procedure disconnecting their two cerebral hemispheres to prevent the spread of seizures from one hemisphere to the other. By sectioning the corpus callosum and the anterior commissure, sensory information in one cerebral hemisphere cannot be transferred to the other hemisphere. Thus the patient's performance with each hand reflects what the contralateral hemisphere is capable of in isolation (i.e., with no input from the ipsilateral hemisphere). So, when such a patient is constrained to construct a block design with his or her left hand, and though both cerebral hemispheres receive visual information (the model to be constructed), it is only the right hemisphere that can direct the performance of the left hand.

The left hand and right hand constructions of commissurotomized patients are presented in Figures 1 and 2. Though the patient in Figure 1 was many years postsurgery, his performance with his left hand is remarkably similar to the patient who was only 3 weeks postsurgery (see Figure 2). Both patients, when using their left hand (or right hemisphere in isolation), never broke the configuration, that is, they preserved the 2 × 2 matrix, or contour of the design (see column 1 of Figure 1, and column 2 of Figure 2). Their productions, however, do not correspond to the model. These patients working with their left hand (relying exclusively on the contribution of the right hemisphere) are remarkably similar to patients with significant left hemisphere lesions (LHL), whether they work with their left or right hand. Their LHL necessitated greater reliance on the contribution of their relatively spared right hemisphere, which results in productions that preserve the contour but are not comparable to the model.

The block designs produced by the commissurotomized patients when they used only their right hand, or isolated left hemisphere, were strikingly different from their constructions with their left hand (see column 3 in Figures 1 and 2). In none of the constructions (except for

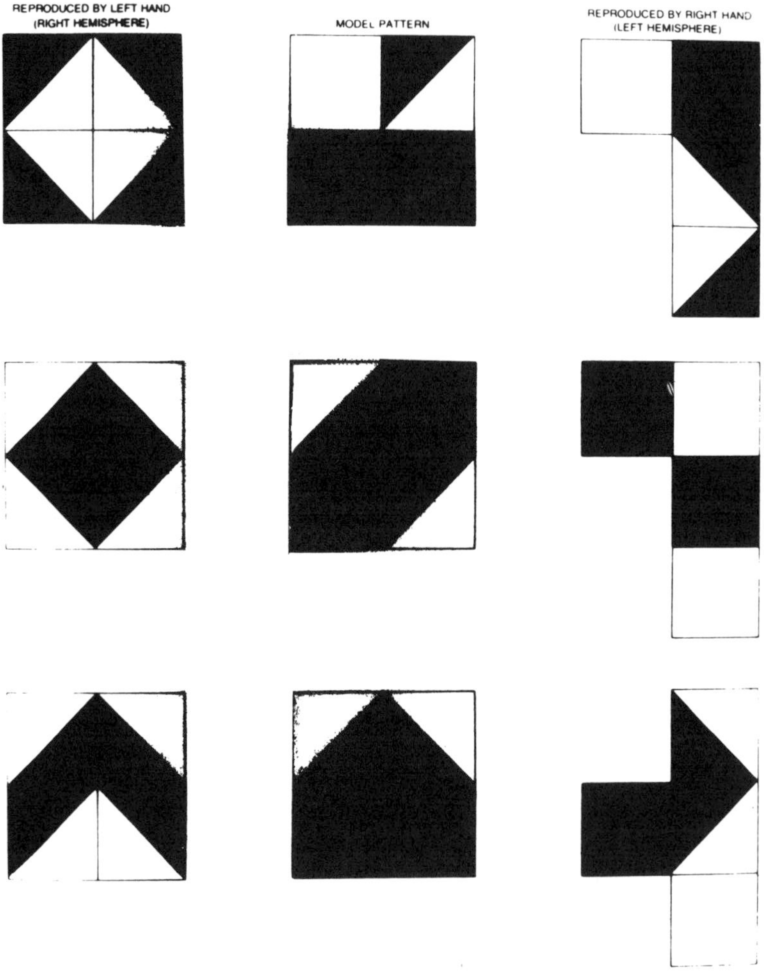

Figure 1. Unimanual block designs of a commissurotomized patient demonstrating the distinctive role of each isolated cerebral hemisphere.

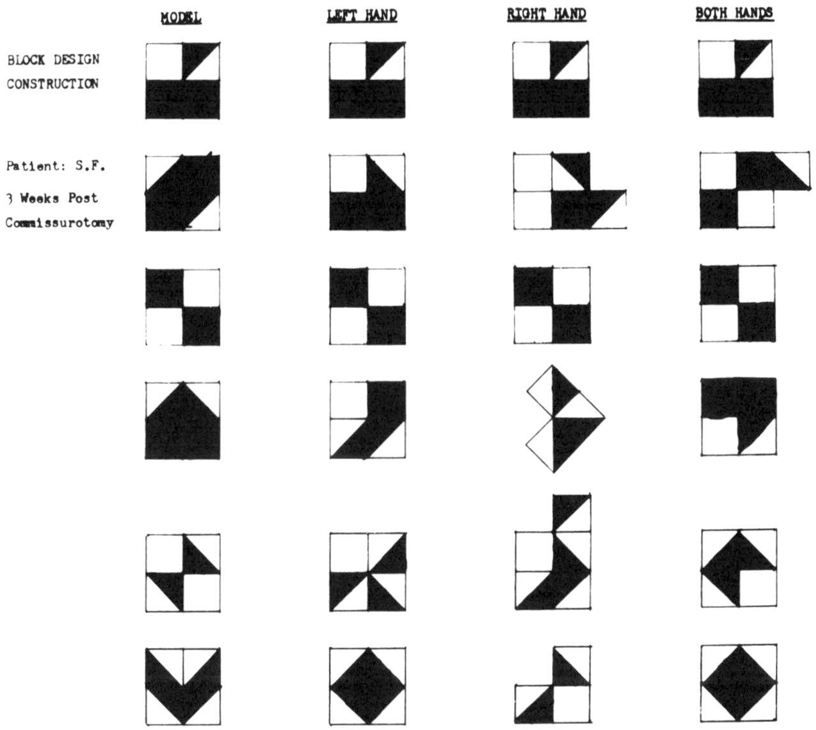

Figure 2. Block designs produced unimanually and bimanually by a commissurotomized patient evaluated by Robert Novelly at the West Haven Veterans Administration–Yale Epilepsy Surgery Program.

the 1st and 3rd design in Figure 2) is the 2 × 2 matrix preserved. Note also that there is a pile-up of blocks at the extreme right of the design (i.e., in the right hemiattentional field), the hemiattentional field contralateral to the left hemisphere that is exclusively mediating the performance of the right hand. I return to this finding when discussing the roles of the two cerebral hemispheres in hemispatial attention. These right hand constructions, when the right hemisphere's contribution is not available to the commissurotomy patient, are remarkably similar to the productions of patients with severe right hemisphere pathology.

There are two additional performance features that are noteworthy in Figure 2. First, designs 2 and 5 (done with the right hand) have an extra block. In the standard administration of the WAIS-R Block Design subtest, the examiner presents the exact number of blocks necessary to construct the design, thus limiting if not precluding the likelihood of the occurrence of this pathognomonic sign. In our modification of the WAIS-R as a neuropsychological instrument (Kaplan, Fein, Morris, &

Delis, in press), we have 12 blocks on the table from which the patient can select the blocks he or she needs. And finally, it is noteworthy that when the commissurotomy patient (see Figure 2) was allowed to use both hands, he relied more heavily on the use of his left, nonpreferred hand (i.e., his right hemisphere). Galin and Ornstein (1972) have found that normal control subjects show greater EEG activity in the right hemisphere when they are constructing block designs. It may well be that normal subjects rely more heavily on the right than the left hemisphere (though in the normal integrated brain both cerebral hemispheres contribute, one more than the other as a function of the task demands and stimulus parameters).

The problems that attend achievement scoring (e.g., the needless loss of relevant diagnostic information) are clearly presented in Figure 3. The three top solutions were correctly completed within the time limit and each received a score of 4 points. A young right-handed control subject placed the first block in the upper left, and on this design, worked systematically from left to right with no errors enroute to the solution. On the other hand, the patient with a right frontal lesion began his design in the lower right and worked from right to left. It should be noted that right-handers most characteristically work from left to right (draw lines from left to right, etc.). Even Israelis, who read from right to left, draw lines from left to right, and construct block designs from left to right, if they are right-handed. Left-handers, however, show a tendency to work from right to left, to draw right to left, and so forth. Because the anomalous dominance of left-handers makes it very difficult to sort out their brain and behavior relations (Geschwind & Galaburda, 1987), all the examples used here were taken from the protocols of right-handers. Returning to Figure 3, it can be seen that the patient with a left frontal lesion began on the left side of space, but probably not for the same reason as the young normal control subject. Enroute to the final solution, he made a perseverative error in the upper right corner, which he self-corrected within the allotted time to obtain full credit.

Incorrect responses that all receive a score of zero may run the gamut from eating the blocks (in a confusional state), all the way to a flawless, systematic but slow construction (completed in 65 seconds, or 5 seconds over the time limit) of a nondemented patient with Parkinson's Disease. The three incorrect final solutions (see Figure 3) all received a score of zero, despite the fact that they are prototypic of patients with different kinds of focal lesions. The two patients with right hemisphere lesions (RHL) broke the configuration (violated the 2×2 matrix), but the patient with the frontal or anterior lesion, with posterior structures in both cerebral hemispheres spared, retained the physiognomic "V-ness" of the chevron-like figure. Pulled by the saliency of the lower point, he first placed a single divided color block at the bottom, capturing the most critical feature of the chevron, and then placed a solid color block on either side of it. Pulled by, or focused on, the salient colored figure, a second stimulus parameter, the ground, was ignored. The patient with the more posterior, right parietal lesion also broke the configuration, but neither figure nor ground are evident. The pile-up of blocks on the right side of the design was noted in the performance of the commissurotomy patients when they worked with the right hand

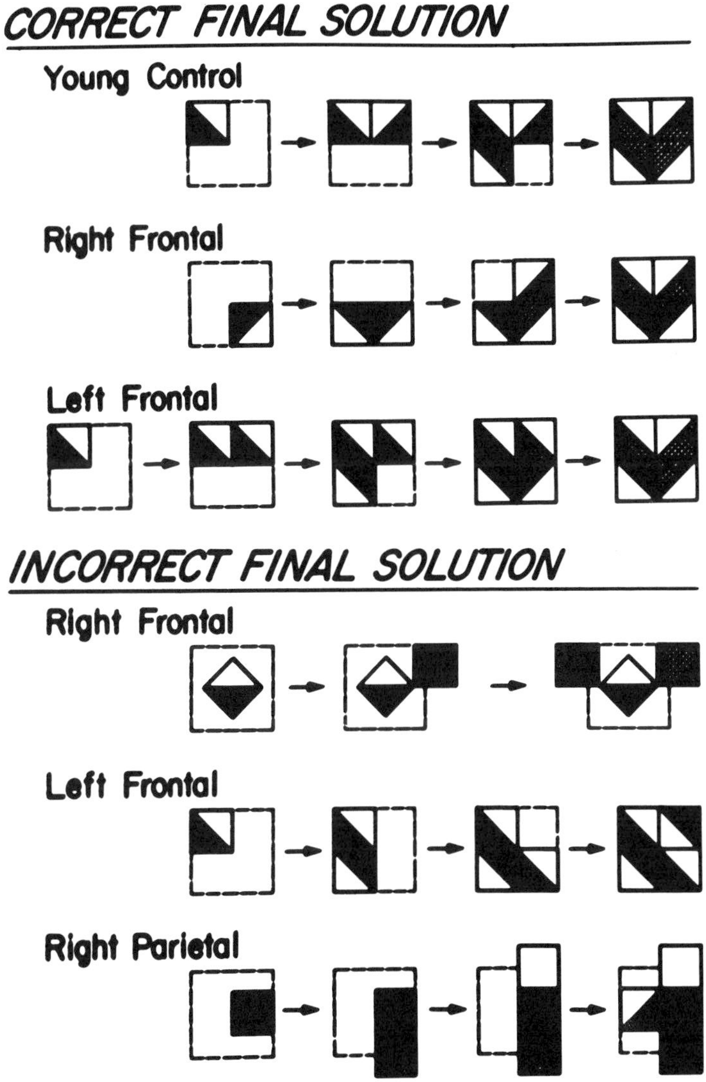

Figure 3. Sample flow charts of performance on the Block Design Subtest of the WAIS-R demonstrating differential strategies employed in correct and incorrect block design productions.

and had no input at all from the right hemisphere. Again we note that the patient with the LHL preserves the configuration, starts the design correctly on the left side, but is totally incorrect on the right side.

We studied the block design performance of 22 patients with pure focal, lateralized cortical lesions (verified by CT Scan), 11 with LHL, and 11 with RHL (Kaplan, Palmer, Weinstein, & Baker, 1981). We found that the RHL patients broke the configuration significantly more often than the LHL patients. In fact, there were no LHL patients who had more than one broken configuration as a final solution, and the one that did occur was typically secondary to getting into set. Because we keep flow charts of the performance of the patients, tracking and recording the order and nature of the block surface placement, we were able to determine the following: LHL patients begin working on the left side, the side contralateral to the nonlesioned right hemisphere, whereas RHL patients begin to work significantly more often on the right side of space (i.e., the hemiattentional field contralateral to the noncompromised left hemisphere); the errors that LHL patients made occurred significantly more often in the right hemiattentional field contralateral to the lesion, whereas the RHL patients made significantly more errors in the left hemiattentional field. We therefore predict that a patient with a focal lateralized lesion will have a preferential starting position in the hemiattentional field ipsilateral to the lesion, and will make more errors in the hemiattentional field contralateral to the lesion.

To monitor the course of recovery (or decline), comparisons over time may be made with regard to frequency counts for the occurrence of broken configurations, starting position, and number of errors. Absolute scores, with a greater range than the standardized score permits may be obtained by crediting each correctly positioned block, hence the score on a 2×2 design could be anywhere from 0 to 4, and on a 3×3 design the range would be from 0 to 9 points. Correct blocks could also be tallied for each of the quadrants. In this way we are less likely to conclude that a given intervention did not have any impact on constructional ability than if we had used standardized scoring, given that the zero scores mask the improvement. Furthermore, we allow the patient to work without time constraints. In this way we have an opportunity to monitor processing time as well as separating out motor speed from visuoconstructive ability.

In an effort to be cost effective, many clinicians have abbreviated their testing by either taking alternate items in a given test or selecting what are thought to be critical items. Satz and Mogel (1962) proposed an abbreviation of the WAIS for clinical use by taking every other item. This cannot be done with impunity on the Block Design subtest. It was pointed out to me by Walsh (1985) that the odd-numbered block design items of the WAIS contain more grid information (i.e., wherever 2 blocks meet there is a discontinuity of color). The even-numbered designs, on the other hand, have absolutely no implicit grid information; there is contiguity of color, either red or white, between any two blocks. If indeed the even-numbered items were given to RHL patients, they would be greatly disadvantaged. Because such patients have a tendency not to deal with the whole, but rather to work in what Paterson and Zangwill (1944) call a "piecemeal" approach, block by block, the task would be far more difficult than if he or she had been given the odd-numbered items. Given the entire test, scatter would be noted, with the patient performing more poorly on alternate items. Alternating between the two split halves of the test, however, to monitor the progress of a patient would be quite misleading, to say the least.

Object Assembly

The relevance of particular stimulus parameters of puzzles vary as a function of age. The easiest object assemblies for children are the horse and the apple (Wechsler, 1974). These puzzles have virtually no detail but are rich in contour (the right hemisphere specialty). As the child linguistically matures and his or her left hemisphere becomes more focally organized, the more difficult puzzles require greater attention to detail for the solution. As the individual ages, he or she relies less and less on contour, and more and more on feature analysis (the left hemisphere contribution to the task). For the adult, the two easier puzzles are rich in internal detail, and the two more difficult assemblies, the hand and the elephant, are virtually devoid of internal detail. These become more and more difficult for an individual as he or she progressively ages. Thus developmentally, individuals start out more competent in processing contour information. Think of the young child and all of his or her complex sensory–motor transactions with the environment (i.e., negotiating all kinds of complex spatial situations); in older age, people have greater and greater reliance on feature analysis and verbal encoding of information.

While flow-charting the object assembly problem-solving behavior of patients with lateralized cerebral lesions, it was noted that LHL patients were attempting to use edge alignment strategies (focus on the contour), whereas RHL patients were trying to match up surface lines (focus on detail). As a consequence RHL patients had less difficulty on the WAIS-R profile (rich in facial feature detail) than the LHL patients. We created two experimental puzzle assemblies (Kaplan et al., in press), a circle and a cow (Figures 4 and 5, respectively), to study edge alignment behavior (focus on contour) more closely.

Both puzzles are white on white and differ only in the saliency of contour. The circle, an interlocking puzzle, can only be solved effectively by an edge alignment strategy. This strategy cannot be utilized at all to solve the cow puzzle in which each juncture is equal; any given part of the puzzle fits equally well into any of the arcs or openings.

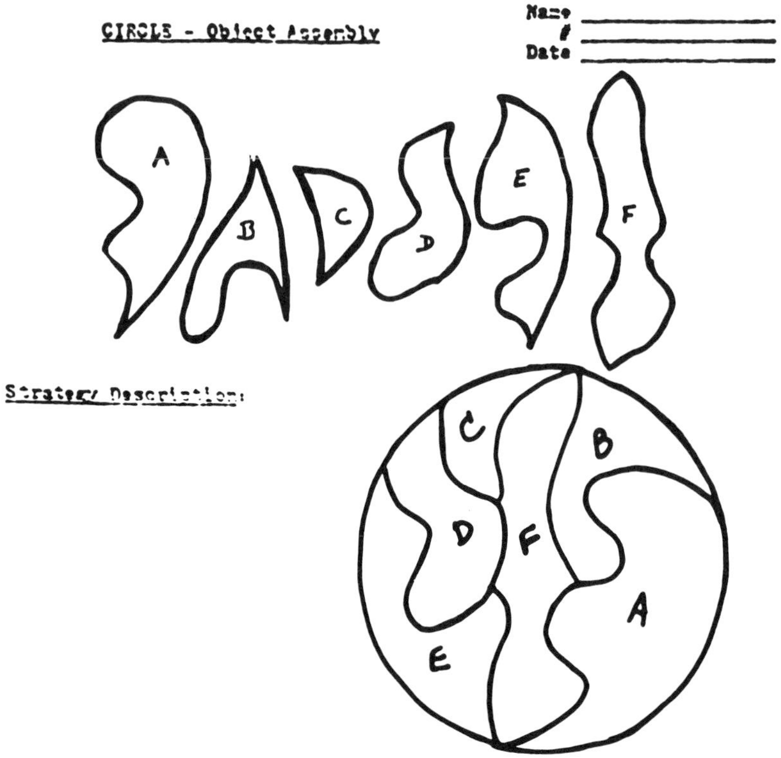

Figure 4. Experimental object assembly of a circle, a task that lends itself to edge alignment strategies.

We found, as we expected, that LHL patients complete the circle more often and more rapidly than they do the cow. Patients with right anterior lesions, focusing on and identifying the segments (e.g., legs, head, etc.), have relatively greater success with the cow than with the circle. Right posterior lesion patients have difficulty with both puzzles.

The interaction between a focus on features or contour and hemiattentional space provides important information with regard to both cognitive processing and designing interventions to optimize behavior. A mental object assembly task such as the Hooper Visual Organization Test (Hooper, 1957) illustrates this interaction well. The first and easiest item of the Hooper Visual Organization Test is readily identified as a fish (see Figure 6).

RHL patients, however, who are relying on their nonlesioned left hemisphere, are pulled to partial information in the right hemiattentional field. Their prototypic response is that it is "a flying duck" based on the fact that the tail of the fish is in the upper right side of the figure and

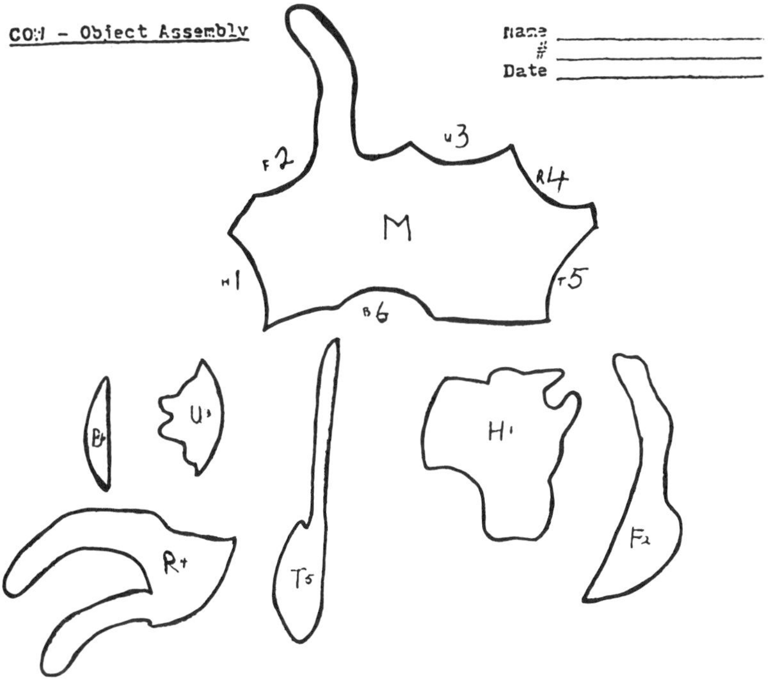

Figure 5. Experimental object assembly of a cow, a task that cannot be solved by edge alignment strategies.

Figure 6. First item of the Hooper Visual Organization Test. Reprinted by permission of Hooper (1957).

indeed looks like the head of a duck, whereas the head of the fish, more salient for the correct identification, is in the left hemiattentional field. To check this out, we asked our photographer to reverse the picture (see Figure 7).

With the salient information (the fish head) in the right hemiattentional field, RHL patients, as well as the elderly, now were more likely to identify the fish. It is abundantly clear that analysis of stimulus parameters can provide important information about how these parameters may be manipulated to induce a better performance.

Visual Confrontation Naming

Word-finding difficulty occurs in virtually all patients who have lesions involving the language area of the left hemisphere. The particular way that this difficulty manifests itself varies as a function of the region in the language zone that has been affected and the resulting aphasic syndrome (Goodglass & Kaplan, 1983). Some of the types of errors aphasic patients may make are phonemic paraphasias (i.e., the inadvertant substitution, addition, deletion, or reversal of phonemes, e.g., *mahonica* for *harmonica*); verbal paraphasias (i.e., substituting another word for the intended word, e.g., *accordion* for *harmonica*); and circumlocutions (i.e., describing the target, e.g., "it's the thing that you blow"). Word-finding ability is most directly tested by presenting the patient with a pictured object and recording latencies and verbatim

Figure 7. Right–left reversal of the first item of the Hooper Visual Organization Test. Adapted by permission of Hooper (1957).

responses. One such test, the Boston Naming Test, consists of 60 line-drawn objects of graded difficulty (Kaplan, Goodglass, & Weintraub, 1983). Because all aphasics have word-finding difficulty, an achievement score alone (the total number correct) would not be diagnostically helpful. A poor score, however, might not even differentiate between a patient with a lesion in the language zone of the left hemisphere and one with a lesion in the right hemisphere. An RHL patient and an LHL patient might make the same number of errors but for very different reasons.

The RHL patient's nonaphasic misnaming is perceptually based. As I stated earlier, a patient with a right frontal lesion may be pulled to what is most salient in a stimulus. The reeds of the harmonica, pictured in Figure 8, are salient on two counts; the reeds are black and there are many of them. Being so pulled, characteristic RHL responses are "a double-decker bus," "a garage," "a factory." All of the misnaming errors are based on an incomplete perceptual analysis of the stimulus. The patients do not have a naming problem. Based on his or her percept, the patient has accessed his or her lexicon correctly.

In Figure 9, we again see the relevance of the spatial location of the salient information for identification of the stimulus (recall the fish in the Hooper Visual Organization Test). The salient information for the tongs appears in the lower left quadrant, the portion of the visual field that would be disturbed in a patient with a right parietal lesion. Such a patient might say it was a coffin because, in fact, if you do not attend to the bottom part of the tongs, then what you see is the shape of a coffin. For the naive clinician, such a response might raise the question of depression. Similarly, such aphasic paraphasias as "my mother came to see me today" when in fact it was the patient's wife who had visited, may be misinterpreted as "the patient is feeling infantilized, dependent." Paraphasic responses are variable; on another occasion the patient might have made a phonemic substitution and said "my fife," or provided another verbal paraphasia "my son." Clearly one should exercise caution and not generalize from isolated responses.

Figure 8. The harmonica stimulus item of the Boston Naming Test. Reprinted by permission of Kaplan, Goodglass, and Weintraub (1983).

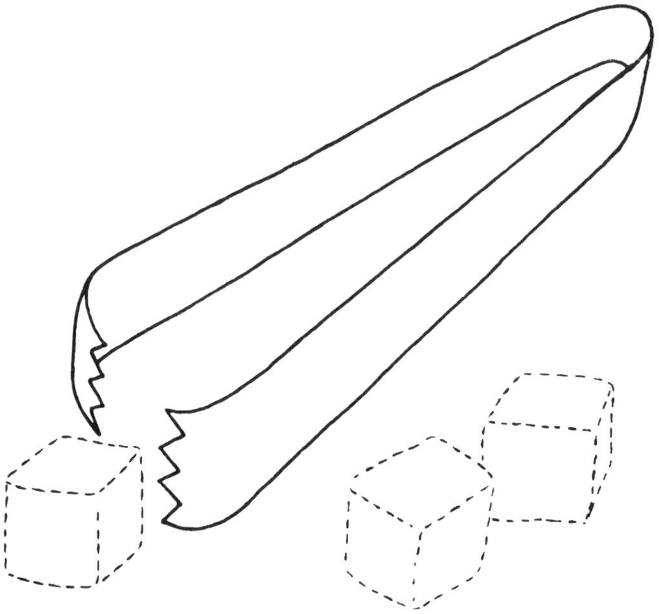

Figure 9. The tongs stimulus item of the Boston Naming Test. Reprinted by permission of Kaplan, Goodglass, and Weintraub (1983).

A left hemi-inattention in an RHL patient may obviously also result in such reading problems as missing the words or parts of words to the left. For example, an RHL patient with neglect might read the word *women* (as it might appear on the door of a ladies' room) as *men*. If one were testing for reading comprehension, one might erroneously be lead to the interpretation that the patient had an alexia.

In the process approach to neuropsychological assessment, the focus on the strategies that the patient spontaneously employs to compensate for his or her cognitive problems can be very informative. If we assume that a given lesion has resulted in some kind of deficit associated with the particular locus of the lesion, we must also assume that the responsive behavior emanates not from the "hole" but from the regions of available brain. Certainly the visuospatial constructions illustrated earlier indicate that both cerebral hemispheres are engaged in visuospatial processing; therefore, LHL patients rely on the contributions of the nonlesioned right hemisphere, and vice versa. It should therefore not be surprising that the right hemisphere's capacity to appreciate contour would play a role in reading, a task presumed to be relegated to the language region of the left hemisphere. Without reading further in the text, try to determine the word that is spatially represented in

Figure 10. Each rectangle represents a lower case letter; the word is 8 letters long.

When I have presented this to large audiences, there are generally more men than women who recognize (read?) this word without any cue. When cued that it is an animal, many more members of the audience identify the word. If you still do not know the word, you can find it at the end of the reference list.

Given this illustration, and our knowledge that LHL patients preferentially process contour information, we could hypothesize that LHL patients would read words printed in lower case more effectively than words printed entirely in capital letters. Nancy Helm-Estabrooks and I designed a study to test this hypothesis. Preliminary results appear to confirm our expectations.

Digit Symbol

Most tests are multifactorial (i.e., they require a number of preserved skills). The Digit Symbol subtest of the WAIS-R is a good example of a multifactorial task. In order to rapidly transcribe symbols that are paired with digits in a reference key, the patient must have at least (a) adequate motor speed (the score is based on how many symbols are transcribed in 90 seconds), (b) paired associate learning (if the digit symbol pairs are learned, time does not have to be wasted on continually checking the reference key), and (c) the ability to scan back and forth and to and from the reference key. To parce out and document which factor or combination of factors may be contributing to a poor performance, the administration of the Digit Symbol subtest has been modified by having the patient continue until the end of the third row, rather than terminating the test at 90 seconds. The examiner keeps note of the number of symbols transcribed every 30 seconds (an increase in the number of

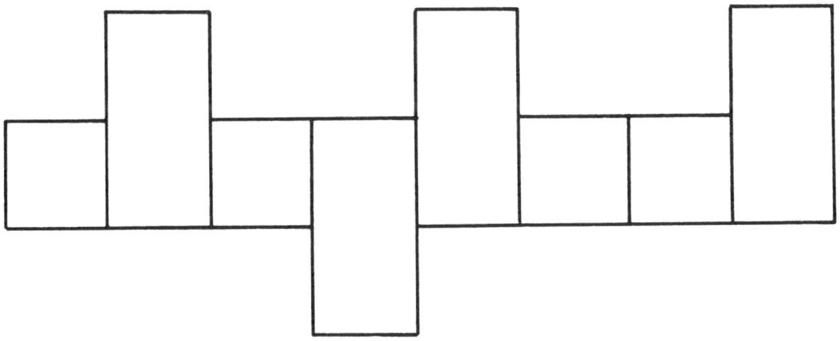

Figure 10. The contour of a word printed in lower case.

symbols indicating some learning, a decrease suggesting fatiguing). To test the extent to which there was incidental learning of the digit symbol pairs, the fourth row is exposed and, in the absence of the reference key, the patient is asked to draw as many symbols as he or she can recall that are associated with the given digits (Kaplan et al., in press). To measure motor speed, the patient is presented with a straight symbol copy task, again with the examiner noting the number of symbols drawn every 30 seconds and noting whether the patient is speeding up or slowing down over time. Finally, the integrity of the patient's ability to scan is evaluated by administering a verbal cancellation test (the letter *A* embedded in an array of random letters) and a nonverbal cancellation test (a geometric figure randomly embedded among other figures; Weintraub & Mesulam, 1985).

On a multifactorial test, such as the Digit Symbol subtest, the same score may be attained by a number of patients with diverse lesion loci, or distinctive neurological syndromes. When the factors are more or less isolated and individually tested, differential diagnosis is facilitated, and a far better understanding of the underlying problems of a given patient emerges. For example, patients with motor persistence have inordinate difficulty on the Digit Symbol subtest because of overwriting. Their performance on the symbol copy test is obviously comparably impaired. For these patients, so much cognitive energy has been expended at the motor level that learning of the digit symbol pairs is precluded (4 or less symbols recalled). Parkinsonian patients with bradykinesia (generalized motor slowing) may be inordinately slowed on the Digit Symbol subtest, and slowed on copying the symbols, but may have normal incidental learning of the digit symbol pairs (6 to 9 symbols recalled). Similarly, RHL patients with left hemi-inattention may obtain poor Digit Symbol scores secondary to their scanning difficulty (evident on the visual cancellation tests) and yet have normal incidental learning of the associated pairs.

Visual Attention

The letter and geometric figure cancellation tests of Weintraub and Mesulam (1985) are sensitive measures of hemispatial attention and provide rich information for the understanding of dysfunctional visuospatial processing. For example, LHL patients typically start on the left side, systematically scan, and even in the presence of a right visual field cut, tend not to omit targets on the right side, and tend to be more accurate and faster at detecting geometric figures than at detecting letters. RHL patients, however, preferentially start on the right side, scan erratically, tend to omit targets on the left side, and tend to be less accurate at detecting the geometric target than at detecting the letter *A*. The hemispheric differences in scanning and hemispatial attention were dramatically demonstrated with the Wada Test (Wada & Rasmussen, 1960), which involves injecting amobarbital to temporarily suppress all functions in one cerebral hemisphere. When neurosurgery is being contemplated, this technique of temporarily isolating a cerebral hemisphere permits the assessment of the functions that are spared and impaired in each of the cerebral hemispheres. Spiers (1987), employing a slightly enlarged and somewhat simplified version of the letter cancellation test just described, tested a series of patients, during the Wada procedure, who were candidates for temporal lobectomies. He found profound neglect for contralateral space only when the right hemisphere was amobarbital-suppressed. These patients, regardless of the side of their seizure focus, turned their heads to the right, their eyes deviated to the right, and they identified the target letter *A* only at the extreme right side, frequently pointing to the right of a target (sometimes off the stimulus card and onto the examiner's sleeve). Though the patient's attention could be briefly redirected toward the left on the stimulus card, and some targets identified, there was not only a marked tendency to shift back to the extreme right side, but there was also a significant amount of perseveration, at the far right (i.e., multiple identifications of the same target letter). When the amobarbital injection was to the left hemisphere, there was no neglect for targets in the right side of space, and no perseveration on the left side of space. The neglect for the left side of space, and "getting stuck" on the right side when the left hemisphere was tested in isolation, was also noted in the commissurotomy patients when their left hemispheres were tested in isolation (recall the pile-up of blocks when constructions were done with the right hand), as well as in RHL patients. Though these dramatic findings are certainly not seen in LHL patients, we have noted scanning problems in association with posterior left hemisphere lesions. For example, a patient with an alexia without an agraphia (a lesion in the left occipital lobe and in the splenium) may start to scan for the letter *A* on the left side but make aborted attempts to continue into the right side. When the left side has systematically been completed, the patient may then take twice as long to cancel the remaining targets on the right side. These tests would be ideal for computer presentation. The targets could be touched with a light pen, and the computer could record the sequence of identifications, the time between each identification in relation to the quadrant it was in, the total time for the first half and for the second half of the test, omissions, displacements, and false positives.

Visual Memory

The multiple factors that are involved in processing visuospatial material have to be addressed before one can attribute a flawed reproduction of a stimulus to a memory problem per se. The first stimulus of the Visual Reproductions subtest of the Wechsler Memory Scales (Wechsler, 1945, 1987) serves as an excellent example of how important it is to parse out the factors that may be involved in the memory for designs. For example, after a 10-second exposure to the first design (see Figure 12), a patient could produce a flawed drawing because he or she had misperceived the stimulus, or because the patient did not have the visuomotor capacity to reproduce what he or she had indeed perceived correctly, or because the patient could not remember it adequately, despite good perception and no visuomotor problem.

To parse out these various factors, the standard administration of the test is altered as follows: (a) as the patient is drawing the design after the 10-second exposure, the examiner keeps a flow chart of the sequence in which each line is drawn as well as the direction; (b) following the drawing of the last immediately recalled design, a multiple choice recognition task is introduced (see Figure 12) for each of the stimuli (foils chosen from actual productions by RHL and LHL patients); (c) immediately after the last multiple choice recognition for the last design, each of the stimuli is presented consecutively for direct copy; (d) after a 20-minute filled delay, the patient is asked to reproduce the designs he or she had seen earlier, the examiner again carefully recording the sequence and direction of the drawn lines; (e) another multiple choice recognition test is administered, and finally; (f) a straight matching condition is administered (using the original individual stimuli with each of the relevant multiple choice recognition strips). Examining a patient's visual reproductions in this manner obviously can be very helpful in determining the impact that such factors as encoding, retrieval, visuomotor ability, and perceptual functioning have on performance. Thus, if a patient fails to adequately reproduce a design that he or she has just seen but can recognize it and has no problem copying the design except for a segmented approach, a retrieval problem secondary to deficient encoding may be postulated. If a patient's impaired immediate recall, copy, and delayed recall are all comparably flawed, but both multiple choice recognition tests are unimpaired, one may assume that visuomotor dysfunction is implicated rather than a memory problem.

The visuospatial constructional strategies employed by patients with focal lesions, that were discussed earlier, are clearly evident in the reproductions of LHL and RHL patients. Typical responses of brain-damaged patients are presented in Figure 11. LHL patients tend to maintain the configuration (the X shape), but have difficulty orienting the global figure and tagging the features (flags). The errors on this design are mainly rotations. RHL patients, on the other hand, tend to reproduce all the features or components, but have difficulty integrating them.

The Effects of Aging on Information Processing

The effects of aging on information processing have been reported to be greater on visuospatial tasks than on verbal ones (Hochanadel &

Kaplan, 1984). In a process-oriented cognitive screening of over 2,500 Framingham Heart Study respondents, between the ages of 55 and 89 (Kaplan, 1980), a relation between the level of cognitive functioning and the strategies employed in visual reproductions was noted (see Figure 13). The elderly, who were found to be above the median on a cognitive screening test, showed preserved configural processing making only the types of rotational errors observed in LHL patients with relatively preserved right hemisphere functions (see the "high" scoring patients' drawings in Figure 13). The flawed visual reproductions of the elderly who performed below the median level on the cognitive screening test are remarkably similar to the productions of the patients with known right hemisphere lesions (see the "low" scoring patients' drawings in Figure 13). There is a striking similarity between the nature of the errors in the "normal" elderly and the patients with structural lesions (compare Figures 12 and 13).

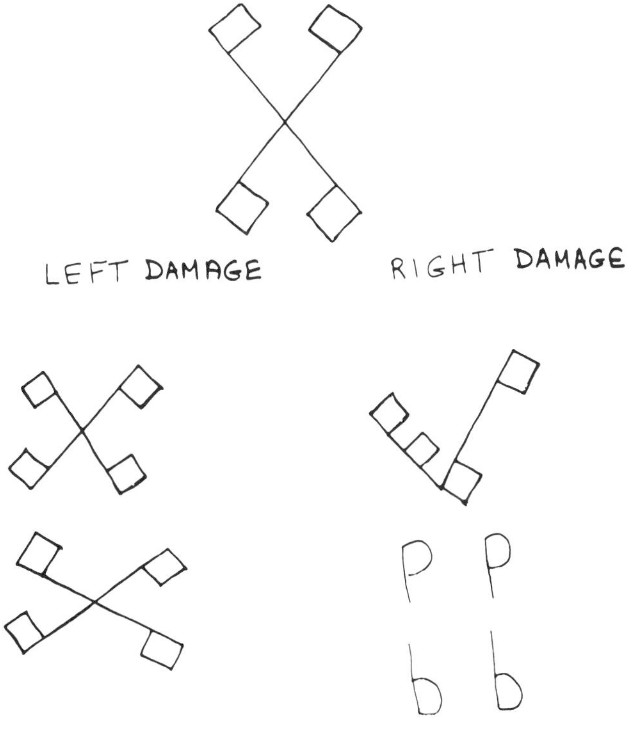

Figure 11. Visual reproduction errors in patients with lateralized lesions.

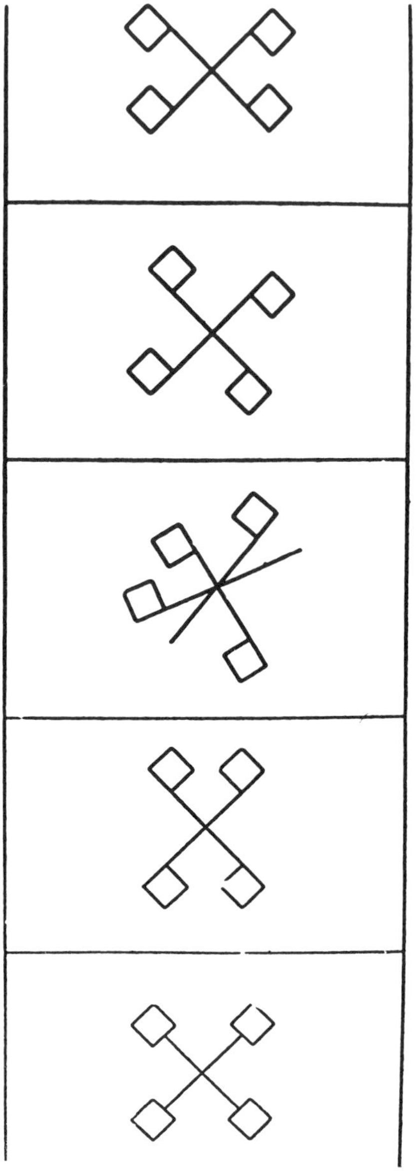

Figure 12. Multiple choice recognition task for the first Wechsler Memory Scale-Revised Visual Reproduction item. Reprinted from Wechsler (1987) by permission.

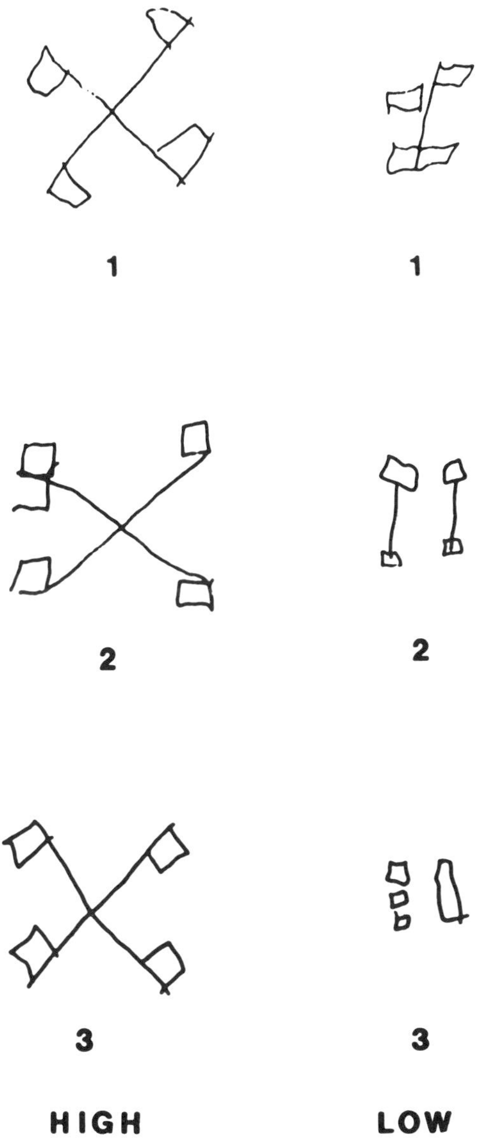

Figure 13. Visual reproduction errors of elderly with "high" and "low" scores on a neuropsychological screening test. Reprinted by permission of Kaplan (1980).

It would appear then that as people age they may become more reliant on the contributions of the left hemisphere for feature detection, feature analysis, verbal encoding, and so forth, and less reliant on the contributions of the right hemisphere (configural aspects). Until recently, there has been no neuroanatomical evidence to support a hypothesis of asymmetrical hemispheric aging. Kemper has found CT scan age-related gyral atrophy in the superior parietal lobule, greater in the right hemisphere than in the left (personal communication, March 7, 1988).

The monitoring of the strategies employed by the elderly in their reproductions of the first Wechsler Memory Scale design led to another finding of interest. Veroff (1980) went through the flow charts of all the reproductions that received full credit for being correct, and recorded the proportion of those correct responses that were executed using the sequential strategy of first drawing the major configural component (the X shape) and adding the "squares" next. This strategy may be said to draw on the contribution of both cerebral hemispheres, probably leading with the right. In any case it is the most efficient strategy, demanding the storage of the least number of elements.

Men and women are significantly different with regard to how they reproduce visual stimuli, and their vulnerability to aging (see Figure 14). Between the ages of 55 and 64 there is not a sex difference: Men use the sequential strategy about 82% of the time; women 85% of the time. After the age of 65, however, there is a significant sex difference. Although men are producing correct designs, they are not using the major structural component strategy; how they are proceeding remains to be determined, but they are not performing as women are, or as LHL patients who rely on the contribution of the right hemisphere are. After the age of 75, the men who were performing above the median on the cognitive screen were producing less configurally based drawings than the men who were a decade younger but were below the median on the cognitive screen. Women, on the other hand, continue to use the sequential configural strategy on into their 80's (with almost 100% of their correct solutions configurally sequenced). It is very seductive to attribute this finding to sex differences in the degree of lateralization of hemispheric functions. Before we can assume that women consistently, across ages, perform as they do because they are more bilaterally organized for visuospatial processing than men are, it will be necessary to examine the nature of the strategies that men are employing to obtain a final correct reproduction.

Clock-drawing

Requiring a patient to draw a clock has long been in the repertoire of the neurologist's bedside examination for the assessment of cognitive

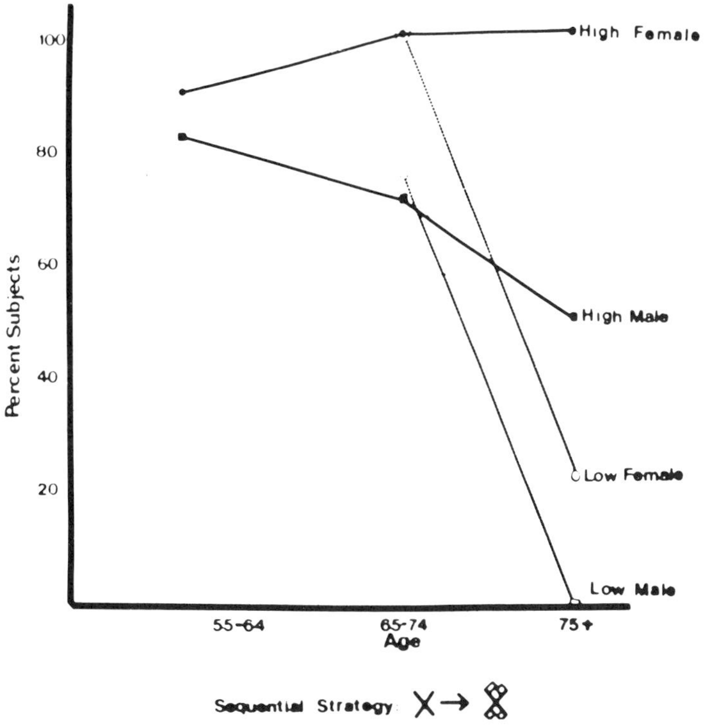

Figure 14. Percentage of correct responses with sequential strategy in elderly men and women. Reprinted by permission of Veroff (1980).

impairment. They have typically asked the patient to set the hands of the clock to 20 after 8 (presumably to have one hand in each parietal hemifield, thus having an opportunity to check for the presence of neglect). Because there is no 20 on a clock face, it is relatively easier to recode the 20 and to focus on minutes, than it would be for the clock-setting of 10 after 11. In fact I chose the setting of 10 after 11 because it would be a more demanding task for patients with right frontal lesions who tend to be pulled to the sensory perceptual features of a stimulus.

Examples of the clock-drawings of the elderly in the Framingham Heart Study underscore the distinctions described earlier between the reproductions of the higher cognitively functioning elderly and those elderly falling below the median on the cognitive screen. Figure 15 illustrates the worst errors that were made by the cognitively higher functioning elderly. The "frontal" features that we so commonly see in patients with lesions in the right "frontal system" are characteristic of this group of elderly individuals. For example, the patients may set the hands at 10 and at 11; they may get confused between the lengths of

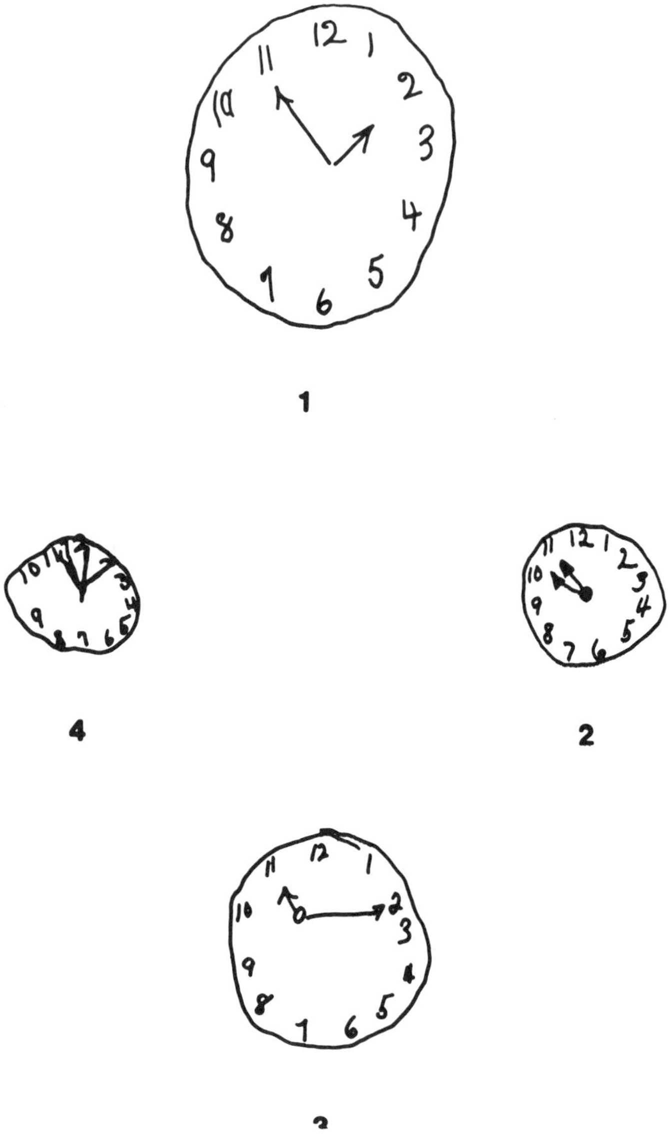

Figure 15. Clock drawings by elderly subjects with high scores on a neuropsychological screening test. Reprinted by permission of Albert and Kaplan (1980).

the hour and minute hands, and place hands emanating from above center (closer to the location of the number the hand is pointing to). In Figure 16 we see the more dramatic, severe errors of the elderly who performed below the median on the cognitive screening test. Example 2 looked like the product of an RHL patient with a left quadrantanopsia. A review of the medical history indicated that indeed there had been a right parietal vascular episode. The bottom clock was drawn by a woman who was considered to be suffering from a progressive dementing process. Note the predilection to write the command; the relatively preserved comprehension of the verbal command; and the significant perseveration in the motor execution, along with the spatial dysfunction. Clocks 1 and 2 are characteristic of the frontal pull noted in RHL patients with frontal system dysfunction, with Clock 2 the most literal translation of the command.

Most often patients are either asked to draw a clock to command or to copy a drawing of a clock. Because there may be a dissociation based on the task demand (i.e., drawing to an oral command versus copying a visually presented model) it is recommended that a patient be required to draw a clock under each condition. Figure 17 shows the differences between drawing to command and to copy as a function of the locus of the lesion. Clocks A and B were drawn by a patient with a right parietal lesion (Clock A was drawn under the copy condition, Clock B was drawn under the command condition). If this patient had been required to only draw a clock to command, the inattention for the lower left quadrant (the parietal field) might have gone unnoticed. Similarly if the patient with the right temporal lesion had only been required to copy a clock (see Clock C) the absence of the global contour and the question of a left upper inattention (see Clock D, which was drawn under the command condition) might have been missed. The differences in the quality of the drawings as a function of task demand and lesion locus argue for distinctive brain and behavior relations, that is, mediation by temporal structures for drawings to command and mediation by parietal structures for drawings to copy.

My colleagues and I (Freedman, Kaplan, Delis, Shulman, & Winocur, in press) have developed an objective scoring system for a comprehensive analysis of clock-drawing. In addition to providing normative data on normal adults sampled from a wide age range, findings in patients with focal lesions, Alzheimer's disease, Parkinson's disease, and psychiatric disorders are presented.

Buccofacial Apraxia

Apraxia has been defined as the inability to perform a learned movement to command, which cannot be accounted for by a motor, sensory, or

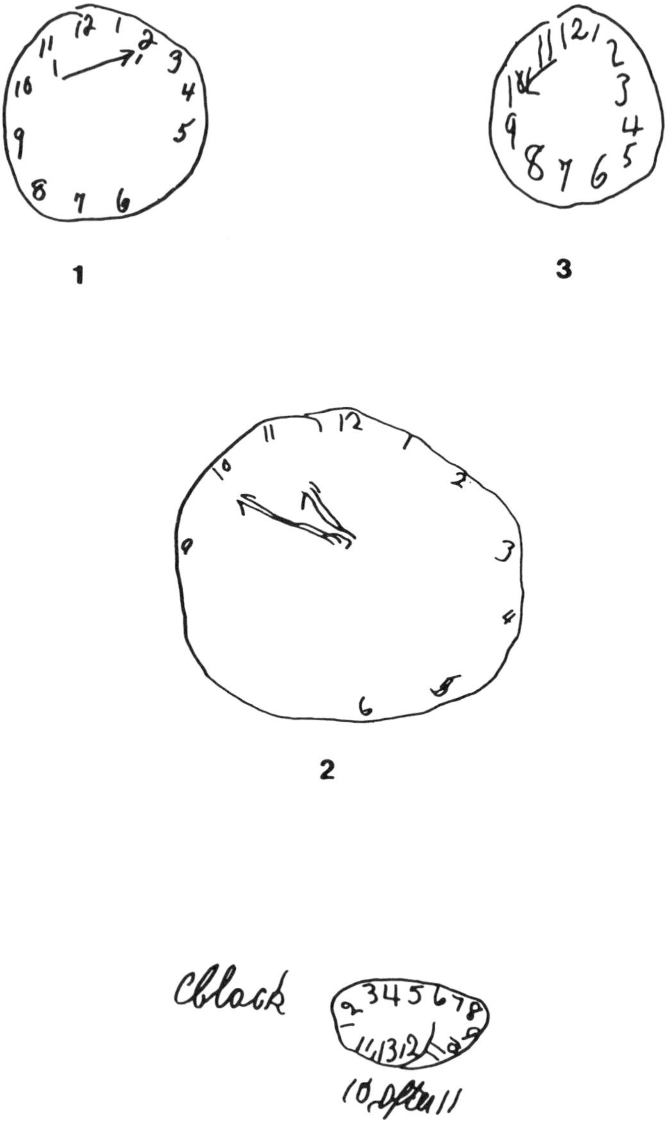

Figure 16. Clock drawings by elderly subjects with low scores on a neuropsychological screening test. Reprinted by permission of Albert and Kaplan (1980).

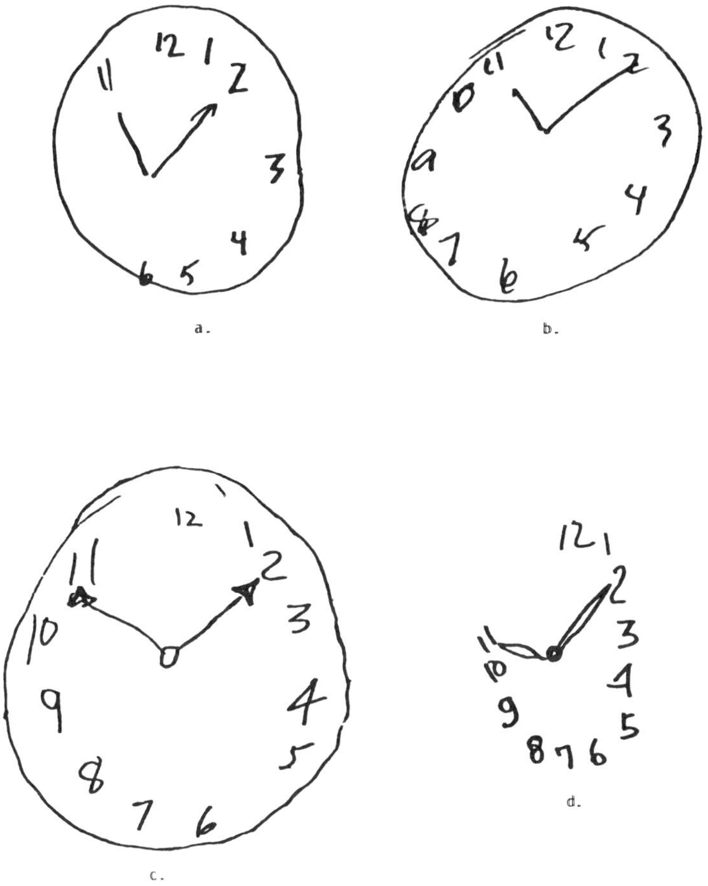

Figure 17. Differences in clock drawings as a function of task demand and locus of lesion.

auditory comprehension impairment. Buccofacial apraxia is an inability to follow such commands as "cough," "pretend to blow out a match," and "smile," despite evidence that these behaviors are unimpaired in the context of real action. Apraxia commonly occurs in conjunction with an aphasia secondary to a lesion in the left hemisphere (for the anatomy, see Geschwind, 1975). The inability to produce a symmetrical smile on verbal command, or to produce a symmetrical smile in imitation of the examiner smiling, stems from an inability to exercise cortical control. Such a patient, however, is capable of producing a perfectly symmetrical smile in response to a humorous situation or a joke, via the limbic system. The reverse holds true as well. A subcortical lesion may result in impaired spontaneous natural contextual responses, which may be overcome by cortical control. This dissociation with regard to diverse structures mediating the same behavior has relevance for the process approach as well as relevance for rehabilitation.

Rey Complex Figure

The Rey Complex Figure (Osterrieth, 1944) is widely used to assess perceptual organization and memory (see Figure 18). The complexity of the figure lends itself to a process analysis. The examiner monitors the patient's performance with a detailed flow chart reproducing the patient's sequence during the copy of the design as well as during the drawings from memory, immediate and delayed.

A patient with a left frontal lesion and right hemiplegia is obliged to draw with his or her left nonpreferred hand. Given that the patient will rely more heavily on the contribution of the relatively spared right hemisphere, and given that the use of the left hand will activate the right hemisphere, it is not surprising that the patient begins the copy in the upper left and captures the outer contour of the figure with one continuous line (see Figure 19). The outer contour is retained in the immediate (Figure 20) and delayed (Figure 21) conditions, while internal details particularly on the right side (contralateral to his lesion) tend to progressively drop out. The left side of the design shows some reduplicated lines which persist over time.

The copy of the complex figure shown in Figure 22 was produced by a patient who suffered a left fronto-temporal gunshot wound. The copy contains the structure, albeit executed in a segmented fashion, as well as all the internal components. Much of the internal detail has dropped out immediately after the copy (Figure 23), and after a 20-minute filled delay, all that is left is the contour and the major structural lines (Figure 24). This patient, with a lateralized left hemisphere lesion, has a selective visuospatial memory problem which is referable to the role that the left hemisphere plays in visuospatial processing.

The copy done by a patient with a right parietal lesion (Figure 25) is of great interest because the breakdown in contour and organization and integration of those parts is limited to the hemiattentional field contralateral to the lesion. The right side (contralateral to the relatively preserved hemisphere) is much better organized than the left side, and shows contour and coherence of parts.

The next two copies of the Complex Figure (Figures 26 and 27), are the result of a relatively rare natural experiment. Figure 26 shows the rather well drawn, though somewhat laterally expanded complex figure produced by a patient with a very small LHL in Broca's area with some extension into white matter. Two years later, he suffered another stroke,

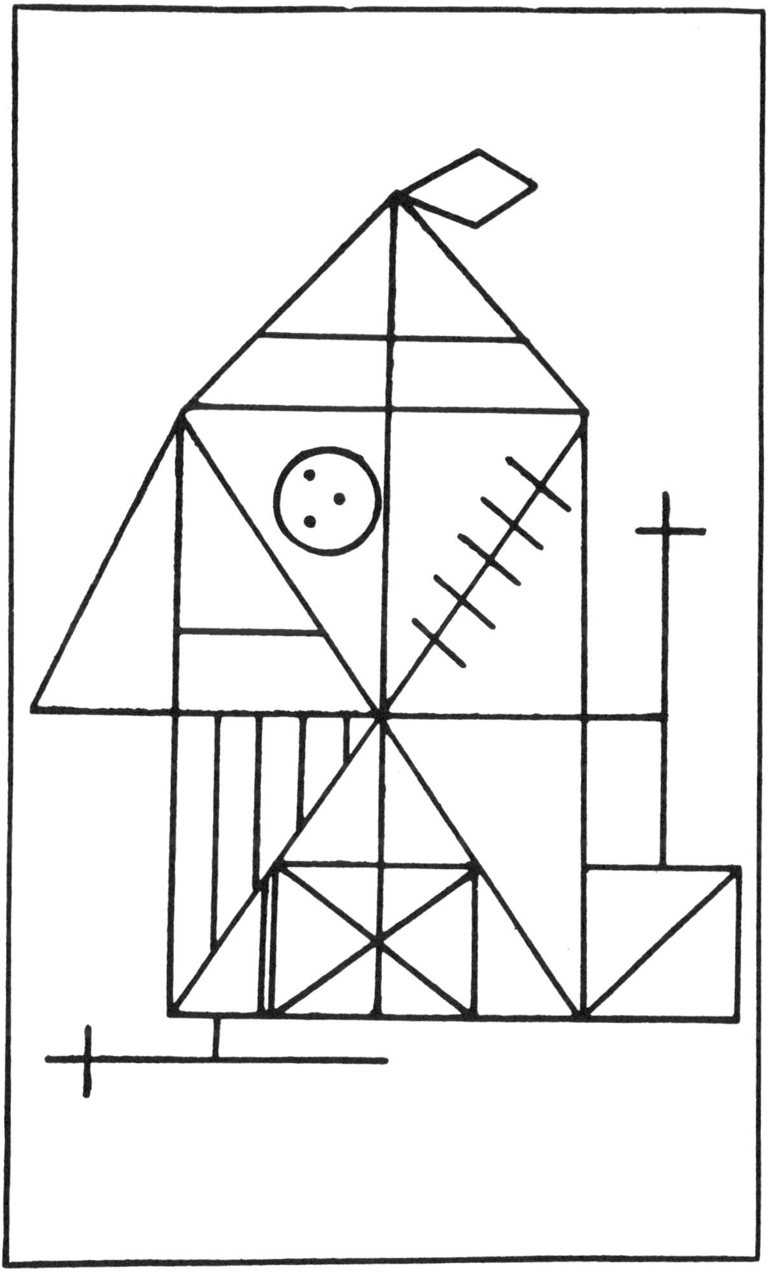

Figure 18. Rey Complex Figure. Reprinted by permission of Osterrieth (1944).

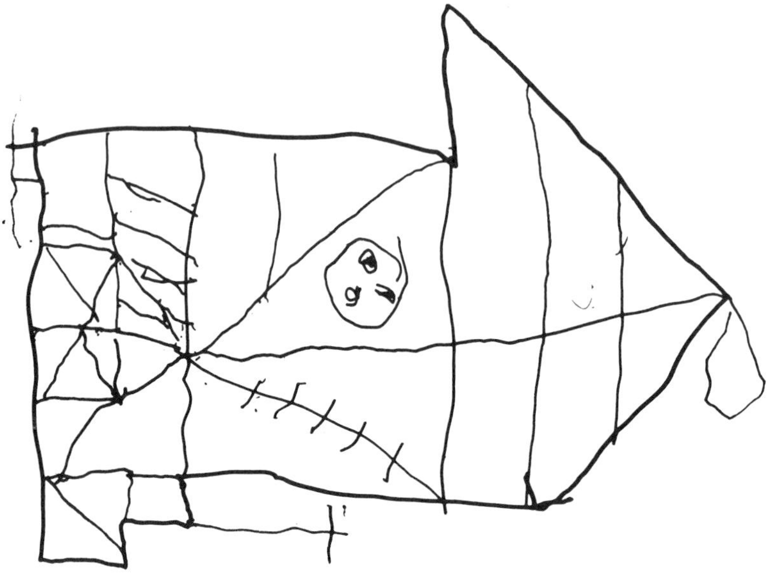

Figure 19. Copy of the Rey Complex Figure by a patient with a left frontal infarct.

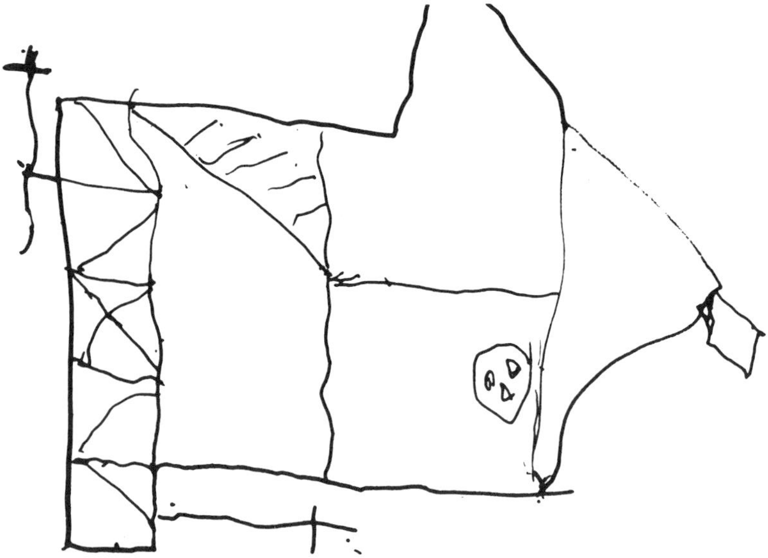

Figure 20. Immediate recall of the Rey Complex Figure by the patient with the left frontal lesion.

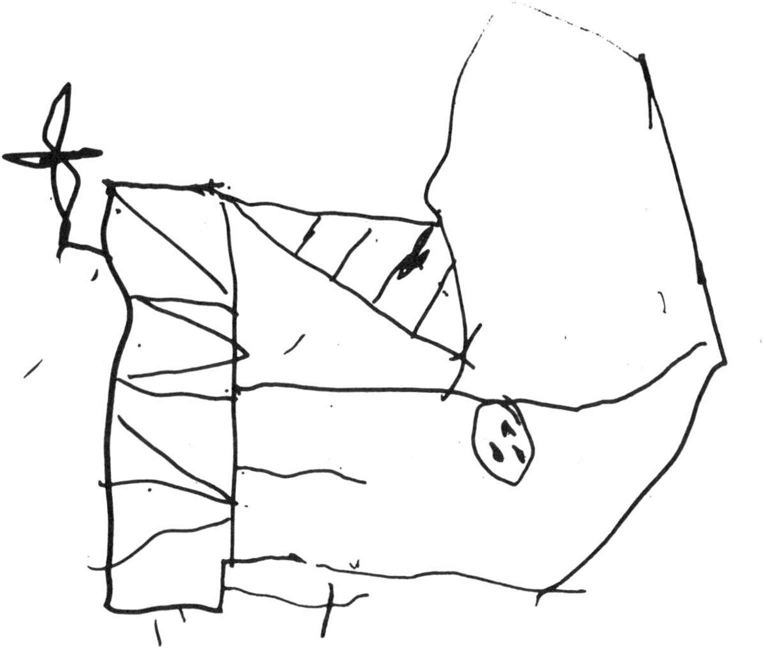

Figure 21. Delayed recall of the Rey Complex Figure by the patient with the left frontal lesion.

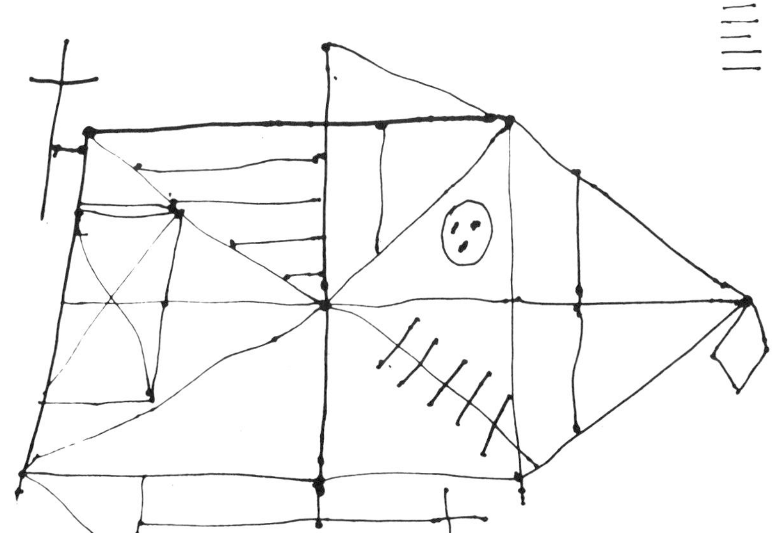

Figure 22. Copy of the Rey Complex Figure by a patient with a left frontotemporal missile wound.

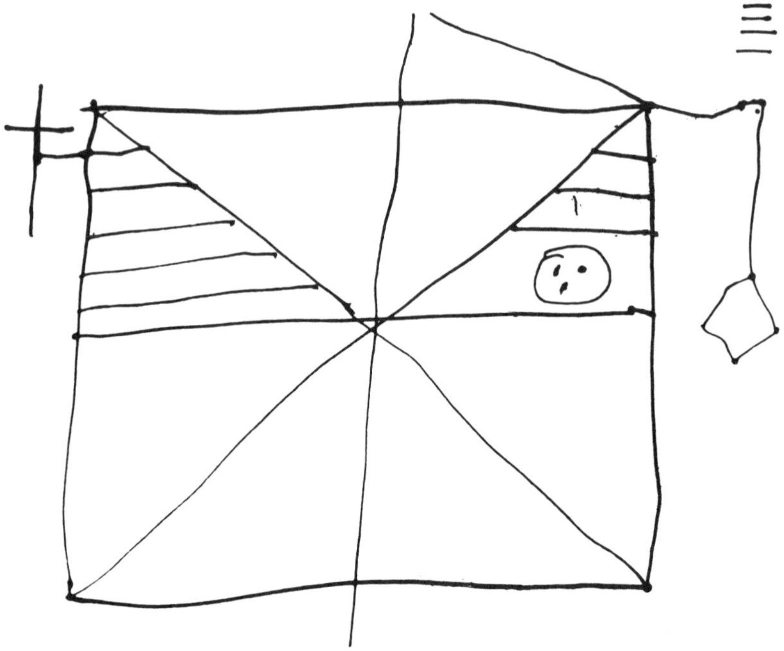

Figure 23. Immediate recall of the Rey Complex Figure by the patient with the left fronto-temporal injury.

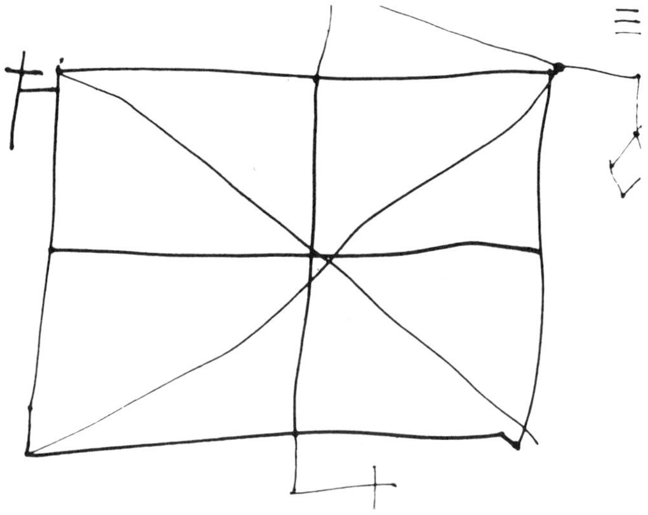

Figure 24. Delayed recall of the Rey Complex Figure by the patient with the left fronto-temporal injury.

Figure 25. Copy of the Rey Complex Figure by a patient with a right parietal lesion.

this time in the right hemisphere. In Figure 27, we see the left neglect and the major role that the left hemisphere is now playing.

Until fairly recently the scoring of the Rey–Osterrieth Complex Figure has been rather achievement-oriented, that is counting the presence of lines (see Lezak, 1983). Waber and Holmes (1985) devised a scoring system that attempts to capture and quantify the drawing process in children.

Most studies using the complex figure have neither reported sex differences nor handedness differences. Weinstein (1987), using the Waber and Holmes scoring system, found an interaction between handedness and academic major in a population of college women. The best copies and drawings from memory were done by left-handers with a math/science major; the poorest drawings of the complex figure were made by right-handed, non-math/science majors, with no familial history

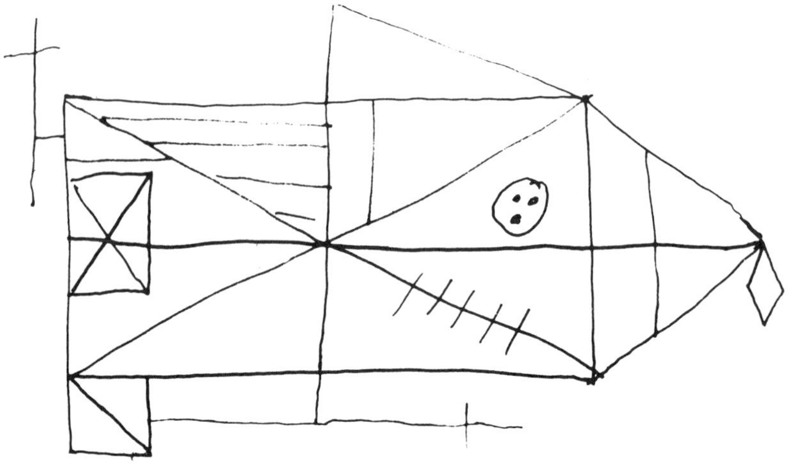

Figure 26. Copy of the Rey Complex Figure drawn by a patient after his first stroke (left hemisphere).

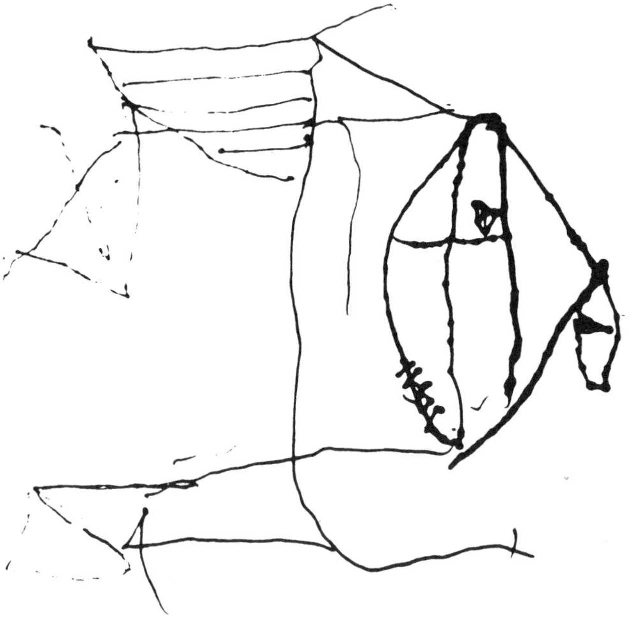

Figure 27. Copy of the Rey Complex Figure drawn after the patient's second stroke (right hemisphere).

of sinistrality. It was of interest that right-handers, with left-handed first degree relatives, performed more like left-handers than right-handers. This study should be replicated with a comparable male population.

Based on research in cognitive science, and our knowledge of brain and behavior relations, Delis, Kiefner, and Fridlund (in press) studied the performance of patients on a relatively factor-free test of visual information processing—the Global–Local Test. Large letters and figures (global form) composed of smaller letters or figures (local form) were presented two at a time (see Figure 28), one letter and one figure, counterbalanced for side of presentation, with multiple learning trials. Memory for the stimuli was tested by recall and recognition. A copy condition concluded the test.

LHL patients showed global form recall and preferentially processed the stimuli in their left hemiattentional field (i.e., the side contralateral to their right hemisphere; see Figure 28). In sharp contrast, RHL patients showed local form recall at the expense of the global form (see Figure 29).

Figure 28. Global–local stimulus figures drawn from memory by an LHL patient.

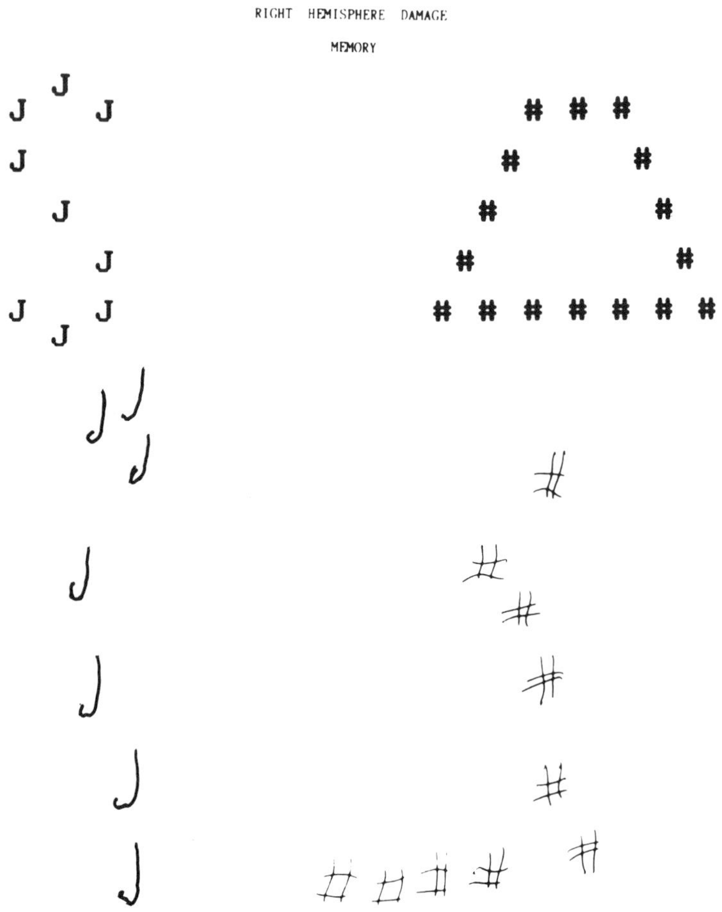

Figure 29. Global–local stimulus figures drawn from memory by an RHL patient.

The power of the process approach to neuropsychological assessment presented in this chapter has been demonstrated mainly with visuospatial examples. It should be clear, however, that the focus on process, the parsing of factors on multifactorial standardized tests, the systematic testing of limits, and the development of experimental procedures to permit a better understanding of the role of individual variables, task variables, and stimulus parameters in brain and behavior relations is applicable to all types of content (e.g., verbal and nonverbal), all modalities of input and output (e.g., auditory, visual, sensory, and motor). Scoring systems have been developed so that patients may be followed over time, and rehabilitation efforts evaluated more effectively than most available scoring procedures allow. The focus on process and how best to optimize performance informs other disciplines engaged in rehabilitation. Perhaps the most important benefactor of this approach is the patient.

References

Albert, M. S., & Kaplan, E. (1980). Organic implications of neuropsychological deficits in the elderly. In L. W. Poon, J. L. Fozard, L. S. Cermak, D. Arenberg, & L. W. Thompson (Eds.), *New directions in memory and aging* (pp. 403–432). Hillsdale, NJ: Erlbaum.

Boll, T. J. (1981). The Halstead-Reitan neuropsychology battery. In S. B. Filskov & T. J. Boll (Eds.), *Handbook of clinical neuropsychology* (pp. 577–607). New York: Wiley.

Christensen, A. (1975a). *Luria's neuropsychological investigation: Text.* New York: Spectrum Publications.

Christensen, A. (1975b). *Luria's neuropsychological investigation: Manual.* New York: Spectrum Publications.

Delis, D. C., Kiefner, M. G., & Fridlund, A. J. (in press). Visuo-spatial dysfunction following unilateral brain damage: Dissociations in hierarchical and hemispatial analysis. *Journal of Clinical and Experimental Neuropsychology.*

Freedman, M., Kaplan, E., Delis, D. C., Shulman, K., & Winocur, G. (in press). *Clock-drawing: A neuropsychological analysis.* New York: Oxford University Press.

Galin, D., & Ornstein, R. (1972). Lateral specialization of cognitive mode: An EEG study. *Psychophysiology, 9,* 412–418.

Geschwind, N. (1965). Disconnection syndromes in animals and man. *Brain, 88,* 585–644.

Geschwind, N. (1975). The apraxias: Neural mechanisms of disorders of learned movement. *American Scientist, 6,* 188–195.

Geschwind, N. (1979). Specializations of the human brain. *Scientific American, 241,* 180–199.

Geschwind, N., & Galaburda, A. M. (1987). *Cerebral lateralization.* Cambridge, MA: The MIT Press.

Geschwind, N., & Kaplan, E. (1962). A human cerebral deconnection syndrome. *Neurology, 12,* 675–685.

Goodglass, H., & Kaplan, E. (1983). *The assessment of aphasia and related disorders (2nd ed.).* Philadelphia: Lea & Febiger.

Hochanadel, G., & Kaplan, E. (1984). Neuropsychology of normal aging. In M.L. Albert (Ed.). *Clinical neurology of aging* (pp. 231–244). New York: Oxford University Press

Hooper, H. E. (1957). *Hooper visual organization test.* Los Angeles: Western Psychological Services.

Kane, R. L. (in press). Standardized and flexible batteries in neuropsychology: An assessment update. *Advances in Neuro-psychology (Vol. 4).* New York: Plenum.

Kaplan, E. (1980). Changes in cognitive style with aging. In L. K. Obler & M. L. Albert (Eds.), *Language and communication in the elderly* (pp. 121–132). Lexington, MA: Heath.

Kaplan, E. (1983). Process and achievement revisited. In S. Wapner & B. Kaplan (Eds.), *Toward a holistic developmental psychology* (pp. 143–156). Hillsdale, NJ: Erlbaum.
Kaplan, E., Goodglass, H., & Weintraub, S. (1983). *The Boston naming test.* Philadelphia: Lea & Febiger.
Kaplan, E., Fein, D., Morris, R., & Delis, D. C. (in press). *The Wechsler Adult Intelligence Scale-Revised as a neuropsychological instrument.* San Antonio: The Psychological Corporation.
Kaplan, E., Palmer, E. P., Weinstein, C., & Baker, E. (1981). *Block design: A brain-behavior based analysis.* Paper presented at the annual European meeting of the International Neuropsychological Society, Bergen, Norway.
Lezak, M. D. (1983). *Neuropsychological assessment (2nd ed.).* New York: Oxford University Press.
Luria, A. R. (1980). *Higher cortical functions in man (2nd ed.).* New York: Basic Books.
Milberg, W. P., Hebben, N., & Kaplan, E. (1986). The Boston process approach. In I. Grant & K. M. Adams (Eds.), *Neuropsychological assessment of neuropsychiatric disorders* (pp. 65–86). New York: Oxford University Press.
Osterrieth, P. A. (1944). Le test de copie d'une figure complexe. *Archives de Psychologie, 30*, 206–356.
Paterson, A., & Zangwill, O. L. (1944). Disorders of visual space perception associated with lesions of the right cerebral hemisphere. *Brain, 67*, 331–358.
Satz, P., & Mogel, S. (1962). An abbreviation of the WAIS for clinical use. *Journal of Clinical Psychology, 18*, 77–79.
Spiers, P. A. (1987). *Unilateral neglect following intracarotid injection of sodium amytal and the cerebral organization of directed attention.* Unpublished doctoral dissertation, Clark University, Worcester, MA.
Veroff, A. E. (1980). The neuropsychology of aging: Qualitative analysis of visual reproductions. *Psychological Research, 41*, 2590–2598.
Waber, D. P., & Holmes, J. M. (1985). Assessing children's copy productions of the Rey-Osterrieth Complex Figure. *Journal of Clinical and Experimental Neuropsychology, 7*, 264–280.
Wada, J. A., & Rasmussen, T. (1960). Intracarotid injection of sodium amytal for the lateralization of cerebral speech dominance. *Journal of Neurosurgery, 17*, 266–282.
Walsh, K. (1985). *Understanding brain damage.* Edinburgh: Churchill Livingstone.
Wechsler, D. (1945). A standardized memory scale for clinical use. *Journal of Psychology, 19*, 87–95.
Wechsler, D. (1974). *Wechsler Intelligence Scale for Children-Revised.* New York: The Psychological Corporation.
Wechsler, D. (1981). *Wechsler Adult Intelligence Scale-Revised.* New York: The Psychological Corporation.
Wechsler, D. (1987). *The Wechsler Memory Scale-Revised.* San Antonio: The Psychological Corporation.
Weinstein, C. S. (1987). *Delineation of female performance on the Rey-Osterrieth Complex Figure.* Unpublished doctoral dissertation, Boston College, Newton, MA.
Weintraub, S., & Mesulam, M. M. (1985). Mental state assessment of young and

elderly adults in behavioral neurology. In M. M. Mesulam (Ed.), *Principles of behavioral neurology* (pp. 71–123). Philadelphia: F. A. Davis.

Werner, H. (1937). Process and achievement: A basic problem of education and developmental psychology. *Harvard Educational Review*, *7*, 353–368.

Werner, H. (1956). Microgenesis and aphasia. *Journal of Abnormal and Social Psychology*, *52*, 347–353.

elephant

MICHAEL I. POSNER

STRUCTURES AND FUNCTIONS OF SELECTIVE ATTENTION

Michael I. Posner is a professor of psychology at the University of Oregon, Eugene. He began work in neuropsychology in 1979 when he was a visiting professor in the Department of Neurology at the Cornell University School of Medicine. He worked at Cornell with Drs. Michael S. Gazzaniga and Jerome B. Posner. From 1979 to 1985 he directed the Cognitive Neuropsychology Laboratory at the Good Samaritan Hospital in Portland, Oregon, in collaboration with Dr. O. S. M. Marin. From 1985 to 1988 he was a professor of neuropsychology at the Washington University School of Medicine where he was involved in studies with a group using Positron Emission Tomography led by Dr. Marcus Raichle. During this ten-year period he was concerned with neural systems underlying selective attention.

Posner is a member of the U.S. National Academy of Sciences and has been a recipient of the Distinguished Scientific Contribution Award of the American Psychological Association, the Warren Medal of the Society of Experimental Psychologists, and the Paul M. Fitts Award of the Human Factors Society. He has published extensively in cognitive psychology, neuropsychology, and neuroscience with emphasis on the study of selective attention and its deficits.

MICHAEL I. POSNER

STRUCTURES AND FUNCTIONS OF SELECTIVE ATTENTION

The central problem of clinical neuropsychology is to understand the relation between the performance of tasks in everyday life and the neurosystems that support them. On the one hand, clinical neuropsychologists are faced with neuroimages that provide a picture of the locations of lesions, and on the other hand, they must discuss with patients, relatives, and insurance companies, likely deficits in performance that will be seen in daily life.

This chapter attempts to develop a framework within which the relation between cognition and brain systems can be better understood. The basic proposition is that the brain localizes mental operations of the kind studied in cognitive psychology (Posner, Petersen, Fox, & Raichle, in press). This form of localization is quite different than the idea of particular centers important for the performance of entire tasks (e.g., visual imagery or word reading). Rather even simple cognitive tasks involve the orchestration of a network of brain areas. However, each node in the network performs a component operation, thus at one level of analysis there is strict localization of function. This analysis of the relation between cognition and brain systems is a very general one. In

This research was supported by ONR Contract N-0014-86-0289 and by the McDonnell Center for Higher Brain Function. I am grateful to Mary K. Rothbart, Steven E. Petersen, and Jennifer Sandson for examination of earlier versions of this manuscript.

this chapter I discuss it with respect to an understanding of the mechanisms of selective attention.

Selective attention is an old topic within experimental psychology (James, 1890; Titchener, 1908) and most frequently refers to performance when there are conflicts between signals. Attention involves selection of higher levels of processing, including conscious processing, while preventing access of other signals to those same high levels of processing. Selective attention plays an important role in most cognitive tasks including pattern recognition, reading, and mental imagery (see Posner, 1982, for a historical review).

In this chapter I do not deal with the problems of maintaining concentration over time (vigilance) nor with the issues of level of alertness. Instead I concentrate on the mechanisms of selection among competing inputs. Although problems of vigilance and alertness are of importance for clinical neuropsychology, the study of selective attention provides the best current model for working out detailed relations between brain systems and mental operations.

During the last dozen years it has been possible to work out some aspects of the neural structures involved in spatial selective attention based upon work with humans (Posner, Walker, Friedrich, & Rafal, 1984) and alert monkeys (Mountcastle, 1978; Wurtz, Goldberg, & Robinson, 1980). The research has been accomplished by many different investigators, but studies have used similar tasks and have been aided by our increased understanding of the anatomy of the visual system (Cowey, 1985) and to some extent of the frontal lobes (Goldman-Rakic, 1987). Thus something of a common overall view has begun to emerge despite remaining conflicts and uncertainties. This work has been summarized in edited volumes from anatomical, physiological, neuropsychological, and cognitive perspectives (see Berlucchi & Rizzolatti, 1987; Posner & Marin, 1985).

The work on spatial attention may serve as a useful model for understanding the way in which cognition is represented within the nervous system. It already has provided a basis for understanding some functions of selective attention, such as visual pattern recognition (Prinzmetal, Presti, & Posner, 1986; Treisman, 1986) including the recognition of visual words (Petersen, Fox, Posner, Mintun, & Raichle, 1988; Posner & Presti, 1987). Research on spatial attention provides a basis for understanding deficits of attention found in such diverse disorders as schizophrenia, depression, and closed head injury.

In this chapter, I trace a general framework for connecting cognitive and neural systems of selective attention. I also review the effects of unilateral brain lesions on the cognitive operations of visual spatial orienting, citing studies that show how damage to this system affects pattern recognition. Next I review evidence relating attention to language and attention to visual locations in order to construct a general picture of the structure of the attention system. Finally, I apply our knowledge about the structure and function of attention to a condition whose organic basis is unknown—schizophrenia.

A Framework for the Connection Between Cognitive Systems and Neurosystems

It is useful to view the connection between cognitive systems and neurosystems in terms of a very general framework (Posner, 1986). This framework involves five levels of analysis shown in Table 1. At the highest level are tasks of daily life. Cognitive scientists have developed a number of computational models for tasks such as visual imagery (Kosslyn, 1980), reading (Rumelhart & McClelland, 1981), and typewriting (Rumelhart & Norman, 1982). These tasks provide a view of the computations necessary for any electromechanical system to perform the cognitive tasks described. Some of these computational models consist of subroutines that operate on symbolic representation, labeled here as *elementary operations*. They resemble the types of operations studied by cognitive experiments of the last twenty years (Posner, 1978). Each operation can be specified in terms of the input to the operation and its output. Sample operations include match, store, zoom, compare, engage, and move. These operations sometimes serve as labels on the box models of information flow that dominate textbooks of cognitive psychology.

In recent years a new form of computational model has arisen in several areas of psychology (see McClelland & Rumelhart, 1986, for a review). In these parallel distributed or connectionist models, perfor-

Table 1
A General Framework for Levels of Analysis in Connecting Cognitive Tasks of Daily Life to Neural Systems

Level of Analysis	General Examples	Covert Orienting Task Examples
Task	Reading, speaking, imagery	Covert orienting
Elementary operations	Next, scan, name, zoom	Disengage, move, engage
Component analysis	Facilitate pathway, inhibit pathway	Facilitate location
Neural system	Processing negativity, blood flow, lesions	Midbrain (superior colliculus), parietal lobe
Cellular activity	Selective enhancement	Light sensitive cells

mance in terms of elementary operations is not directly discussed but instead facilitations and inhibitions between levels are referred to. Fortunately, as we have learned to measure elementary operations in chronometric experiments, we find that they can be specified in terms of component facilitations and inhibitions in performance. In my own work I have often attempted to describe mental operations in terms of these time-locked facilitations and inhibitions (Posner, 1978; Posner & Snyder, 1975) in reaction time. Methods for making such measurements have been described and have been widely applied (Jonides & Mack, 1984; Neely, 1977; Posner, 1978; Taylor, 1977). A great deal is known about how such measures can be taken and what pitfalls there are in using them (Jonides & Mack, 1984). The use of the words *facilitation* and *inhibition* in connectionist models and in the description of the components of elementary mental operations are biased to make one inquire as to whether such patterns are related to the activity of populations of nerve cells that might perform the computation. To what extent do our findings on facilitation and inhibition in the performance domain and in connectionist models relate to changes in populations of nerve cells? This relation is a central question for the neuropsychology of cognition. If it is possible to move from the level of facilitation and inhibition in performance to the level of neurosystems, one can then see how it is possible to go from an understanding of lesions in an area of the nervous system to predictions about normal cognition.

The study of visual spatial attention has been extremely important to this enterprise. Visual spatial attention can be studied in people and in alert monkeys. The presence of an animal model provides an opportunity to determine whether results obtained from performance studies of normal humans converge with those using single cell methodology. Insofar as this link can be established, it is possible to move from the general study of neurosystems, as can be done in human beings in the studies I describe here, to the study of individual nerve cells.

Facilitation and Inhibition in Visual Spatial Attention

In attempting to work out a complex system such as selective attention, it is important to study experimental situations or "model tasks" that define what is meant by the phenomenon and allow us to study it in simple forms. An important aspect of selective attention is orienting to a source of visual signals. In this area, similar model tasks have been used in studies of animals, normal humans, and patients (Berlucchi & Rizzolatti, 1987; Posner & Marin, 1985). The importance of studying covert shifts of attention is the hope that the mechanisms involved in these shifts of attention will help us understand more general problems of selectivity in other modalities and in memory.

A very simple model task is illustrated in Figure 1. At the start of each trial (Time 1 in Figure 1) the subject is fixated at the center of the screen. One of the two squares located to the left or right of fixation brightens (Time 2 in Figure 1). This draws the subject's attention to the cued location. A target is then presented (Time 3 in Figure 1) at varying intervals following the cue that occurs either at the cued location or on the side opposite the cue. In order to be sure that any effects are due to attention shifts and not to the brightening of the box a second form of cueing is used. In this form an arrow is presented in the center box indicating the box in which the target is most likely to occur. Thus any difference in reaction time between the cued and uncued side could not be due to brightening the box.

Many experiments have now been performed with both of these forms of cueing. The results for these tasks uniformly show an advantage for the cued location over the uncued location that is closely time-locked to the occurrence of the cue. This relative facilitation has been measured in reaction time (Posner, 1980), probability of correct detections for near-threshold stimuli (Bashinski & Bachrach, 1980), and increased electrical activity at the cued location in comparison with the uncued location (Mangun, Hansen, & Hillyard, 1986).

Two interrelated issues in interpretation of these findings remain in dispute. First, is the relative facilitation of the cued location a genuine improvement of information coming from the cued location or a re-

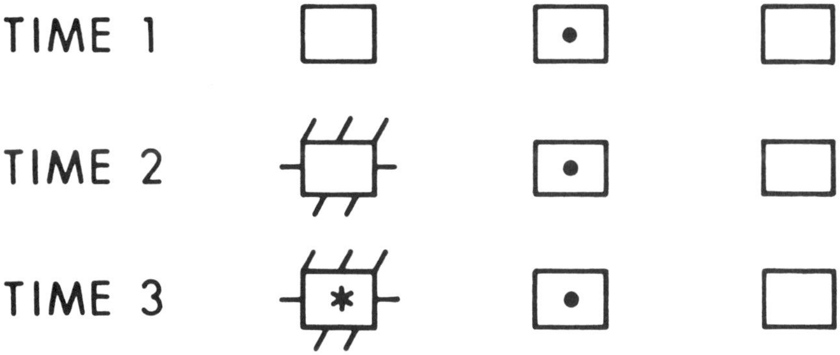

Figure 1. A model task of peripheral cueing to study covert shifts of visual–spatial attention. The top row (Time 1) shows the cathode ray tube at the start of each trial. The subject fixates on the dot in the center of the screen. The second row (Time 2) indicates a brightening of the left box (about 5 degrees from fixation) designed to draw the person's attention while the eyes remained fixed in the center. The third row (Time 3) occurs at varying intervals following the brightening and indicates a clear target figure presented in the box. The subject responds as rapidly as possible to the target. Shown is a valid trial because the target occurs on the cued side. On invalid trials the target occurs on the opposite side. For null trials no cue is presented.

duction or inhibition of information coming from all other locations? Second, what is the extent of the facilitated area? Most experiments seem to be consistent with the idea that facilitation occurs not only at the attended location but also in a gradient over a range of adjacent locations (Downing & Pinker, 1985; Rizzolatti, Riggio, Dascola, & Umilta, 1987). The size of the area facilitated depends in part on the degree of eccentricity from the fovea and in part upon the complexity of the information in the visual field. How large a part of the visual field is represented by the focus of attention? This has been a widely disputed issue. For example, Hughes and Zimba (1985) have argued that attention acts simply by inhibiting the hemifield to which one is not attending. Others have found a facilitation localized to the neighborhood of the target and increasing with eccentricity from the fovea, with an inhibition stronger once one has crossed the midline (Downing & Pinker, 1985). These disputes indicate the complexity of the overlapping processes that accompany a shift of attention.

My basic approach to these complexities has been to develop a functional model that can both account for these findings and conform to other properties associated with attention. According to this functional viewpoint (Posner & Cohen, 1984), three basic components are involved when attention is summoned by a cue located in the neighborhood of a likely target. These components combine to determine the net increase in efficiency at the cued location. First, the cue increases alertness because a target is now expected. It is known from previous work that alertness is not spatially selective (Posner, 1978) and works to potentiate all targets following the cue. Second, the cue initiates a spatially selective movement of visual attention to the cued location. Such attention shifts are not fully automatic in the sense of being unavoidable (Posner, Cohen, Choate, Hockey, & Maylor, 1984), but they occur with little effort if the subject does nothing to avoid them (Jonides, 1981).

Third, the occurrence of a cue in the periphery initiates two forms of inhibition. The first, called *cost*, is a consequence of orienting attention to the cue. Once attention is engaged at the cued location, all other locations will be handled less efficiently (inhibited) than if no such orienting had occurred because one must first disengage from the cued location before moving to targets at other locations. This form of inhibition is spatially selective only in the sense that it is not present within the focus of attention. A second form of inhibition also occurs. This is called *the inhibition of return* (Posner & Cohen, 1984). The inhibition of return depends upon the act of orienting to a spatial location (Maylor, 1985), but it is most clearly shown if one summons attention to a location and then returns it to a neutral location. The efficiency of the previously cued location is reduced with respect to comparable locations in the visual field for several seconds. The overlap between facilitation due to orienting of attention and the specific inhibition of a cued location helps to explain conflicts in the literature. Sometimes a cued location is handled more efficiently than other locations, sometimes less efficiently, depending upon the balance between the facilitation due to orienting of attention and the inhibition due to the reduction in efficiency of returning attention to an already cued location.

Are there any ecological advantages to this very complex constellation of internal events by a cue? Our theory rests on our finding that the relative facilitation obtained from a peripheral cue moves with the eyes as though it were mapped in retinal coordinates (Posner & Cohen, 1984). This effect is not on the retina because it can be obtained in stereoscope. However, it preserves the coordinates of the retina as do many visual images at cortical levels. Inhibition of return on the other hand, does not move when the eyes do; it behaves as though it were dependent on the coordinates of the environment. When we move our eyes, the objects of the world appear to maintain their locations, thus many psychological phenomena maintain the coordinates of the environment as we move about it. It seemed to us of basic importance that one of our effects (facilitation) is retinotopic and the other (inhibition of return) is environmental in this sense.

The facilitation effect serves to give priority to targets during a visual fixation. It allows people to give momentary priority to an object in the visual field as, for example, when a person carefully examines the nose within a face. If the task demands high acuity, he or she is likely to move his or her eyes to the examined location and thus, produce a reorienting of attention back to the fovea. In reading, for example, the reduction of acuity with eccentricity may be the cause of the eye movement (Morrison, 1984). Attention allows a temporary emphasis outside of the fovea, and it is crucial as a guide to the occulomotor system to tell people where to move the eyes next.

My colleagues and I speculate that inhibition of return evolved to maximize sampling of novel areas within the visual fields. Once the eyes move away from the target location, events occurring at that environmental location are inhibited and one is less likely to move the eyes back to them (Posner, Choate, Rafal, & Vaughn, 1985). This reduces the effectiveness of an area of space in summoning attention and serves as a bias for favoring fresh areas in which no previous targets have been presented. The long-lasting nature of inhibition of return ensures that two to three eye movements are biased against a return. The organization of facilitation and inhibition outlined previously seems to represent an exquisite functional adaptation to the needs of the visual world.

In Figure 2, the top of the figure indicates the occurrence of a visual cue. The bottom indicates a set of partially sequential but overlapping mental operations induced by the cue. According to this diagram, the cue produces a non-spatially specific alerting effect that serves to interrupt ongoing performance. The cue also leads to calculation of its

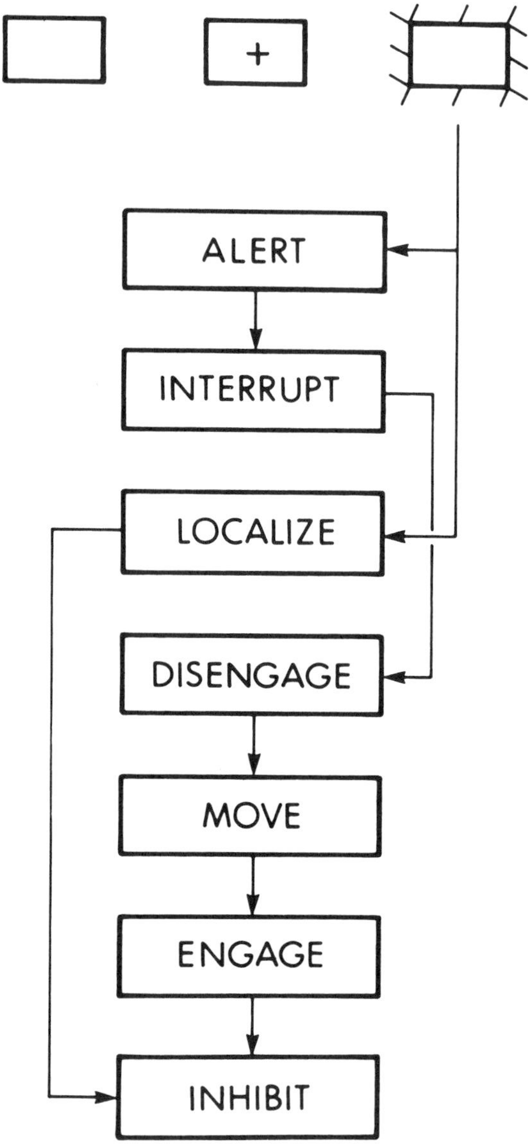

Figure 2. The top row indicates the model task described in Figure 1. The boxes indicate mental operations thought to occur as the result of the cue. The disengage, move, engage, and inhibit operations involve portions of the posterior visual spatial attention systems as described in the text. The alert and interrupt operation involve functions that relate to the anterior attention system. Reprinted from Posner, Inhoff, Friedrich, and Cohen (1987) by permission.

coordinates and in turn produces a disengagement of attention, a movement to the location of the cue and subsequent engagement of the target. If the subject's attention is withdrawn from the cue to another location, the inhibition at the target location, called the inhibition of return, can be measured. Single cell recordings in monkeys and the study of patients with restricted neurological lesions can be used to examine the neurosystems that support each of these operations. The basic argument developed in the next section is that widely separated neurosystems are involved in the computation of these various mental operations.

Deficits of Orienting from Focal Lesions

Several areas of the monkey brain have cells in which firing rates are enhanced selectively when the monkey's attention is directed to targets in their receptive fields (Wurtz, Goldberg, & Robinson, 1980). In one of these areas, the superior colliculus, the selective enhancement occurs only when attention is directed overtly via eye movement. In a second area, the posterior parietal lobe, selective enhancement occurs when attention is directed overtly or when the monkey is required to maintain fixation while attending covertly to a peripheral stimulus. The third area of selective enhancement lies between the midbrain and cortical projections in the thalamic nuclei known as the pulvinar (Petersen, Robinson, & Morris, 1987). Selective enhancement appears to be restricted to these three areas. The single cell results allow us researchers to ask about the relation between modulation of cellular activity and patterns of facilitation and inhibition found in our work with humans. In this sense they provide an opportunity to connect the last row of Table 1 (cellular level) with the facilitatory and inhibitory performance changes described for visual spatial orienting. These connections are fundamental to our effort to see if the nervous system localizes the components of cognitive operations.

There is a long clinical history documenting the finding that lesions of the posterior part of one hemisphere can cause a severe deficit in reporting information on the side of space opposite the lesion (DeRenzi, 1982). Neglect of visual information contralateral to the lesion occurs most strongly when patients are confronted with simultaneous lateralized visual stimuli. Under these conditions stimuli contralateral to the lesion are frequently not reported (extinguished). The phenomena of neglect can arise from unilateral lesions of the midbrain and thalamus as well as from a variety of cortical lesions. However, clinical observations seem to suggest parietal lesions on the right side as the most frequent area of damage leading to neglect and extinction (DeRenzi, 1982).

In recent years a number of these parietal patients have been studied in experiments using cues such as those described in the previous section (Baynes, Holtzman, & Volpe, 1986; Morrow & Ratcliff, 1987; Nagel-Leiby, Buchtel, & Welch, 1987; Posner, Cohen, & Rafal, 1982; Posner, Walker, et al., 1984; Posner, Inhoff, et al., 1987). The studies have been uniform in showing a particular type of deficit present in patients with right parietal lesions. These patients have a general advantage in reaction time for those targets that occur ipsilateral to the lesion in comparison to those that occur contralateral to the lesion. However, for many parietal patients there is little or no difference between the two types of targets if they follow a cue at the same location (valid trial). When attention is drawn to either side, these patients have nearly equal ability to detect the target at the cued location. Thus the ability to engage the target once attention is properly directed is not necessarily interrupted by parietal lesions although it is affected in many patients.

Striking results occur on trials when attention is cued to the side of the lesion and the target is presented to the side opposite the lesion (invalid trials). In some cases, targets show extinction; that is, targets are missed entirely by the subject (Posner, et al., 1982). In other cases, targets are not completely excluded from consciousness, but show greatly delayed reaction time, sometimes two or three times the normal reaction time. The results suggest that this elevation in latency is simply a less severe form of complete exclusion from consciousness. Patients who miss signals completely when they remain present in the field only briefly will report them when they remain present but with greatly increased latency. The idea that a latency increase is a less severe form of difficulty than extinction fits with the account of covert orienting in normal humans discussed previously.

The pattern of increased reaction time to contralateral targets following miscues does not depend upon the miscue being ipsilateral to the lesion. Indeed, the increases in reaction time occur in both visual fields when the subject has to produce a covert movement in a contralesional direction from the cue to the target (Ladavas, 1987; Posner, Inhoff, et al., 1987). For patients with right parietal lesions, leftward movements from cue to target are longer than rightward movements to the same target. These findings suggest that the main deficit in parietal patients occurs in the disengage operation. It may be instructive to review the logic. On validly cued trials there is only a modest difference in reaction time on the two sides. Moreover, the improvement in reaction time following a valid cue appears to be about the same on the two sides of the field. We argue that this reduction is due to a shift of attention, thus many parietal patients (those with no difference in valid reaction times between the two visual fields) are able to shift attention equally well to the two sides. However, once attention is engaged either at fixation or in either visual field, reaction times (RTs) to targets that lie in a contralesional direction are greatly elevated for even those patients with no differences on valid trials. Why should this be? Why should contralesional targets be at so great a disadvantage following a cue at another location? We reason that it must be because the parietal lesion has a special affect on disengaging attention.

This specific deficit in the disengage operation for contralateral targets found in parietal patients has been confirmed in a number of experiments (Baynes, et al., 1986; Morrow & Ratcliff, 1987). There are several remaining complexities, that have not been successfully resolved. Using a central cue, Nagel-Leiby et al. (1987) found differences between men and women and in some cases, frontal patients showed more severe deficits than parietal patients. In addition, Morrow and Ratcliff (1987), who confirmed our basic result with right parietal patients, have found little deficit in left parietal patients and also found a similar pattern to the right parietal patients in one frontal lobe patient. The unique status of the parietal lobe that appeared clear in our earlier work seems somewhat in question. The issue may be partly resolved by the widespread effects that occur immediately following a lesion. For some months following an insult to the nervous system, there may be widespread changes in glucose utilization and blood flow over the entire hemisphere (Deuel & Collins, 1984). It is possible that some of the reports from other areas may have arisen because the patients were tested too early. The deficits we have reported persist even when patients are tested years after the stroke. Morrow and Ratcliff (1987) have traced these recovery effects for some months following lesions.

Another reason for finding these effects in frontal patients may be because the spatial attention system is not an isolated module that operates independently of other levels of control. Thus lesions of the frontal lobe may affect the spatial attention system along with a variety of other systems because it influences command systems necessary to allow for the disengagement process. It is not completely clear whether lesions of the left parietal lobe produce an identical pattern with the same strength as lesions of the right parietal lobe. These comparisons are, of course, always between subjects and thus can involve many sources of error not found in the within-subject comparisons on which we have mostly relied.

Forms of Neglect

Clinically, neglect occurs after a wide variety of lesions. This may be in part because many of the reports of neglect are from studies of patients who are acutely ill and may have widespread metabolic problems following the initial insult. We have so far found only three groups of patients who show systematic deficits in visual spatial orienting even after relatively long periods of time after the lesions. These correspond to areas that give selective enhancement in single cell studies of alert monkeys. The reaction time patterns in these three forms of "neglect" are shown in Figure 3. It shows the reaction times to valid and invalid trials at short intervals between the cue and the target and divides them according to whether the target occurs in the field that is usually neglected (right panel) or the one that has no evidence of neglect (left panel). In the case of parietal lesions the neglected field involves the area of space contralateral to the lesion.

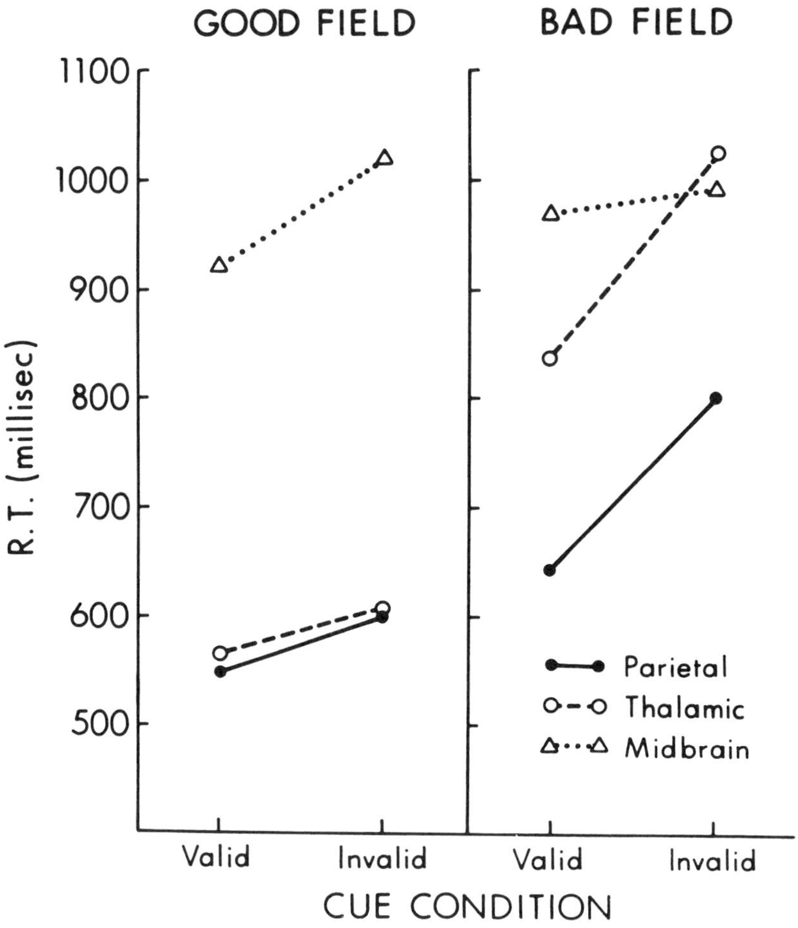

Figure 3. Three forms of neglect. The left panel shows performance when targets are in the nonneglected visual areas, the right panel when they are in the neglected visual areas. Data are always from cue to target intervals of 100 ms or less.

A second group of patients have progressive supranuclear palsy, with lesions of the midbrain, including the superior colliculus and surrounding areas. These patients showed a unique deficit in eye movements, having great difficulty making voluntary eye movements, particularly in the vertical direction. Impairment develops more slowly for horizontal movements. These patients often come to the neurologist's attention because they neglect the lower part of the visual field. In the case of these patients we have systematically compared attention movements in the vertical direction with those in the horizontal direction (Posner, Choate, et al., 1985). The results for these patients are very striking and completely different for those found for parietal patients. As can be seen from Figure 3, these midbrain patients have very long reaction times. The long reaction times may be due to the widespread reticular lesions along with the deficits that we have described. However, in the horizontal direction there is clear evidence of a validity effect. Even at short intervals, valid trials are systematically faster than invalid trials. Thus orienting to horizontal targets appears relatively normal. However, in the vertical direction, the validity effect does not emerge until much later. There is no evidence of a validity effect at the fast probe interval shown in Figure 3 but usually by half a second a validity effect has emerged.

These data are very different from the parietal patients who show a greater than normal validity effect in the neglected field at the earliest intervals. Because the emergence of a validity effect is due to a shift of attention to the cued side, the findings from the midbrain patients suggest a specific delay in their ability to move attention to the target. Hence, if enough time is given following the cue, the vertical and horizontal directions both show validity effects. It appears that the deficit in the midbrain patients is in their ability to move attention covertly in the direction that has the largest eye movement deficit.

An additional finding with supranuclear palsy patients is that they lose the inhibition of return in the vertical direction. Although they can move attention to a vertical cue if given sufficient time, they do not show the reduced tendency to return attention to a previously cued location (Posner, Choate, et al., 1985). This loss of inhibition of return was unique to these midbrain patients and is not found in control groups with cortical or other subcortical lesions. It fits quite well with the functional theory that identifies inhibition of return with the tendency to move the eyes to novel locations. Deficits in the move and inhibit operations provide more evidence in favor of the idea that specific neurosystems influence different aspects of the set of computations necessary to induce orienting of visual spatial attention.

A third form of neglect has been found following thalamic lesions that may involve the pulvinar (Rafal & Posner, 1987). As can be seen from Figure 3, these patients show another pattern of performance deficit, especially long reaction times for the invalid trials on the side opposite the lesion. This effect is similar to that found in parietal patients, although the deficit on invalid contralesional trials does not appear to last as long following the cue in the thalamic patients. Striking in the thalamic patients is that the increase in RT is also quite large for valid trials on the side contralateral to the lesion.

This constellation of deficits for both valid and invalid trials could be consistent with a purely visual defect. However, careful ophthalmologic testing of these patients, particularly in their six-month follow-up, showed no evidence of ophthalmologic deficits. The second explanation would be a specific deficit in their ability to engage attention on the side contralesional to the target. This would suggest that these patients cannot use attention to make processing as efficient as it could be when targets are contralesional. This supports the idea that thalamic lesions produce a specific deficit in the engage operation and it provides some support for a theory of the special role of thalamic areas in control of the attentional spotlight (Crick, 1984). In Crick's view, the thalamus is the area of the brain most likely to be involved in the search of the complex visual field for targets. A deficit in the engage operation would be consistent with this theoretical view.

Figure 3 summarizes three patterns that we have found present for posterior lesions related to aspects of poor RT performance to targets contralateral to the lesion. These include parietal lesions and the disengage operation; thalamic lesions and the engage operation; and midbrain lesions and the move operation. The results do not show complete separation. For example, parietal patients frequently show engage deficits and thalamic lesions produce disengage deficits as well. The known anatomy and close physiological connections of these areas would lead to the expectation that the three are in close contact. For covert orienting to occur, all these operations must be performed. One assumes that the disengage operation begins the sequence, information is then sent to the midbrain to move attention to an already calculated location and when that is completed, it is possible for the system to work through thalamic sites to engage targets. An important point is that the thalamus (particularly the lateral pulvinar) represents an area allowing contact between parietal systems responsible for spatial attention and systems of the brain known to be responsible for pattern recognition. It is clear that patients with lesions of the parietal lobe do show deficits in the pattern recognition process and I present evidence of this effect in the next section.

Functions of Spatial Attention in Pattern Recognition

According to recent views of the neurophysiology of vision, there are two major systems extending from the primary visual cortex. The first extends from area Vl (striate cortex) to the inferotemporal cortex and is involved in the recognition of objects. The second extends from area V1 into the parietal lobe and is more responsible for localization of information and as I have discussed previously, for visual spatial attention (Mishkin, Ungerleider, & Macko, 1983). It is important to ask whether deficits in visual selective attention influence the pattern recognition process, and if so, in what way?

We have developed two different strategies to evaluate this issue. First, cueing in normal humans can be used to control orienting of attention, and can then explore the effects of such cues on pattern recognition. Second, patients with deficits in visual spatial attention due to specific lesions can be studied. It is possible to ask both whether the cueing known to be responsible for covert visual orienting influences pattern recognition and also whether the presence of lesions in areas related to visual spatial attention influences pattern recognition. The answer to both questions seems to be yes and provides us with information on the relation of attention to pattern recognition.

According to one recent theory, visual spatial attention has the role of integrating visual features into conjunctions (Treisman, 1986). Individual features of objects such as color, orientation, or motion are to some extent registered in separate spatial maps in the monkey cortex. This registration occurs in parallel across the entire visual field. If an object differs from its background by a single feature, it is possible for a person to respond to the presence of that feature rapidly and efficiently without attending to individual items in the field. If, however, the judgment requires the integration of features into a conjunction, such as looking for a red *T* in a field of *T*s and other red objects, spatial attention is needed and a more serial search is conducted. If normal subjects are cued to a location eccentric of the fovea, both feature and conjunction search are conducted more efficiently at the cued location. However, the affect on conjunction search is far stronger than the effect for feature search (Prinzmetal, et al., 1986; Treisman, 1986). This suggests that although attention can effect the registration of features, it plays a more important role in the recognition of conjunctions.

Similarly, it is possible to study the effects of lesions of the visual spatial attention system on the visual search process. It is well known clinically that right parietal lesions produce a relative neglect of information on the side of space opposite the lesion. Researchers have shown that both right and left parietal lesions have clear effects on visual pattern recognition (Friedrich, Walker, & Posner, 1985). Subjects were presented with two strings of letters, one above the other. The letter strings were identical half the time and half the time differed by a single letter. This difference could be in the beginning of the string, in the middle, or at the end of the string. The subject's task was to press one key if the strings were identical and another if they were not. Subjects were free to move their eyes, and the letters remained present in the visual field until they responded. Left parietal patients showed extreme difficulty when the discrepant letter was at the end of the letter string. Reaction times were nearly 800 ms longer for differences found at the end than at the beginning. Moreover, the subjects frequently missed differences at the end. On the other hand, right parietal patients were slower and made more errors when the differences were at the beginning. This task is an attention demanding spatial search task and shows quite clearly the pattern recognition deficits in the parietal patients. The ability to organize and recognize differences on the side of space opposite the lesion is greatly impaired even when they can take the time to move their eyes and examine the stimulus in detail. These were patients tested a long time after their strokes and they showed little evidence of clinical neglect or extinction. Despite the general recovery, the visual search task showed clear deficits.

An important distinction in the study of pattern recognition is between automatic and attended processes. By exploring automatic processes we can examine the operations for which attention is not needed. One process that has been a candidate for automatic processes is the ability of a visual word presented on the fovea to contact its visual, phonological, and semantic representations in memory (LaBerge & Samuels, 1974; Marcel, 1983; Posner, 1978). The advantage of an integrated word, even in comparison to individual letters, has been an important theme in cognitive psychology and in recent connectionist models of visual word processing (McClelland & Rumelhart, 1986). It thus became of considerable interest when Sieroff and Michel (1987) reported that patients who showed profound extinction of individual short words when they are presented simultaneously to the right and left visual field showed no evidence of extinction with tachistoscopic presentation of a single word across the fovea, even when it covered the same visual angle as the word pair. Patients with both right and left parietal lesions showed clear evidence of extinction to simultaneous words but even right parietal patients showed little evidence of extinction of the single foveally presented word.

We compared the perception of single eight letter strings (Sieroff, Pollatsek, & Posner, 1987) that either formed words or not. Tests of ten right parietal patients presented at bedside with 3″×5″ cards showed that the patients missed the first few letters of nonwords, but not of words (see Figure 4). This result was confirmed by tachistoscopic testing of right and left parietal patients who were tested a long time after their stroke. The results showed that the recognition of the letters in nonwords appeared to depend upon an intact visual spatial attention system, but for words the lesion did not produce any spatially specific deficit. These results fit with the findings in cognitive psychology that word perception is superior to nonword perception. One reason given for the superiority of words is that recognition of visual words might have top down assistance from a visual lexical dictionary (McClelland & Rumelhart, 1986).

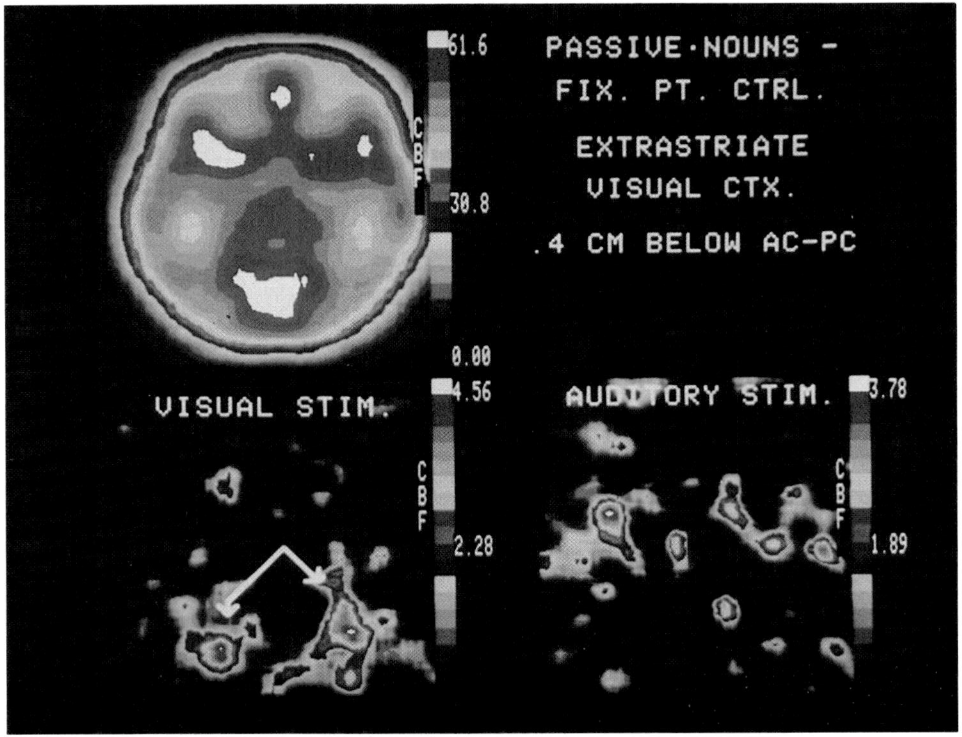

Figure 5. Subtracted positron emission tomographic images of cerebral blood flow. The stimulated tasks involve passive reception of visual or auditory words at the rate of one per second. The control condition is passive fixation with no stimulation. Both conditions involve an average of 40 seconds. Fix pt cntr is the fixation point control condition in which subjects remain fixated but receive no information during the scan. Extrastriate visual ctx is the cortical area activated in the visual scan. It is indicated by arrows. AC-PC is the anterior commissure to posterior commissure line that is the common reference used to define the anatomical coordinates of the areas of blood flow. CBF is the cerebral blood flow. The diagram color indicates the amount of change in blood flow from the control condition.

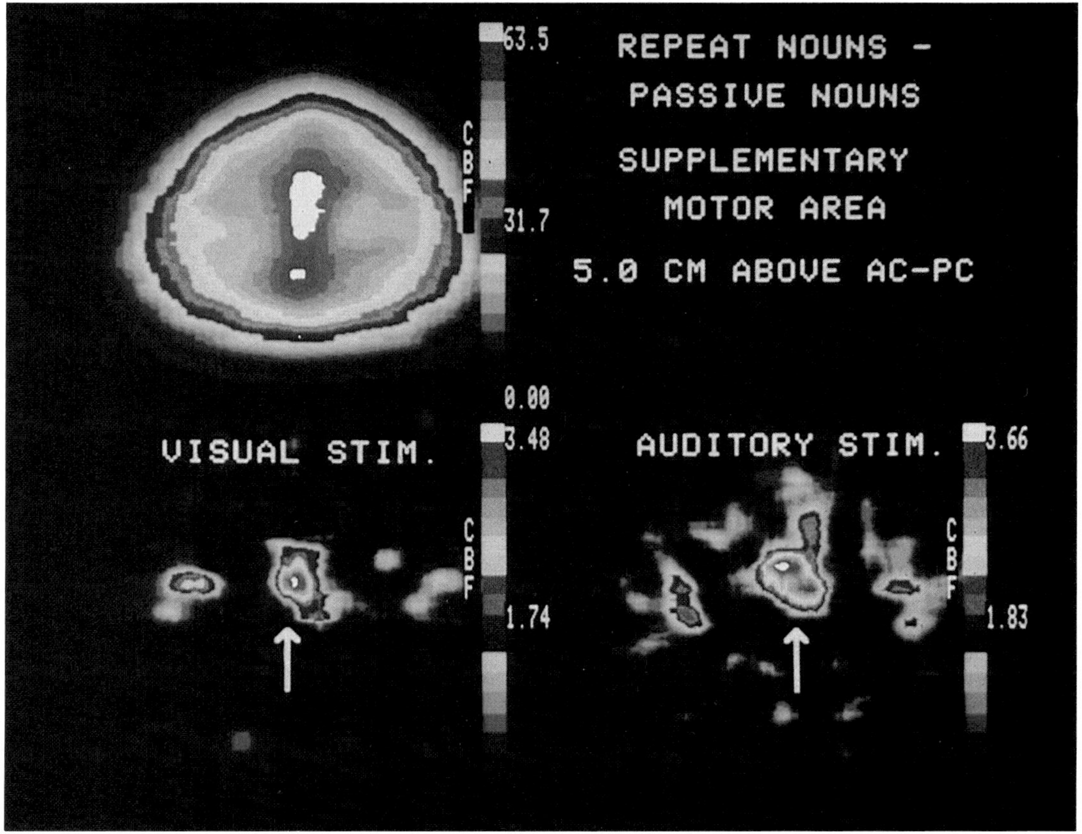

Figure 6. Subtracted PET images of cerebral blood flow. The stimulated task involves repeating visual or auditory words. The control condition is a passive reception of the same stimulation.

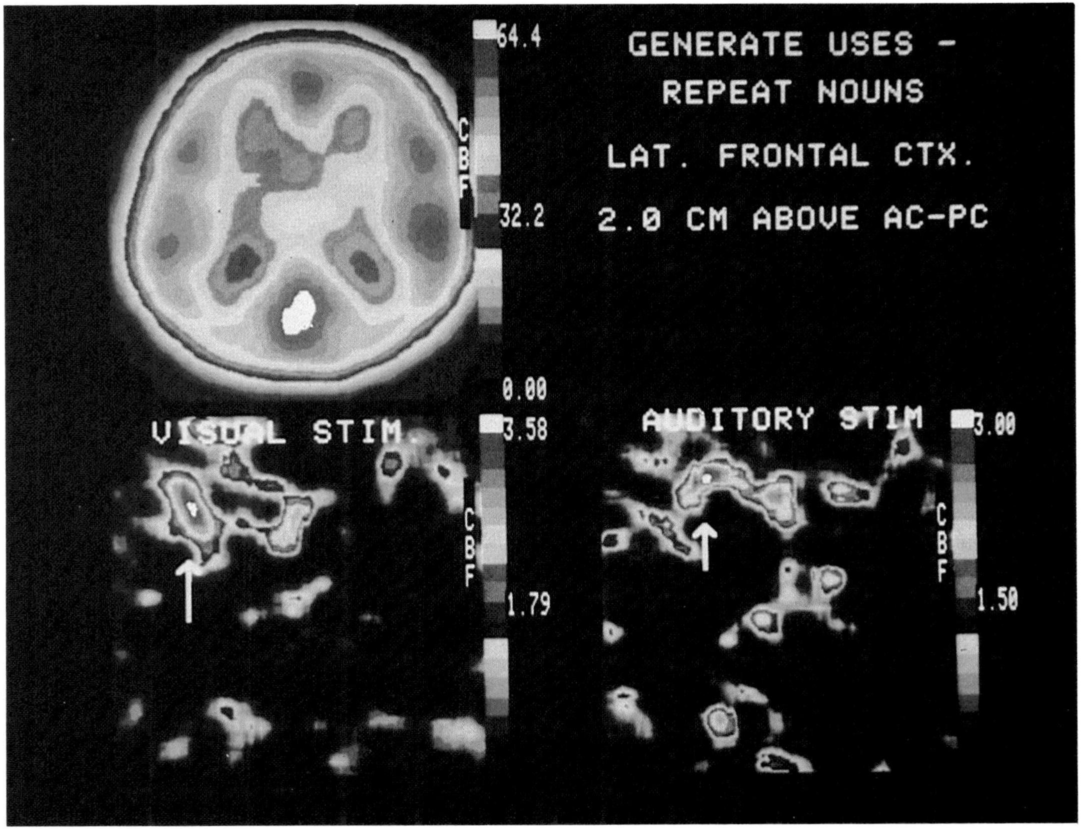

Figure 7. Subtracted images of cerebral blood flow. The stimulated state is generating aloud the use for each presented noun stimulus. In the stimulated state each word is presented as described in Figures 5 and 6. The control state is repeating aloud each noun as described in Figure 6. The subtraction is thought to represent areas unique to the semantic nature of the task (see Petersen, Fox, Posner, Mintun, & Raichle, 1988, for more details).

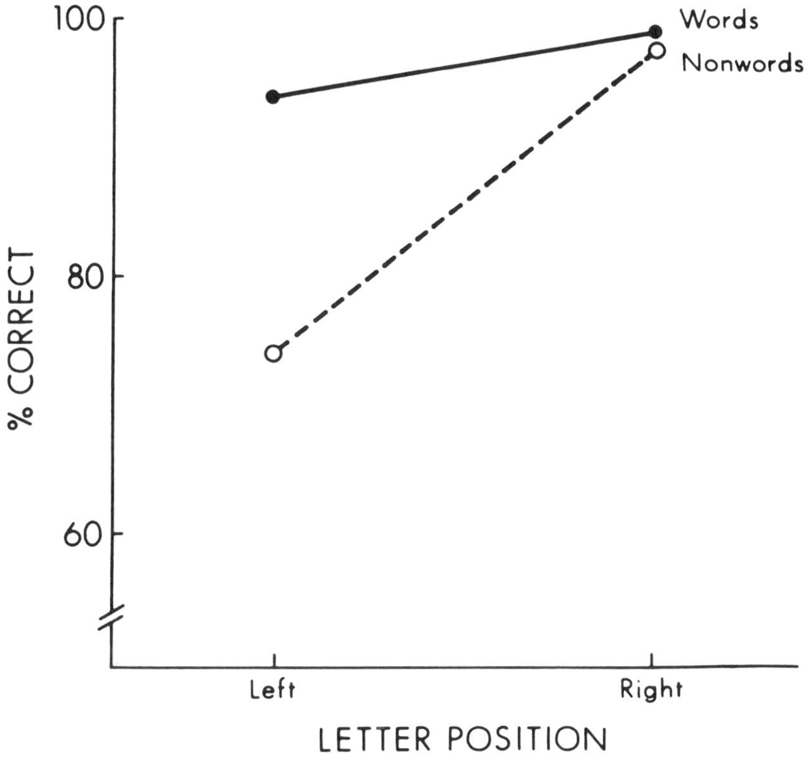

Figure 4. Performance of ten right parietal patients on word and nonword strings presented to them on cards shortly after their lesion.

The cueing method can also be used to bias visual spatial attention in normal humans (Sieroff & Posner, 1987). Thus it should be possible to confirm our patient results by looking at the processing of normal subjects with attention drawn covertly either to the left or right end of strings of letters. To do this, we first presented a digit for 50 ms below the position in which would follow the first or last letter of a 100 ms exposure of a letter string. The results with the normal subjects were similar to those found with the patients. For words, biasing of attention to the beginning or end made little difference in the parts of the string correctly reported. For random letter strings, the subjects systematically missed information on the side of the word away from the cue. The more word-like the letter string, the less the effect of the cue on the subject's report.

These experiments show quite clearly that visual spatial attention deficits produced by parietal lesions can have very strong effects on pattern recognition. They also suggest that both formation of conjunctions and reports of stimuli making nonword strings are greatly affected by attention. However, for word strings, there is little or no effect of damage to the spatial attention system nor of shifts of spatial attention in normal humans. Foveal words appear to have automatic access at least to a visual lexicon.

Recent studies of normal humans using Positron Emission Tomography (PET) to study regional cerebral blood flow during visual language tasks, have provided additional evidence for the rapid packaging of individual letters into word forms (Petersen, Fox, Posner, Mintun, & Raichle, 1988). In these studies subjects in separate blocks (a) watched passively while nouns were presented visually once each second, (b) pronounced the nouns, and (c) generated uses (verbs) to the nouns. During 40 seconds of the task, regional blood flow was assayed by the use of PET. A subtractive technique allowed examination of the neural systems active when either watching words passively or actively responding to them. The passive visual task activated areas of the prestriate cortex as far anterior as the occipital temporal boundary (see Figure 5, color photo inserted in this volume). This activation is very different from that found with auditory words (see Figure 5). When the subject was required to pronounce the words or to generate uses for the words, two parts of the anterior cortex (frontal lobe) were activated. One part was left lateralized and seemed specifically related to language (see Figures 6 and 7, color photos inserted in this volume). The repetition task appears to activate areas near and superior to the classic Broca's area. These areas appear to relate to the generation of the articulatory code of the visually presented word. The generate task activates areas more anterior on the lateral surface that appear to be related to the semantic operations in achieving the use of the presented word. The areas activated in the use generation task for visual and for auditory words are in close proximity but appear separate (Petersen, Fox, Posner, Mintun, & Raichle, 1988). The second set of anterior areas are on the medial surface and do not necessarily seem to be language related. These areas include the supplementary motor area and the cingulate cortex. We believe these areas may be parts of the anterior focal attention system that is discussed in the next section. Roland (1985) has reported several areas that seem to accompany almost all forms of cognitive activity. The areas to which he refers appear to be somewhat more anterior to the ones we have found active, but differences in our techniques may account for anatomical differences. In any case there do appear to be several candidate areas that may be involved in coordination of attention to visual, spatial, and language information.

The fact that no posterior area other than in the occipital lobe was activated by visual words, whether the subjects were passive or active, suggests that the visual analysis of words must take place within the occipital lobe. This result fits with several findings within the psychological literature. First, it fits well with the previously described results in which subjects with right parietal lesions extinguished the left side of nonwords but not of word strings. The lesion result suggests that the distinction between words and nonwords must be made rather early in the nervous system. Second, models of interactive computations (McClelland & Rumelhart, 1986) require intimate feedback from higher levels to lower ones. The rich feedback available in the occipital lobe would make an ideal basis for this system.

Third, many cognitive studies with letters and words conducted in the late 1960s and early 1970s (see Posner, 1978, for a review) argued that visual codes of letters and words had access to output systems. When subjects were required to indicate whether a letter or word pair were physically identical, they could do so independently of the names or semantics of the items shown. Nonetheless, words were responded to faster than nonwords. This would require the ability to route visual input to output mechanisms without having to go through phonological, or semantic systems. As further support for this idea, we (Posner, Sandson, Dhawan, & Shulman, in press) asked subjects to make lexical decisions about whether or not a string of letters made a word. They did the lexical decision task either alone or while also shadowing a verbal message. We found that priming of the target by an identical immediately prior string (identity priming) was not reduced by shadowing while semantic priming was generally reduced by shadowing. This result supports the idea that physical priming involves visual spatial pathways and their connection to the output system (in this case manual), while semantic priming involves systems in which visual and auditory input is intermixed.

Although many previous anatomical theories of visual word reading had relied upon information reaching the angular gyrus or Wernicke's area (Geschwind, 1965), in current cognitive literature the use of a purely visual code as a means of accessing semantic memory is discussed (see Carr & Pollatsek, 1985, for a review). These PET studies confirm the idea that visual spatial attention is not needed for pattern recognition of individual words outlined in this section, but also suggest the importance for anterior areas in higher levels of attentional control of language. It is these higher levels of control that I discuss in the next section.

Common Systems of Attention to Language and Visual Space

In this chapter I have been using two cognitive systems to examine control by attention. These are a visual spatial attention and an attention system that processes language information. The two systems can be viewed in terms of a hierarchy of attentional control systems as shown in Figure 8. Visual spatial attention can be seen as part of a system

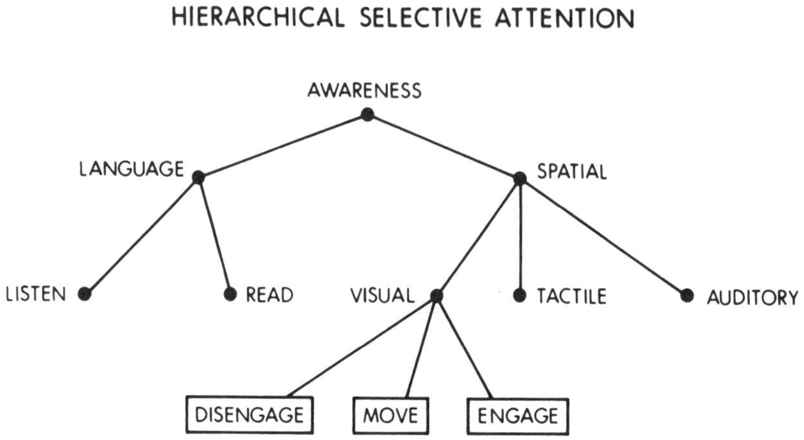

Figure 8. A hierarchically distributed view of selective attention to spatial and language stimuli.

involving orienting to sensory information. We know that parietal lesions can impair orienting to tactile and auditory information as well as to visual information. Moreover, impairments in different forms of sensory orienting are independent in the sense that auditory and visual extinction are not correlated among patients with parietal lesions (DeRenzi, Gentilini, & Pattacini, 1984; Sieroff & Michel, 1987). Similarly, we found that a cue that draws attention to a spatial location was ineffective when the person did not also know the modality of the target (tactile or visual). These findings suggest separate neural systems within the parietal lobe responsible for attention to visual, tactile, or auditory modalities.

On the other hand, it is possible to compare the relative influence of modality (auditory vs. visual) with the influence of the type of cognitive system (spatial or language) in the control of attention. The two cognitive systems correspond to the two major branches of Figure 8. In a series of studies with normal humans (Posner & Henik, 1983) and patients (Walker, Friedrich, & Posner, 1983) we have used a conflict between spatial and linguistic events to study this issue.

In these experiments subjects were instructed to respond either to the visual words *left* or *right*, to the location of these words on the screen, to visual symbols (arrows pointing to the left or right), or to auditory words (*left* or *right*) that might be presented to the left or right ear. In different experiments manual or vocal responses have been used. In work with normal humans (Posner & Henik, 1983), we compared irrelevant dimensions using either the same cognitive system but a different modality than the attended event with those in the same modality but a different cognitive system. When a person is to deal with a visual or auditory word, the extent of facilitation or conflict in RT from words in the opposite modality is much greater than from spatial locations in the same modality. For example, the auditory word *right* interferes more with processing the visual word *left* than does the location of the visual word on the screen. Stimuli from the same cognitive system, even when they involve different sensory modalities, interact strongly. This motivates the common nodes for language and for space independent of modality (see Figure 8).

Reading is one task that clearly involves both language and spatial attention because eye movements and higher level semantic codes are both involved. However, the choice of language and spatial attention was designed to allow for the possibility that above the spatial processing needed for foveating visual words, the control mechanisms for the two systems might be quite separate. So far we have shown that the visual spatial attention system includes the posterior parietal lobe and areas of the thalamus and midbrain. We now ask whether this visual spatial attention system is an independent module that operates on its own or whether it operates in relation to a more complex attentional system that is also involved in the processing of, for example, auditory language.

One way to examine this task is to ask normal subjects and patients with parietal lesions to perform a language task and at the same time, to respond to cues and targets occurring at varying locations in the visual field (Posner, Inhoff, Friedrich, & Cohen, 1987). For patients this required a very simple language task in which they listened to twenty words, one every second, and counted the number of times the words contained a particular phoneme. While listening to these words, visual cues appeared at two locations in the field and we measured the speed of pressing a key to targets following those cues. The language task retarded the ability of a cue to draw the subject's attention to a location in visual space. These patients showed large validity effects (advantage of the cued location over the uncued one), by 100 ms when performing the spatial task alone, which under dual task conditions no validity effect was found until 500 ms. The same results can be obtained with normal subjects; however, they require a more complicated task than the very simple phoneme monitoring task used with patients. For example, a similar retardation of the cueing effect can be obtained if the subjects are required to count backwards by three (Posner, Cohen, et al., 1984).

As expected, the dual task increases reaction time to the visual spatial processing task. However, it does more than merely increase reaction time, it also retards the validity effect. This suggests that the ability to orient attention is retarded when the person is engaged in a language task. Language tasks interfere with some of the operations necessary to shift visual spatial attention to a cued location. Thus visual spatial attention is not an independent module but shares operation with a more general attention system also involved in the processing of language.

Can we say more about the interaction between visual attention and language processing? The use of patient populations does allow us to show that the interaction between visual spatial attention and language attention does not involve the parietal visual attention system. This conclusion stems from the finding that the parietal lobe lesion produces a deficit in the disengage operation. Patients would have to show a specific slowing on invalid contralateral targets when processing language, if language used the same parietal system. However, when engaged in the language task, patients show little difference in reaction time between targets that are ipsilateral versus contralateral to the lesion. Apparently the disengage deficit is local only to visual spatial attention and is not a general disengage deficit. The results of the PET scanning data support these findings because we find no common posterior areas that are involved in auditory and visual language processing. Thus if one seeks an area that deals with language processing (both in its visual and auditory form), and in visual spatial attention (see Figure 7), one must move to anterior parts of the brain. Whatever system is involved in processing visual spatial and language information must lie in the frontal lobes or their related subcortical areas.

The area of the frontal lobes are currently a very active area of research within neuropsychology. Good summaries of this work are available (Goldman-Rakic, 1987). It is well known that lesions of this area can produce devastating effects on human thought and behavior that in one review has been likened to producing a person whose thought and behavior lacks coherence (Duncan, 1986). One result of including frontal lobe function in the ability to allocate attention to visual space is to reconcile the existing conflicts in the literature. Even if the basic visual spatial attention system is posterior, as we have argued, its control system may lie within the frontal lobes and affect both language and spatial function. Thus findings that neglect can be obtained from frontal lesions may have to do with the command functions that act to allow the posterior areas to function (see Figure 2). The common finding in experimental psychology that much of our attentive behavior is closely related to motor performance (Allport, 1980) fits with the idea that attentional systems lie in close proximity to systems controlling motor output.

Although I believe that midline systems that we have found activated in our PET scanning experiments (see Figures 7 and 8) are likely to be part of the focal attention system of the frontal lobe, we do not yet have definitive studies that have localized the different computations that are performed within the control structures found in the frontal areas. The relation of computational models of executive function to the complex anatomy of the frontal lobes still remains in the future, although a beginning of this kind of thinking has arisen, particularly on the role of the dorsolateral prefrontal cortex in inhibiting conflicting responses (Diamond, 1987). One must keep in mind the lessons learned from the posterior attention system that such systems involve widely scattered cortical and subcortical sites. As we seek to understand the anterior attention control systems it is likely that we will discover many anatomically distinct areas are involved.

Applications to Putative Disorders of Attention

The implication of the framework that has organized this chapter is that deficits in mental function must be described both in terms of the elementary operations impaired and of the neurosystems affected. To develop this theme we have been dependent upon cases in which the damaged anatomical area can be observed by neuroimaging. This is traditional neuropsychology. There are many putative disorders of attention, however, in which the underlying neural damage is unknown. These disorders are said to be attentional in the relatively loose sense that they seem to involve the ability of the person to concentrate, to interact appropriately with the environment, and do not seem to be simply due to sensory, motor, or general cognitive damage. Four disorders in this category are depression, schizophrenia, closed head injury, and attention deficit disorder. In each of these, a disorder of attention is indicated and although there are ideas about the organic basis of the disorder it still is unknown.

I would like to use schizophrenia as a model illustrating how the framework developed in this chapter may serve to guide research relating cognitive and neural systems. My interest in schizophrenia began with a study using Positron Emission Tomography in never-medicated schizophrenics (Early, Reiman, Raichle, & Spitznagel, 1987) showing a left basal ganglia abnormality. This anatomical result, together with the widely held belief that schizophrenia was a disorder of attention (Mirsky & Duncan, 1986), led us (Posner, Early, Reiman, Pardo, & Dhawan, in press) to examine the operations of visual spatial attention among schizophrenics. The hypothesis was that there would be a right visual field deficit (because of the left hemisphere abnormality found in PET) that would occur under conditions in which attention had first been drawn to the left visual field (because of the attentional nature of the disorder). We used our standard visual cueing method (see Figure 1). Our initial results were with 12 patients diagnosed as schizophrenic. They were of mixed types although most had suffered from the disorder only a short time. Three of them were studied prior to medication. The results were quite favorable to our hypothesis. In Figure 9 we show data from the model task described in Figures 1 and 2. We included some trials in which no peripheral cue was presented (null trials) that were intermixed with the valid and invalid trials. It is clear that normal subjects show no important differences between visual fields, whereas both

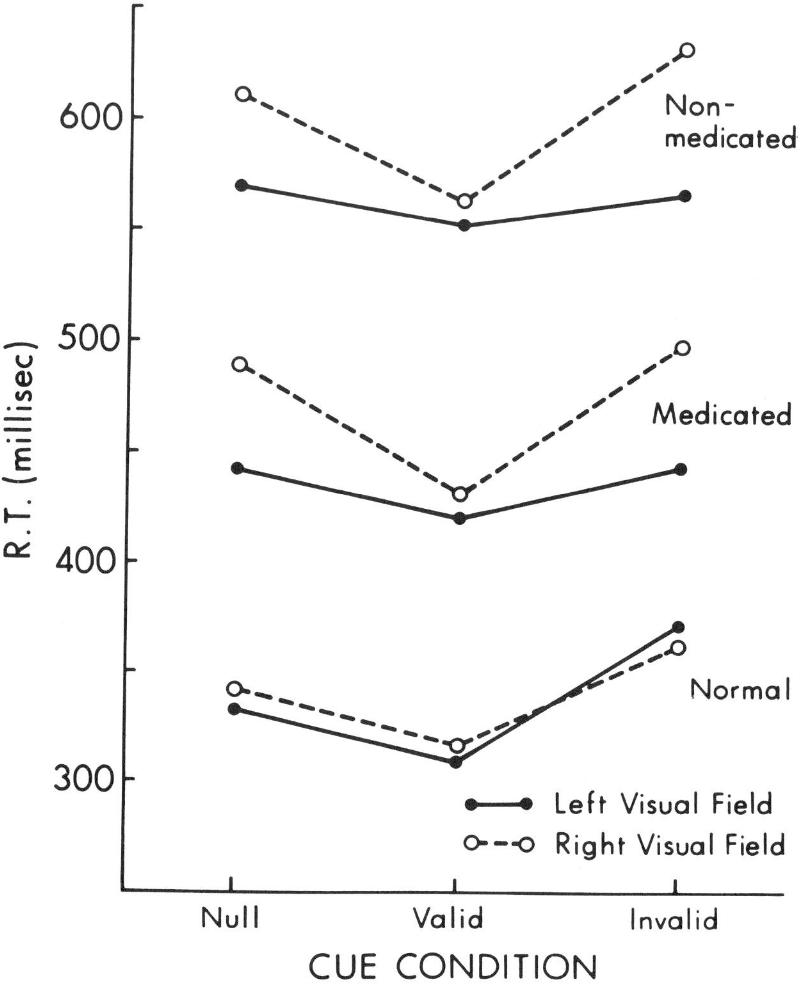

Figure 9. Reaction times of never-medicated schizophrenics, medicated schizophrenics, and normal humans in the model cueing task for visual spatial attention. All data are from the 100 ms target to cue interval. See Posner, Early, Reiman, Pardo, and Dhawan (in press) for more details.

medicated and unmedicated schizophrenics have longer RTs to left visual field targets in the invalid and null cue conditions.

The advantage of using this simple task for the study of schizophrenia is that the attention deficit can be observed within a subject. The subject's performance in the left visual field and right visual field can be compared within the exact same task format. This result elim-

inates such explanations as lack of motivation, fatigue, and other general reasons that schizophrenics might differ from normal humans in overall task performance.

What might be the anatomical and psychological explanation underlying such a right visual field deficit of attention? One possibility is that a deficit of the parietal lobe accounts for the visual spatial abnormality shown in Figure 9. In this case a separate anterior deficit would be needed to account for the problems with language processing that are documented in the literature. There are known pathways that connect the posterior parietal cortex with lateral frontal areas and these tend to involve the basal ganglia as well (Alexander, Delong, & Strick, 1986). Another possibility is a deficit involving the anterior attention system common to spatial and language processing. One reason that a deficit in the common anterior attention systems seems likely is that schizophrenics who report auditory hallucinations appear to be somewhat more likely to show stronger visual spatial deficits. Moreover, Bick and Kinsbourne (1987) have shown that auditory hallucinations seem to be related to self-generated voices by the patients. Our work with normal humans has suggested that it is possible to create a right visual field deficit somewhat similar to that found in schizophrenics by having them shadow auditory messages while responding to visual spatial cues.

It has been known for some time that schizophrenics have difficulty in selecting and holding a set (Weinberger, 1986). Weinberger (1986) has shown severe deficits in the Wisconsin Card Sorting Task. His work with blood flow shows that the Wisconsin Card Sorting Task seems to be related to an area of the frontal lobe called the dorsolateral prefrontal cortex. This is an area of the brain that when lesioned in monkeys produces severe deficits in tasks involving conflicts between previously rewarded acts and current information (Goldman-Rakic, 1987). The mediation of conflict between competing signals is a basic aspect of attentional control. To study this form of conflict we used the word-arrow conflict task I described previously. We had previously shown that patients with right hemisphere lesions tend to respond well to the words but poorly to the arrows and the reverse for left hemisphere lesions. Unmedicated schizophrenics, like left hemisphere-lesioned patients, show a very large advantage for the arrow.

Both the word-arrow conflict results and Figure 9 point to an anterior left hemisphere deficit that is attentional because of its strong interaction with cues. Although the exact nature of the disorder of attention involved in schizophrenia remains a puzzling mystery, our results provide markers that seem to relate both to the laterality of the disorder and to its attentional nature. Within subjects markers for the schizophrenic syndrome provide us with new methods for investigating the nature of this disorder and perhaps tying it to the underlying anatomy of the attention system. The ability to specify the mental operations should open up new ways of linking human disorder to the underlying physiology. Our results support the general framework of this chapter and may aid in the search of theory-driven hypotheses about the nature of other putative disorders of selective attention. This chapter has attempted a very general empirical approach to the neuropsychology of selective attention and of its disorders. The approach uses both cognitive and anatomical data to develop a structural model of the neural systems involved in selecting an item for awareness. The major general conclusion is that the nervous system localizes cognitive operations in widely separated neural systems that are then orchestrated in performance.

To study disorders of attention one may seek links at the level of impairment of mental operations. For example, we find that schizophrenia impairs the ability to shift attention to an event in the right visual field and impairs the selection of a spatial cue. Or one may seek to link impairments in neural systems to individual operations, as in the assertion that right parietal lesions impair the ability to disengage attention to deal with a target located in a leftward direction. It is also possible to indicate the functional significance of an impairment, as for example when it is asserted that a parietal deficit impairs the ability to read.

Our analysis relates diverse methods such as cognitive experiments with normal humans, study of brain injury and mental disorders, and use of neuroimaging techniques. Although our description of attention remains incomplete at both the computational and neural systems levels, it already provides a basis for understanding some putative deficits in terms of their effects on the structures and functions of what we now regard as a cognitive system for the selection of information.

References

Alexander, G. E., Delong, M. R., & Strick, P. L. (1986). Parallel organization of functionally segregated circuits linking basal ganglia and cortex. *Annual Review of Neuroscience*, *9*, 357–381.

Allport, D. A. (1980). Attention and performance. In G. Claxton (Ed.), *Cognitive psychology: New directions* (pp. 112–153). London: Routledge & Kegan Paul.

Bashinski, H. S., & Bachrach, V. R. (1980). Enhancement of perceptual sensitivity as the result of selectively attending to spatial locations. *Perception and Psychophysics*, *28*, 241–248.

Baynes, K., Holtzman, J. D., & Volpe, B. T. (1986). Components of visual attention: Alterations in response pattern to visual stimuli following parietal lobe infarction. *Brain*, *109*, 99–114.

Berlucchi, G., & Rizzolatti, G. (Eds.). (1987). Selective visual attention. *Neuropsychologia*, 25A.

Bick, P. A., & Kinsbourne, M. (1987). Auditory hallucinations and subvocal speed in schizophrenic patients. *American Journal of Psychiatry*, *144*, 222–225.

Carr, T. H., & Pollatsek, A. (1985). Recognizing printed words: A look at current models. In D. Besner, T. G. Weller, & G. E. MacKinnon (Eds.), *Reading research* (pp. 2–73). New York: Academic Press.

Cowey, A. (1985). Aspects of cortical organization related to selective attention and selective impairments of visual perception: A tutorial review. In M. I. Posner & O. S. M. Marin (Eds.), *Attention and performance XI: Mechanisms of attention* (pp. 14–62). Hillsdale, NJ: Erlbaum.

Crick, F. (1984). Function of the thalamic reticular complex: The search light hypothesis. *Proceedings of the National Academy, 81*, 4586–4590.

DeRenzi, E. (1982). *Disorders of space exploration and cognition*. New York: Wiley.

DeRenzi, E., Gentilini, M., & Pattacini, F. (1984). Auditory extinction following hemisphere damage. *Neuropsychologia, 22*, 733–744.

Deuel, R. M., & Collins, R. C. (1984). The functional anatomy of frontal lobe neglect in the monkey: Behavioral and quantitative 2 DG studies. *Annals of Neurology, 15*, 521–529.

Diamond, A. (1987, April). *Development of progressive inhibitory control of action: Retrieval of a contiguous object.* Paper given to the Society for Research in Child Development, Baltimore, MD.

Downing, C. J., & Pinker, S. (1985). The spatial structure of visual attention. In M. I. Posner & O. S. M. Marin (Eds.), *Attention and performance XI: Mechanisms of attention* (pp. 171–187). Hillsdale, NJ: Erlbaum.

Duncan, J. (1986). Disorganization of behavior after frontal lobe damage. *Cognitive Neuropsychology, 3*, 271–290.

Early, T. S., Reiman, C. M., Raichle, M. E., & Spitznagel, E. L. (1987). Left globus pallidus abnormality in never-medicated patients with schizophrenia. *Proceedings of the National Academy, 84*, 561–567.

Friedrich, F. J., Walker, J., & Posner, M. I. (1985). Effects of parietal lesions on visual matching: Implications for reading errors. *Cognitive Neuropsychology, 2*, 253–264.

Geschwind, N. (1965). Disconnection syndrome in animals and man. *Brain, 88*, 237–294.

Goldman-Rakic, P. S. (1987). Circuitry of primate prefrontal cortex and regulation of behavior by representational analysis. In F. Plum & V. Mountcastle (Eds.), Higher cortical function. *American Physiological Society Handbook of Physiology, 5*, 373–417.

Hughes, H. C., & Zimba, L. D. (1985). Spatial maps of directed visual attention. *Journal of Experimental Psychology: Human Perception and Performance, 11*, 409–430.

James, W. (1890). *Principles of psychology* (Vol. 1). New York: Holt.

Jonides, J. (1981). Voluntary versus automatic control over the mind's eye. In J. Long & A. Baddeley (Eds.), *Attention and performance IX* (pp. 87–207). Hillsdale, NJ: Erlbaum.

Jonides, J., & Mack, R. (1984). On the cost and benefit of cost and benefit. *Psychology Bulletin, 96*, 29–44.

Kosslyn, S. M. (1980). *Image and mind*. Cambridge, MA: Harvard University Press.

LaBerge, D. L., & Samuels, J. (1974). Toward a theory of automatic word processing in reading. *Cognitive Psychology, 6*, 293–323.

Ladavas, E. (1987). Is hemispatial deficit produced by right parietal damage associated with retinal or cravitational coordinates? *Brain, 110*, 167–180.

Mangun, G. R., Hansen, J. C., & Hillyard, S. A. (1986, December). *The spatial orienting of attention: Sensory facilitation or response bias?* (ONR Technical Report SDEPL 001).

Marcel, A. (1983). Conscious and unconscious perception. *Cognitive Psychology, 15*, 238–300.

Maylor, E. A. (1985). Facilitory and inhibitory components of orienting in visual space. In M. I. Posner & O. S. M. Marin (Eds.), *Attention and performance XI: Mechanisms of attention* (pp. 189–204). Hillsdale, NJ: Erlbaum.

McClelland, J. L., & Rumelhart, D. E. (1986). *Parallel distributed processing, explorations in the microstructures of cognition: Vol. 1. Foundations*. Cambridge, MA: MIT Press.

Mirsky, A. F., & Duncan, C. C. (1986). Etiology and expression of schizophrenia: Neurobiological and psychosocial factors. *Annual Review of Psychology, 37*, 291–319.

Mishkin, M., Ungerleider, L. G., & Macko, K. A. (1983). Object vision: Two cortical pathways. *Trends in Neuroscience, 6*, 414–417.

Morrison, R. E. (1984). Manipulation of stimulus onset delay in reading: Evidence for parallel programming of saccades. *Journal of Experimental Psychology: Human Perception and Performance, 10*, 667–682.

Morrow, L. A., & Ratcliff, G. (1987). Attentional mechanisms in clinical neglect. *Journal of Clinical and Experimental Neuropsychology, 9* (Abstract).

Mountcastle, V. B. (1978). Brain systems for directed attention. *Journal Royal Society of Medicine, 71*, 14–27.

Nagel-Leiby, S., Buchtel, H., & Welch, K. M. A. (1987). Right frontal and parietal lobe contributions to the process of directed visual attention and orientation. *Journal of Clinical and Experimental Neuropsychology, 9* (Abstract).

Neely, J. H. (1977). Semantic priming and retrieval from lexical memory. *Journal of Experimental Psychology: General, 106*, 226–254.

Petersen, S. E., Fox, P. T., Posner, M. I., Mintun, M., & Raichle, M. E. (1988). Positron emission tomographic studies of the cortical anatomy of single-word processing. *Nature, 331*, 585–589.

Petersen, S. E., Robinson, D. L., & Morris, J. D. (1987). Contributions of the pulvinar to visual spatial attention. *Neuropsychologia, 25*, 97–105.

Posner, M. I. (1978). *Chronometric explorations of mind*. Hillsdale, NJ: Erlbaum.

Posner, M. I. (1980). Orienting of attention. *Quarterly Journal of Experimental Psychology, 32*, 3–25.

Posner, M. I. (1982). Cumulative development of attentional theory. *American Psychologist, 32*, 53–64.

Posner, M. I. (1986). A framework for relating cognitive and neural systems. *EEG and Clinical Neurophysiology*, Supplement 38, 155–166.

Posner, M. I., Choate, L. S., Rafal, R. D., & Vaughn, J. (1985). Inhibition of return: Neural mechanisms and function. *Cognitive Neuropsychology, 2*, 211–228.

Posner, M. I., & Cohen, Y. (1984). Components of attention. In H. Bouman & D. Bowhuis (Eds.), *Attention and performance X* (pp. 55–66). Hillsdale, NJ: Erlbaum.

Posner, M. I., Cohen, Y., Choate, L., Hockey, R., & Maylor, E. (1984). Sustained concentration: Passive filtering or active orienting. In S. Kornblum & J. Requin (Eds.), *Preparatory states and processes* (pp. 49–65). Hillsdale, NJ: Erlbaum.

Posner, M. I., Cohen, Y., & Rafal, R. D. (1982). Neural systems control over spatial orienting. *Philosophical Transaction Royal Society of London Series B, 2908*, 187–198.

Posner, M. I., Early, T., Reiman, E., Pardo, P., & Dhawan, M. (in press). Asymmetries in hemispheric control of attention in schizophrenia. *Archives of General Psychiatry.*

Posner, M. I., & Henik, A. (1983). Isolating representational systems. In J. Beck, B. Hope, & A. Rosenfeld (Eds.), *Human and machine vision* (pp. 395–412). New York: Academic Press.

Posner, M. I., Inhoff, A. W., Friedrich, F. J., & Cohen, A. (1987). Isolating attentional systems: A cognitive–anatomical analysis. *Psychobiology, 15*, 107–121.

Posner, M. I., & Marin, O. S. M. (Eds.). (1985). *Attention and performance XI: Mechanisms of attention.* Hillsdale, NJ: Erlbaum.

Posner, M. I., Petersen, S. E., Fox, P. T., & Raichle, M. E. (in press). Localization of cognitive operations in the human brain. *Science.*

Posner, M. I., & Presti, D. (1987). Selective attention and cognitive control. *Trends in Neuroscience, 10*, 12–17.

Posner, M. I., Sandson, J., Dhawan, M., & Shulman, G. L. (in press). Is word recognition automatic? A cognitive–anatomical analysis. *Journal of Cognitive Neuroscience.*

Posner, M. I., & Snyder, C. R. (1975). Facilitation and inhibition in the processing of signals. In P. M. Rabbit (Ed.), *Attention and performance V* (pp. 669–681). New York: Academic Press.

Posner, M. I., Walker, J. A., Friedrich, F. J., & Rafal, R. D. (1984). Effects of parietal lobe injury on covert orienting of visual attention. *Journal of Neuroscience, 4*, 1863–1874.

Prinzmetal, W., Presti, D., & Posner, M. I. (1986). Does attention affect feature integration? *Journal of Experimental Psychology: Human Perception and Performance, 12*, 361–369.

Rafal, R. D., & Posner, M. I. (1987). Deficits in visual spatial attention following thalamic lesions. *Proceedings of the National Academy, 84*, 7349–7353.

Rizzolatti, G., Riggio, L., Dascola, I., & Umilta, C. (1987). Reorienting attention across the horizontal and vertical meridians: Evidence in favor of a premotor theory of attention. *Neuropsychologia, 25.*

Roland, P. E. (1985). Cortical organization of voluntary behavior in man. *Human Neurobiology, 4*, 155–167.

Rumelhart, J. L., & McClelland, D. E. (1981). An interactive activation model of context effects in letter perception: Part 1. An account of basic findings. *Psychological Review, 88*, 375–407.

Rumelhart, D., & Norman, D. A. (1982). Simulating a skilled typist. *Cognitive Science, 6*, 1–36.

Sieroff, E., & Michel, F. (1987). In right/left hemisphere patients and the problem of lexical access. *Neuropsychologia.*

Sieroff, E., Pollatsek, A., & Posner, M. I. (1987). Recognition of visual letter strings following injury to the posterior visual spatial attention system. *Cognitive Neuropsychology.*

Sieroff, E., & Posner, M. I. (1987). Cueing spatial attention during processing of words and letter strings in normals. *Cognitive Neuropsychology.*

Taylor, D. A. (1977). Time course of context effects. *Journal of Experimental Psychology*, *106*, 404–426.

Titchener, E. B. (1908). *Lectures on the elementary psychology of feeling and attention*. New York: Macmillan.

Treisman, A. M. (1986). Features and objects in visual processing. *Scientific American, 255*(5), 114–125.

Walker, J. A., Friedrich, F. J., & Posner, M. I. (1983). *Spatial conflict in parietal lesions*. Paper presented to the International Neuropsychology Society, San Diego, CA.

Weinberger, D. R. (1986). The pathogenesis of schizophrenia. In H. A. Nasrallah & D. R. Weinberger (Eds.), *The neurology of schizophrenia* (pp. 397-407). New York: Elsevier.

Wurtz, R. H., Goldberg, M. E., & Robinson, D. L. (1980). Behavioral modulation of visual responses in the monkey. *Progress in Psychobiology and Physiological Psychology*, *9*, 43–83.